KIDOLOGY'S ULTIMATE TOOLBOX FOR CHILDREN'S MINISTRY

EVERYTHING YOU NEED TO BUILD A SOLID CHILDREN'S MINISTRY

KARL BASTIAN

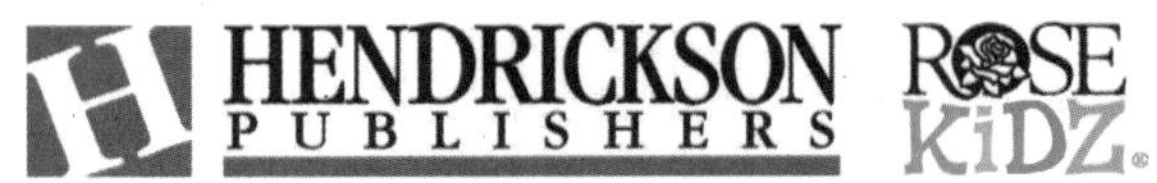

www.hendricksonrose.com

Kidology's Ultimate Toolbox for Children's Ministry

RoseKidz® is an imprint of
Rose Publishing, LLC
P.O. Box 3473
Peabody, Massachusetts 01961-3473 USA
www.hendricksonrose.com

Cover design by Jamie Egglestrom.
Interior design by Drew McCall.
Illustrations by Jamie Egglestrom.

ISBN: 9781628627671
RoseKidz® reorder number R50018
RELIGION/Christian Ministry/Children

Printed in the United States of America

Printed August 2018

Contents

Section Two: Leadership Tools

Section Three: Teaching Tools

Section Four: Training Tools

Section Five: Outreach Tools

KiDOLOGY
.org

Foreword by the Author

Children's Ministry Is Like a Construction Site

You are the foreman of a project that will never be completed.

BUT HELP IS HERE!

You now have the tools you need to thrive in this thrilling environment!

I've said it for years: If you lead a children's ministry, it is critical that you have a realistic perspective of the job you've been entrusted with. If you envision a day when you will gather everyone for a ribbon-cutting ceremony at the grand opening of a perfectly completed children's ministry, you may be in the wrong line of work.

A children's ministry leader's job is never done.

To get a proper perspective on your job, you need to imagine a construction site where the plans are constantly changing; workers routinely come and go; and supplies are often in short supply or you may need to use donated resources. Other unforeseeable circumstances often offset your perfectly detailed plans with very short notice. If this sounds challenging, it is! *But you are up for the challenge!*

But that doesn't mean you aren't up for a little help. And that's where the *Kidology Toolbox* comes in. *Kidology.org* has

You are called to reach and teach kids. You know you are harvesting the ripest spiritual field and that the fruit of your work will far outlast you—and in fact, will impact eternity itself!

been equipping and encouraging children's ministry leaders like you for over twenty years. This toolbox provides ALL NEW, ready-to-use ideas, forms, outlines, and practical blueprints to help you manage your children's ministry like a pro!

For over twenty-five years, I've been leading children's ministries, from small mobile churches to established churches of all sizes in both the city and suburbs. I've learned a thing or two along the way. Many lessons I learned the hard way. The goal of this book is to share those lessons with you. In so doing, you can learn the ropes and discover the secrets to thriving in the never-ending chaos and noise of the children's ministry construction site. Whether you are new or a seasoned veteran, you are about to undertake an exciting ministry expansion as you open up this toolbox loaded with powerful ideas, downloads, and videos.

You are going to learn how to improve your own leadership skills, build a team, take your teaching up a notch, succeed at recruiting and training, and increase your outreach impact. If you use the tools in this toolbox, you are going to impress your boss, volunteers, and parents. And most importantly, you are going to reach more kids for Jesus! Isn't that what it's all about?

So, put on your hard hat, and let's get going!

Because Jesus loves children,

PASTOR KARL BASTIAN

A.K.A. THE KIDOLOGIST

How to Use This Toolbox

The *Kidology Ultimate Toolbox for Children's Ministry* provides you with everything you need to build a solid children's ministry. Each section covers areas of vital interest to children's pastors and directors.

You Can Do It!

This innovative children's ministry guide covers everything you need to know to lead your program:

- Leadership tools and teaching tips
- Recruiting and training volunteers
- Goal setting and team building
- Event Planning and outreach
- Classroom management, learning styles, and MORE!

Here are some suggestions to help you get the most use from your toolbox:

1. Read each section carefully and in the order they are presented.
2. Photocopy the forms, worksheets, and checklists. Many of the pages include a copyright line at the bottom. This indicates that you are free to photocopy these pages.* As these are forms you might use over and over again, or that you might share with others, you might want to make photocopies before you get to Suggestion3 .

3. Write on the pages. There is space allowed to write on the pages in response to questions. But more than that, as you read each section, take notes in the margins.

4. Explore the suggested videos and online resources. Karl Bastian's website, Kidology.org has a wealth of materials and tools to add to your children's ministry toolbox. He has carefully selected several of these tools for you to use. These tools are found at Kidology.org/toolbox

5. Most importantly, pray as you read this book. Pray that the Holy Spirit will guide your steps as you work to build a solid and strong ministry for the children and families in your care.

* For a nominal fee of $2.00 (shipping and handling), the reproducible pages are available as PDFs on a CD-ROM. Email orders@hendrickson.com to order a *Kidology Ultimate Toolbox CD-ROM.*

READY?

LET'S OPEN THE TOOLBOX!

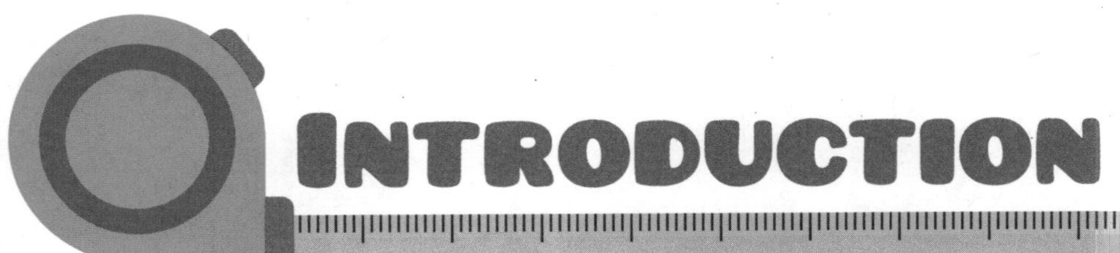

INTRODUCTION

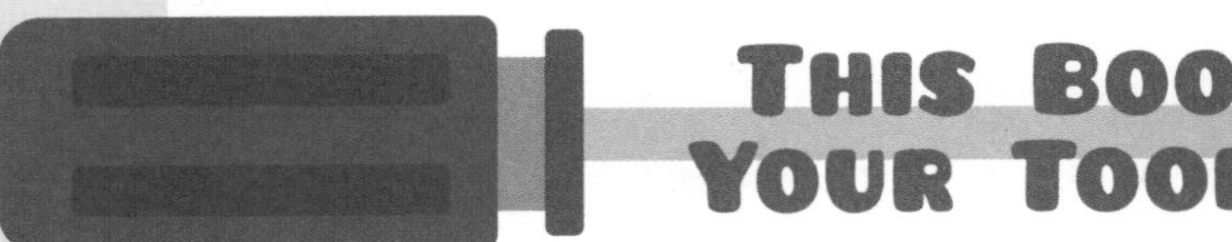

This Book is Your Toolbox!

Under Construction!

I'm glad you picked up this book! Whether you are new to children's or have been at it for a while, you are going to find this toolbox loaded with tools that are going to make your job easier!

It is time to consider your children's ministry as being Under Construction!

You might be starting from scratch. You may want to remodel or build an addition. Either way, there is a good chance you find the task ahead more than just a little daunting.

I have good news! You are not alone. I've had the joy of knowing and getting to meet hundreds of children's ministry leaders over the years. I have yet to meet one who has said to me, "Karl, I've got this thing down. No help needed here. I'm a master at this!" Every leader I have ever met has shared areas where they struggle.

No ministry is easy.

- Small ministries may think, "If only my church was a little bigger, I'd have more volunteers and resources."

- Larger ministries often say, "If only my church wasn't so big, I wouldn't need as many volunteers, and my job would be so much easier."
- Church plants envy the facilities that established churches have.

WATCH THIS VIDEO: Proactive Leadership
Visit Kidology.org/toolbox

- Established churches envy the flexibility that mobile churches have and how quickly they can implement change.
- Churches with little resources wonder what it would be like to have a big budget.
- Large churches in affluent areas long for the dedication and resourcefulness that is found in churches that have far less.

In other words, we all see our own struggles and the things we envy about others. We can fail to see that what we envy simply leads to different problems.

Know what we all have in common? We all share the same mission of reaching kids and families. We all serve the same God who calls, guides, provides, and produces fruit in our ministries.

This book will help you plan, prepare, and improve your ministry, but at the end of the day, it is God who brings about the results. Proverbs 16:9 assures us, "We can make our plans, but the Lord determines our steps." You are not alone! There are children's ministry leaders all across the world facing the same challenges as you, and with God's help, they are seeing lives transformed. You will too!

I love the promise that is given in Galatians 6:9,

So let's not get tired of doing what is good. At just the right time we will reap a harvest of blessing if we don't give up.

Children's ministry isn't for wimps. It is hard work. There are challenges. But easy things are not nearly as rewarding as things that take great effort and energy.

You may not feel qualified for the job. That's OK. God is in the business of using people whose greatest qualification is simply his calling and their willingness to answer and follow. Look at the disciples. They were young; they were inexperienced; at times, they acted immaturely; but they were teachable and through them, God changed the world!

When I was a young leader, my youth pastor would say to me, "Karl, as long as you remain F.A.T., God can use you." He wasn't recommending I gain weight; he was drilling an acronym into my mind and heart. Being F.A.T. stands for being Faithful, Available, and Teachable.

If we are

FAITHFUL to the call God has placed on our life—not giving up when the going gets hard

AVAILABLE whenever and wherever he leads us

TEACHABLE to learn from others and from our mistakes

Then, not only will our ministries always improve, but we will learn, grow, and improve as well.

Whenever I face failure, criticism, or challenges, I still find myself whispering, "Karl, just be F.A.T., and you can do this."

This may surprise you, but God isn't in the business of building children's ministries. He is in the business of building people. Believe it or not, he is more interested in building you than in building your ministry.

This means that God may use struggles and challenges in your ministry to build you. There will be times when you want to fix a problem, but instead, ask yourself, "What is God trying to teach me?" As you learn and grow, the ministry will take care of itself.

YOU CAN DO THIS!

God has called you. He will lead you. He will provide. He will build you as you seek to build your ministry to reach and teach kids for him! Recognize that building your ministry is not the end goal. It is the means to reach God's ultimate goal—building into other lives.

I'm going to share with you a collection of tools that will help you along the way, but at the end of the day, it is God who is going to do the greatest work in you and through you.

As you think of your ministry as being under construction, don't forget that you are under construction, too. Don't expect perfection in the ministry or from yourself. Just work faithfully to see things grow and improve. Remember Philippians 1:6,

[He] who began the good work within you, will continue his work until it is finally finished on the day when Christ Jesus returns.

God isn't finished with you yet. And as you build your children's ministry, he is going to build you!

The Tool of Uniqueness

Only You Can Be You!

While I currently live in beautiful Colorado, most of my life has been spent in the Chicago area. As a child, I enjoyed trips downtown with my grandparents. I loved touring the tall buildings, and I walked almost constantly looking up at all the amazing skyscrapers. While attending Moody Bible Institute in the heart of the city, I took any job in the downtown area

so I could again be in and around these mammoth buildings. A legal messenger job granted me access to see even more grandeur inside these icons of business. My first children's pastor position was at a Chicago church that allowed many more years of life and ministry among architecture that is marveled at and studied around the world.

Chicago was the birthplace of the skyscraper, a term that was originally intended as an insult, but has come to signify a towering masterpiece of steel and glass. In the early years of this booming city, many famous buildings were part of competitions to see which builder could build the most unique structure.

The goal was always focused on both form and function.

- A beautiful building that wasn't practical would soon be torn down.
- A completely functional building that wasn't impressive would be overlooked.

The best buildings offered both—they worked, and they were fascinating to look at, walk through, and work in.

Build to Stand the Test of Time

In children's ministry, we face the same challenge. We need to build ministries that address both form and function. But we also have the opportunity to do something incredibly unique that will stand the test of time.

Too often I see ministries looking at what others are doing and copying it. Too many leaders make the mistake of thinking, "If it worked there, it'll work here, too." The problem is that every ministry situation is different.

Keeping Sharp

Don't start with the problems you need to fix, look higher than that.

The culture, customs, and challenges are different everywhere. Instead, they ought to be asking, "What can I build that is unique?"

Both form and function have to be addressed. You want a ministry that is attractive to everyone who will see it. One that is fun for kids, safe for parents, engaging for volunteers, and effective for church leadership. But you also need a ministry that works. You need policies, structures, training mechanisms, processes, and habits that keep it humming along smoothly.

Embrace Your Uniqueness

You want your ministry to be as special and unique as you are. You want the kids and families who attend your church to feel lucky that they are at your church. Build something unique.

It starts not with blueprints but with prayer. Every towering skyscraper existed first as a dream in the imagination of a builder. You are a builder! But instead of building a skyscraper, you are building lives, and you are building a ministry.

Your first step is to prayerfully ask God, "What would you have me build?" Don't start with the problems you need to fix,. Look higher than that. As you build a ministry that is unique, you'll discover that many of the problems will take care of themselves.

Recruiting gets a lot easier in exciting ministries.

Think about these two things:

- Parental involvement soars when parents are excited about their kids' church experience.
- Giving goes up as attendance grows and enthusiasm increases.

It's time to build something that has never been built before—something that only you can build. Let's get started!

The Tool of Assessment

Before You Begin

This toolbox is going to walk you through a process to help you build an amazing children's ministry. But there is something you need to do first. It's time to check out the Tool of Assessment!

Pre-Construction Survey

Before a building ever gets built, the land it will tower above needs to be chosen and surveyed. Whether you are remodeling a ministry or starting from scratch, it is critical that you take the time to survey the current landscape upon which your ministry is built.

This accomplishes several objectives:

- It will help you evaluate the potential of what can be built.
- It will help you consider what should be built.
- It will give you a benchmark to see in clear terms and to celebrate how much you have built!

Use the following pages, or download the Pre-Construction Survey and fill it out as completely as you can. If anything doesn't apply to your current ministry, just leave it blank.

The first page is mostly statistics about where your ministry is right now. Some of the answers may require some work to answer. You may even need to put some procedures in place to gather the needed information. The effort will be worth it, as this is information you ought to be collecting anyway. Once you set up the means to get this data, you'll be set going forward.

When you are done, save this survey. You'll be referring back to it later. A month from now, six months from now, even a year or two from now, it will become a benchmark that will help you measure your progress. So make it as accurate as you can.

Pre-Construction Survey

Ministry Details

Name of Church:

Name of Children's Ministry:

Website and Social Media Outlets:

QUESTION	NOW	NOTES (Indicate any special situations)	IN 6 MONTHS	IN 12 MONTHS
PROGRAMMING (WEEKLY)				
Total Classes/Groups				
Total Program Hours				
STAFFING				
Children's Ministry Paid Staff				
Volunteer Leaders				
Preschool Volunteers				
Elementary Volunteers				
Total Volunteers				
ATTENDANCE				
Avg. Preschool Last Month				
Avg. Preschool Same Month Last Year				
Increase/Decrease by # and %				
Avg. Elementary Last Month				
Avg. Elem. Same Month Last Year				
Increase/Decrease by # and %				
Avg. Preschool Last 6 Months				
Avg. Elementary Last 6 Months				
Avg. Total Kids Last 6 Months				
SECURITY				
# of Background Checked Volunteers				
TRAINING				
Date of Last Training				
How Many Over Past 12 Months				
GROWTH				
Guest Kids Past 6 Months				
New Families Past 6 Months				

MINISTRY REFLECTIONS

Take a few minutes to reflect on these questions and write down what first comes to mind. Don't over-think, and be honest. This is not a test. These are not what you hope the answers to be, but what they are right now. Being truthful to how things are now will help show the most improvement as you continue to use the tools in this book to build a stronger ministry!

How would you describe your ministry right now?

What are the strengths of your ministry right now?

What are the weaknesses of your ministry right now?

How would you describe the mood of your volunteers right now?

How would you describe the experience of the families who visit your church?

What has been your biggest success so far in your ministry?

What have you tried that has totally flopped?

If you could magically change just one thing to be effective next Sunday, what would it be?

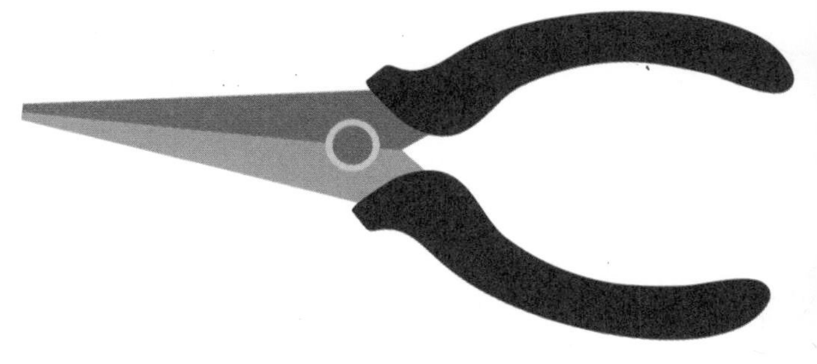

What advice would you give someone in the exact same situation as you?

If someone donated a large sum of money to your ministry, what one thing would you invest it in?

Write out a prayer that reflects your heart for your ministry, its kids, families, and volunteers:

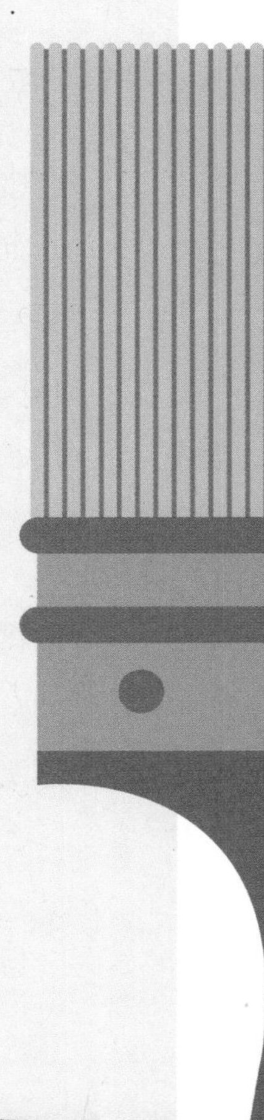

1: Personal Tools

Introduction

Personal Tools

You have been entrusted with the children's ministry of your church. The mere fact that so much of its success or failure depends on you can be daunting—even intimidating. But it also presents a huge opportunity!

Checking Out Who Is in Charge

If you hire a contractor to remodel a room in your house or build an addition, what is your first concern?

- Would you look to see what materials they would use first?
- Would you consider the brands they choose when they purchase materials?

DON'T DO IT!

I know you are considering it, but DON'T SKIP THIS SECTION to get to the practical stuff. This is Section ONE for a reason. Prayerfully and thoughtfully working through this section will make a huge difference in how the rest of this book is applied. You owe it to yourself and your ministry to begin at the starting point—which is here and deals with you.

- Would you ask for plans right away?

No, you'd look at the person you are hiring.

WATCH THIS VIDEO: First Things First
Visit Kidology.org/toolbox

- You'd evaluate whether you could trust them, whether they had adequate training and experience.
- You'd like to know what they had done in the past.
- You might read some reviews from others who have hired them. Too many bad reviews, and likely you'd move on to find someone else, regardless of other impressive credentials.

Who you hire to manage the job is of the utmost importance. In fact, if you trust the contractor, you'll accept their opinions on materials and supplies. You might even accept using less costly materials or less known brands if the contractor assures you the quality is just as good or better.

You Are a Vital Tool

The same is true when you look at building or remodeling a children's ministry. In the past ten years, there has been an explosion in resource providers, curricula, and technology tools for improving a children's ministry. Attend any children's ministry conference, and you can be quickly overwhelmed by the number of tools available. These trade shows, as they are in reality, offer endless tools, and almost any of them will get the job done. Far more important than the tools used is who is wielding the tools.

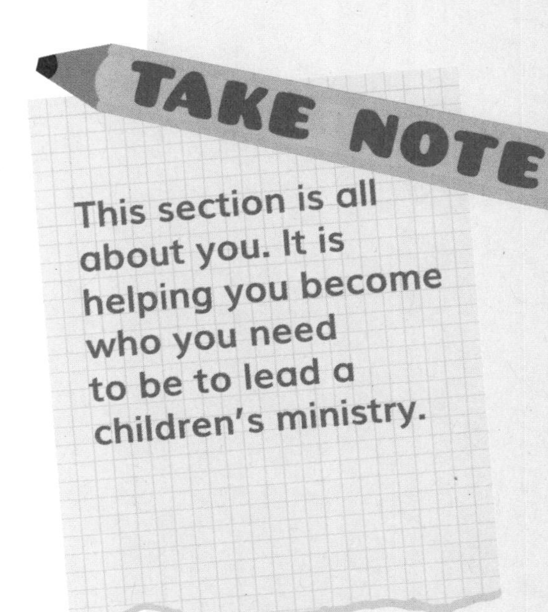

This section is all about you. It is helping you become who you need to be to lead a children's ministry. Ministry is hard. It is exciting, but it is draining. It comes with wonderful perks, but it also features flashes of discouragement.

- For every compliment you get, you'll get complaints as well.
- For every success, you'll have to also manage unrealistic expectations from others.
- At times, you'll wonder if anyone sees the strengths since the attention seems to be focused on the areas that need improvement.

Such is a construction site. It is noisy. It is demanding. And the focus is on the areas that are broken. You need to be strong and healthy and have a realistic expectation yourself, not only on what the ministry can do, but also on how much you should do.

There is an old saying, "You can only take people where you have been." A big part of being a leader is not just leading the ministry, but leading yourself and leading others. As you do, the ministry will naturally, and dare I say more easily, grow as well!

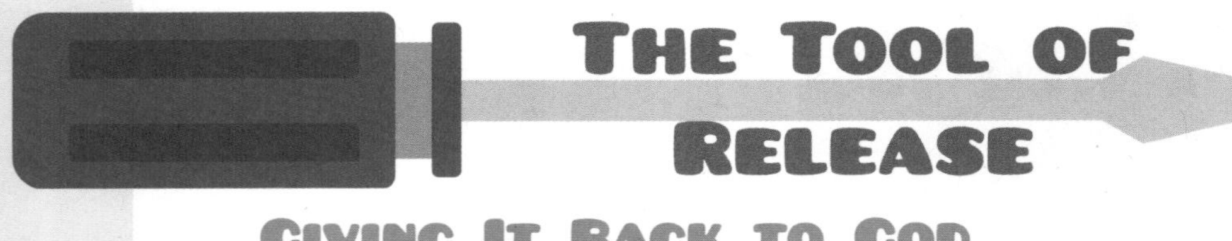

The Tool of Release

Giving It Back to God

Many children's ministry leaders admit to being stressed out over their ministry. Stress has no place in children's ministry!

Seriously, there is no reason to be stressed out over ministry.

None.

I meet a lot of children's ministry leaders, and often they are exhausted, stressed out, worried, and many are on the verge of quitting. I know the feeling, as I have been there. But I have learned the secret to stress-free ministry. It is really quite simple.

Give the ministry back to God.

If this sounds simplistic, it is. But it is also profoundly true. When we get stressed over ministry, there is only one reason.

- It isn't the lack of volunteers.
- It isn't a lack of funds.
- It isn't lack of support from senior leadership.

It isn't anything other than the fact that **we have taken the ministry away from God and made it our own.**

Once we do that, we *ought* to be stressed! There is no way we can create a smooth ministry on our own. Stress is a result of misplaced ownership. Once you discover this secret, it will transform your attitude, personal strength, health, and overall wellness, even in the midst of all the things your ministry may genuinely be lacking.

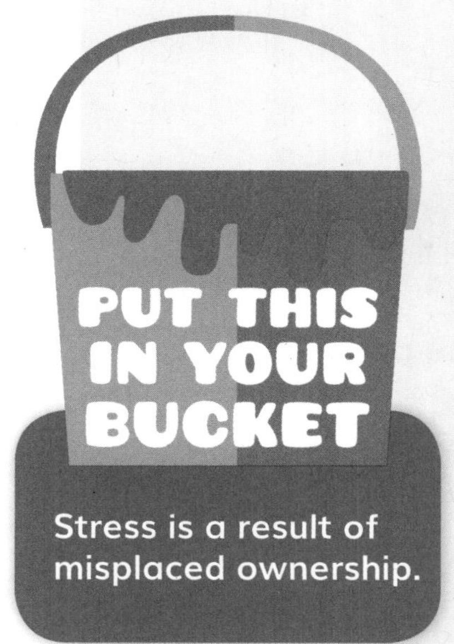

Stress is a result of misplaced ownership.

How do you do this? How do you turn off stress and turn on complete trust in God to run your ministry when there is so much to do?

1. Get it into your head, the ministry is not yours. It belongs to God.

Let me state this as clearly as I can: The children's ministry you lead is *not your ministry*.

This might be something to which you can immediately nod your head and say, "Sure, of course, I know that." However, you have to believe it through and through. Then act on that conviction.

Your ministry belongs to God:

- He started it.
- He will sustain it.
- He is quite capable of running it without you.

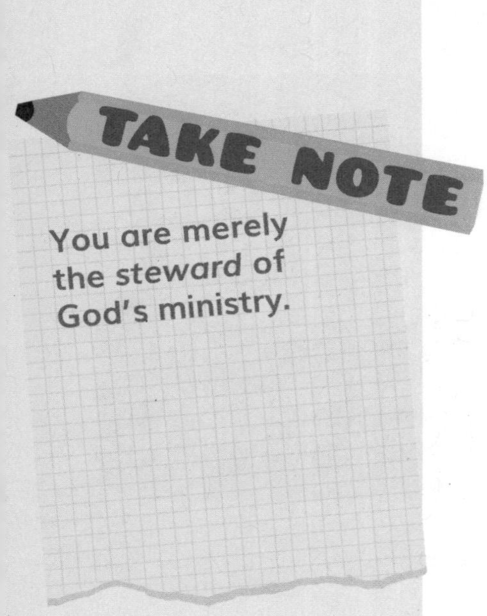

When you stress over your ministry, you take the ministry away from God and make it your responsibility to solve its problems.

As a result, when problems remain unsolved, you feel as if you have failed, or worse, that God has failed you. You operate as though God works for you as a volunteer in your children's ministry, rather than as the very present owner and manager of the ministry.

How you act on and implement this fact can have a profound impact on your ministry.

You Are a Steward of God

This can't be overstated. The day you begin to feel underappreciated, taken for granted, frustrated, or feel like a failure is the day you cease to allow God to run his children's ministry. If you take the ministry from God, you become a hindrance to what he wants to accomplish.

Naturally, I am not suggesting you can just sit in your office and be on social media while God runs the ministry. For a steward, there is work to do, and plenty of it. At the end of day, after you've done your best, the results are up to God.

We often turn ourselves into the protector (or savior) of programs. If God wants a program to launch or continue, he will provide the leadership and workers. If he doesn't, it may be his way of suggesting something. The Bible doesn't lay out programs that we must have, it just calls us to make disciples and reach the lost. Programs are fine as long as they are a means to an end.

For example, Vacation Bible Schools are a wonderful program. Many kids are led to Christ, and they create

DON'T DO IT!

If you take the ministry from God, you become a hindrance to what he wants to accomplish.

lifelong memories for children. But if you can't get a VBS director, instead of despairing, see this as God not raising up a leader. Consider that perhaps it is time to try a new approach to summer outreach.

I could share many stories of times when I let the ministry be God's. And God always did a better job than I could have! The bottom line is if you are stressed over your ministry, you might be out of touch with something God is trying to do in *his* ministry. If he is in something, he will provide!

2. Let others hear you talk about the ministry as God's

When you talk about the ministry as God's ministry and not allow yourself to be the prescription for everything that goes wrong, people will begin to respond.

People will let you do anything you are willing to do. Most people will assume that you can do a better job than they can. Even people who have felt God leading them to do something won't immediately step forward to volunteer.

Out of fear, nervousness, or humility, they will wait to see if anyone else steps up first. If you decide, "Oh, I'll just do it," they will let you. Then you will never know the volunteer of God's choosing. And, you've robbed them of the opportunity to be blessed by serving God's purposes.

Many times, right after I've announced the cancellation of a program because God had not provided a leader, someone has stood up to volunteer. If you truly believe it is God's ministry and you act accordingly, you will see him work in ways you never could!

Maybe it is time for you to give your ministry back to God.

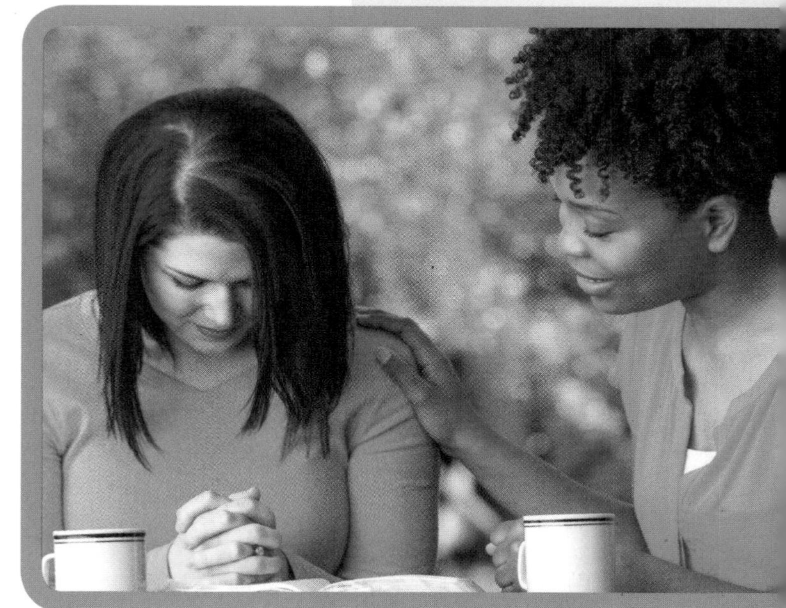

PUT THIS IN YOUR BUCKET

Be Grateful for Your Role.

Often, leaders who are frustrated by an apparent lack of support from their leaders, fail to realize that the existence of their position is a form of support that is often overlooked. Expressions of thanks followed by a need for something to be more effective, will usually work better than accusations about not caring for the children. **It is not so much what you ask as how you ask that gets the best results.**

Here are some steps that might help:

- **Give the ministry back to God in prayer.** Consider writing it out so you can be thoughtful and thorough. Confess acting like it is your job to fix stuff and run everything. Confess it if you have treated God like a volunteer who needed to bless your plans and solve your problems.
- **Thank God for placing you as the steward of his ministry.** Think about all the good things happening, and thank him for them—the children, faithful workers, a heritage of ministry, supportive leaders, and your position.
- **Make a list of the needs in God's ministry and pray about them.** Rather than demanding, "God, do this," or, "God, change that," or, "God, provide this." Ask, "God, what are you doing? These are the needs I perceive, but I'm trusting you to reveal your plans through answers to prayer."
- **After giving the results of these things to God, make a list of the things you can do to work on them as God's steward.** What visits, calls, or announcements can you make? How can you advertise, promote, or communicate the needs? Who can you invite to pray with you, for

NO MORE MAKING TIME FOR FAMILY!

For decades, I always made time for my family. I tried to make the most of days off of work, I planned date nights, and I tried to always be available for important family events and holidays.

What I painfully discovered was that I had it completely backward! I was not supposed to be making time for family, my family was supposed to be my life. What I needed to do was make time for ministry out of my valuable family time. Granted, work will demand a lot of time—but it's a mindset. Am I eager to get back to work, or am I eager to get back to my family?

you, and for these needs? Pick up some tools, and with God's leadership and help, get to work.

As we keep or break the Sabbath day, we nobly save or meanly lose the last best hope by which man rises.

Abraham Lincoln

- **Watch for what God is up to!** For the things that God doesn't seem to be answering, pray and think about what God could be up to. Testing your trust? Suggesting a new strategy? Asking for changes?

You Have a Choice:

Option One: You can lead your ministry feeling overwhelmed with all that there is to do. You'll feel constantly like you are behind and falling short of what you'd like to accomplish. Or . . .

Option Two: You can give the ministry back to God. Work hard with the calm assurance that you can only do what you can do, and the rest is up to God. You'll develop a sense of peace and eager anticipation of what God is going to do as you follow his lead. Watch the amazing things he will do. If something doesn't get done, accept that he is up to something greater and will bring everything to fruition in his perfect time.

The Tool of Rest

Asking Sabbath What?

Why did God rest on the seventh day of creation?

- Was he exhausted?
- Did he need a break?
- Was he brainstorming what he might do next?

It is hopefully pretty obvious that God did not rest because he was tired. He was demonstrating the importance of rest by modeling it from the very first week of creation.

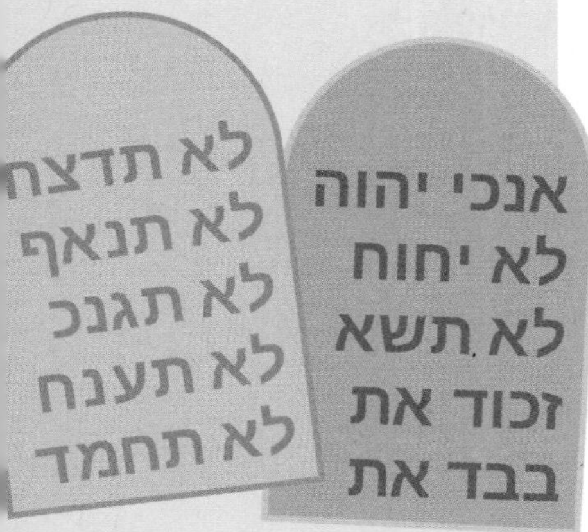

In his loving wisdom, God created a world where rest is an integral part of the overall plan. It wasn't just a necessity, it was a gift. He even included it in the Ten Commandments.

Each Commandment is critical for a happy life. But only two commandments say what to do rather than what not to do. This commandment, to remember the Sabbath and keep it holy, is one of these two proactive commandments. For our own health, God commands that we make rest a regular—in fact, weekly—part of our life.

Violating the Sabbath principle is the number one sin that children's ministry leaders commit. It is often committed without any guilt because they have sacrificed it for the greater good, the hard work of the ministry.

The honest reality is that we need the Sabbath. We need rest. Without it, we end up working unhealthy hours, neglecting

KEEPING SHARP

Have you heard the story of the new lumberjack who, on his first day, bragged about how many trees he could cut in one day? An older, more experienced lumberjack challenged him to a competition. They headed off into the woods. They determined they would both cut all day, meeting only at lunch and at the end of the day to compare how many trees each had felled. "Be prepared to lose!" The young newcomer warned the old timer.

They headed off in opposite directions within earshot of each other. Both set to work. The younger man chopped away and could hear the old timer in the distance working as well. As tree after tree came crashing down, he noticed that from time to time the old timer's ax swings went silent. At lunch, he was eager to see his progress and compare it to the older man's.

They met at noon and exchanged their count. As he had suspected, the younger man had cut far more trees than the older one. Yet the veteran lumberjack seemed unaffected by the news, and after lunch they each continued. Again, the young man heard the elder lumberjack's ax fall silent for portions our families, and neglecting our own spiritual health. We replace our love for God with a love for working for God.

AN EXPERT OPINION

Come to me, all of you who are weary and carry heavy burdens, and I will give you rest. Take my yoke upon you. Let me teach you, because I am humble and gentle at heart, and you will find rest for your souls. For my yoke is easy to bear, and the burden I give you is light.

Matthew 11:28–30

I know this because for far too many years, I had no time for a Sabbath. There was simply too much to do. The end result was a season where I was so empty and depleted that I needed a season out of ministry to heal myself and my family. I determined during that season of rest and restoration that I would never again make the ministry more important than my own spiritual walk, my family, friendships, and, dare I say, other recreational enjoyments that God wanted me to enjoy. Just like the lumberjack below, I need to pace myself.

Making time for rest and honoring the Sabbath takes work. You have to be ruthless about it. You will need to say no to good things. You may even have to disappoint people once in a while.

of time and thought to himself, "I am wearing the old man out, as he is obviously stopping to rest." The young man pressed on to increase his score.

The day wore on, the heat got intense, but the young man continued nonstop to fell tree after tree. When the day was finally complete, they met again to compare their totals. To the young man's great surprise, the older lumberjack had far exceeded the number of trees he had cut.

Dumbfounded, he asked, "How is that possible? I toiled nonstop all day, and I heard you stop constantly to rest. I assumed you were exhausted and needed to stop and recover."

The veteran smiled and replied, "Oh, I did enjoy the rest, but I didn't stop because I was exhausted. I stopped to sharpen my blade."

We have the same choice in ministry. We can work tirelessly as though we are in some competition with other ministries or stop regularly to sharpen ourselves. In the long run, we will be far more successful if we pace ourselves and take time to rest.

But if you prioritize rest:

- You will have more energy.
- You will focus on the things that matter most with the limited availability you have.
- You will enjoy more that life has to offer
- You will be pleasing your Creator who designed you for more than work.

God created you to enjoy life and to enjoy it abundantly!

When is the last time you stopped working and took some time to simply rest? God designed you to work best when you rest well. Determine that you will work only as much as God asks and nothing more. Of course, there are seasons for harder work—special events and week-long outreaches—but there should be exceptions to the normal pace of work, and be balanced by extra rest.

Never forget that Jesus said in Matthew 11:30,

For my yoke is easy to bear, and the burden I give you is light.

If your load feels heavy, it is likely you are attempting more than he is asking of you.

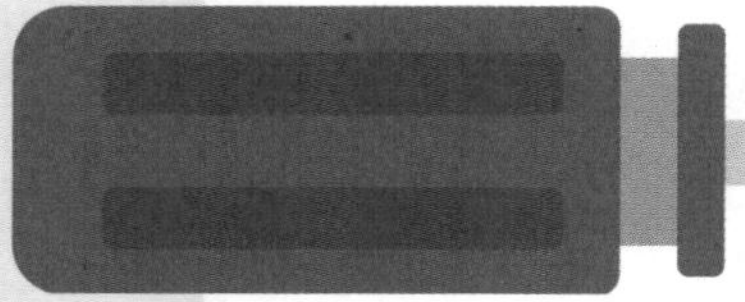

The Tool of Gratitude

Cultivating an Attitude of Gratitude

Why did God rest on the seventh day of creation? When November rolls around, bringing the Thanksgiving holiday, we suddenly find ourselves reflecting on gratitude, perhaps even teaching lessons about it. But November isn't the only time we need to focus on gratitude.

There is never a time in children's ministry when we have everything we want or need. There are always volunteer or resource needs and other desires that we pray for to advance the ministry.

That is simply part of being the overseer of a construction site. This is normal, and it will never cease to be true.

While problems and challenges must be addressed, as leaders, we must make sure that they never overshadow the many things that are going well.

A leader who has not developed an attitude of gratitude will continually be in a state of lacking. They will be frustrated and irritable because their focus is on what they need or want instead of on celebrating what they have.

We have an amazing promise from God in Philippians 4:19:

This same God who takes care of me will supply all your needs from his glorious riches, which have been given to us in Christ Jesus.

A key word in this verse is *needs*. God always provides what we need, when we need it, in the correct amount. When it appears he isn't, we need to adjust our expectations. We often confuse *wants* with *needs*.

I'd love to have a children's ministry overflowing with volunteers. I'd love to have extra money in my budget at the end of the year. I'd love to have more kids than I know what to do with. But when I don't have what I want, I ask myself, "What is God trying to teach me?" Dependence? Trust? Patience? Perhaps there is a new approach he is nudging me to try?

My favorite verse on prayer is also found in Philippians. In fact, just a few verses before the above-mentioned verse. Paul writes in Philippians 4:6:

Don't worry about anything; instead, pray about everything. Tell God what you need, and thank him for all he has done.

This powerful verse contains some hidden nuggets of truth.

TAKE NOTE

List ten things you are grateful for in your present ministry. Try to think of things beyond the obvious. What are some of your unique blessings?

1. ____________________

2. ____________________

3. ____________________

4. ____________________

5. ____________________

6. ____________________

7. ____________________

8. ____________________

9. ____________________

10. ____________________

Do we ever feel anxious in ministry? We do! But this verse clearly tells us that we shouldn't. It doesn't say, "Don't worry about too much," or, "only worry about the big things, don't sweat the little things." No, it says all too clearly not to worry about *anything*. Not about volunteers, budgets, supplies, facility issues . . . anything.

Don't Just Pray about It

Philippians 4:6 then goes on to give the secret to not being nervous or worried: prayer. But it says a lot more than just pray about it. It gives two secrets to prayer that alleviate anxiety.

We aren't just to pray. We are to pray with both *prayer* and *petition*. We are good at petitions. When I teach kids, I say, "Petition is when you ask for stuff." But this verse says by prayer *and* petition.

It separates asking for stuff from prayer. Yes, we are to ask for what we need. Petition is included. But then what is prayer that *isn't* petition? Could that be simply talking to God? And listening to him too? When we talk to God about our ministry, and make space to listen to him, we may find that he changes what we ask for.

Then comes the real gem.

In the normal course of life, we ask for things, and then, *after we get them*, we say thank you. This isn't wrong; it is normal. But in this little verse, tucked into this short book, God places a secret. He says to ask *with thanksgiving*. We are to have an attitude of gratitude even before he answers!

When I show this to kids, I challenge them to try it on their parents. Instead of saying, "Mom, can I go to my friend's house to play?" Say, "Mom, I'd like to go to my friend's house to play, but I just want to say thank you for whatever you decide, as I know you want what's best for me."

Instead of, "Dad, can I have five bucks for some snacks?" Try, "Dad, thanks for how you take such good care of me and give me everything I need. Any chance that might include five dollars for a snack?"

Do you see the difference? One request is self-centered, the other is centered on the giver and accepts whatever answer comes. Not only might a kid get better results from mom and dad, it will change how we ask and receive from our Creator.

Instead of, "God, I'm losing it here. If I don't get more volunteers soon, I'm going to quit."

Try, "God, you know I'm weary. I know you love these children and that this is your ministry. Thank you for giving me this way to serve you and for sustaining me through difficult times. I would love to share this work with some others so they, too, can experience how wonderful your kids are and how fulfilling it is to share you with them. Thank you for being my strength and for building a team around me and these kids. I can't wait to see who you bring next to our children's ministry. If I'm overlooking something or someone, please open my eyes. I want what you want for these children."

Do you see the difference? When we ask with thanksgiving, we are acknowledging:

- That the ministry belongs to God
- That he is in control
- That he will provide for his children

It establishes that we are merely stewards and that God is secure upon the throne and is interested in building us as much as he is in building the ministry.

Before you ask for anything, take time to notice what God has already done, and thank him. Then, by both prayer and petition, present your needs to him with thanksgiving. Guess what happens? Philippians 4:7 verse tells you:

Then you will experience God's peace, which exceeds anything we can understand. His peace will guard your hearts and minds as you live in Christ Jesus.

And that's something every children's ministry leader could use!

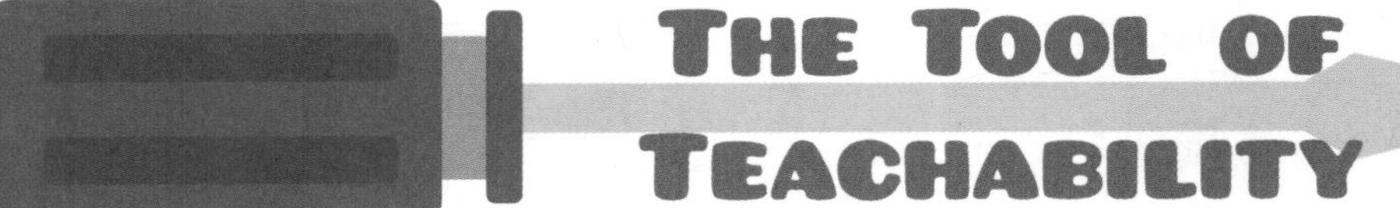

The Tool of Teachability

Handling Personal Criticism

One of the most valuable tools you could ever pick up is one that many overlook. Many neglect to keep it in their toolbox assuming it is only for beginners. The reality is, the longer you are in ministry, the sharper and more useful it needs to get! Teachability is something that comes naturally when we start out, but as we gain experience, it requires effort to maintain.

You may have heard it said, "If you want everyone to agree with you, say nothing," and, "if you want everyone to like you, do nothing." People will not always agree with your decisions. As much as you try to get input, build consensus, and move forward with a team approach, you will face criticism.

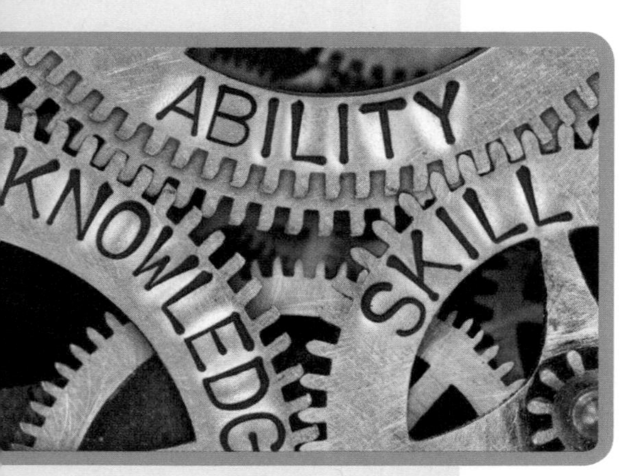

It may come from the leadership above you, the leaders around you, the volunteers who serve under you, the parents, or even random observers who have nothing to do with the children's ministry. Only the children will praise whatever you do. Thank God for the kids!

If we aren't teachable, criticism will discourage us and rob us of the joy that fuels our ministry. Some of the critiques will be fair, but much of it will be ill-informed, unfair, and at times just plain mean. How do

we deal with that? What do you do when the source of the judgment isn't someone you trust or feel has a right to judge?

What is worse is when they make statements without understanding the full situation. Some of what they say may be true, but they miss the broader picture.

Our tendency is to get defensive. The tool of teachability enables a different response.

AN EXPERT OPINION

Let your conversation be gracious and attractive so that you will have the right response for everyone.

Colossians 4:6

Receive It with Grace

First of all, ignore whether or not the person providing the criticism offered it in love or not. As builders, we want criticism! We want any input that will make the ministry bigger or better. So the attitude with which it was given is irrelevant. We can dismiss attitude or delivery with grace.

Even if it is given in anger or for less than noble motivations, we will graciously forgive the person, knowing that God can still use the information to build up the ministry. Choose to thank them sincerely for their feedback. The beauty is that your kind response may surprise them, and that alone may move them toward learning to be more gracious.

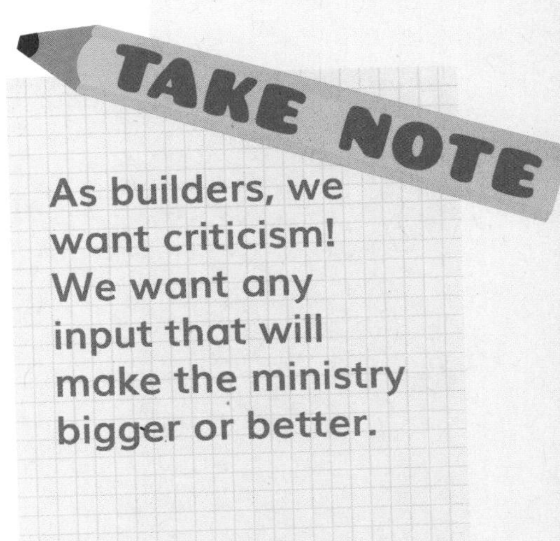

Seek It Out

Don't avoid conflict. Seek out difficult conversations. They won't just go away. We need to resolve them.

Whether:

- Someone says something negative directly to us
- We hear a disparaging remark secondhand

- We get a zinger email
- Someone makes a passing comment on Sunday morning

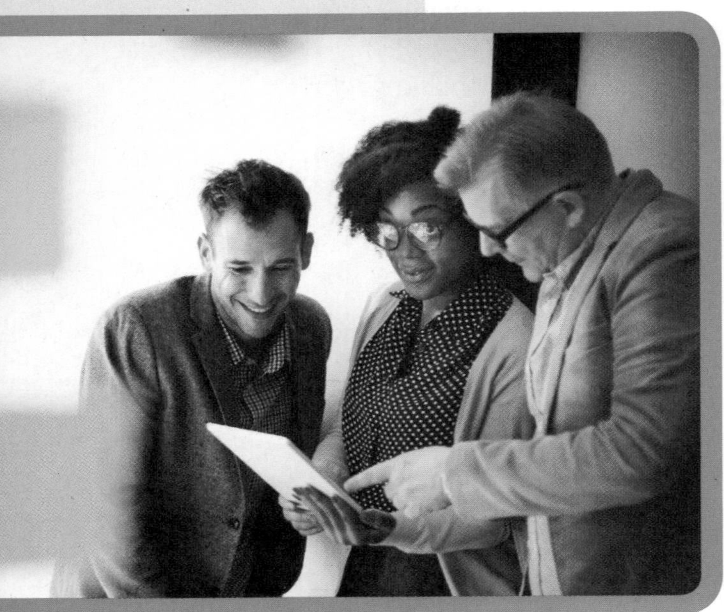

We should ask to meet to discuss it. Never attempt to resolve conflict over text message or email. Even a phone call isn't ideal. In-person confrontation is best. Not only can you hear the tone of voice, but you can see facial expression and even body language. (A real hug trumps an emoji any day!)

If disrespectful criticism happens publicly, politely ask for a private conversation later and refuse to engage at the moment. If you sense it will be contentious, invite a third person, who is mutually respected by both of you, to join the conversation—perhaps a fellow leader or staff member. Avoid including the senior pastor as it usually escalates the situation and can appear as a power play rather than as a neutral party.

In your meeting, be sure to start by asking questions. Make every effort to listen more than you talk. Your natural desire is to be understood. Instead, the goal is for you to understand and to learn. My father often encouraged me, "Even if they are ninety-eight percent wrong and only two percent right, learn the two percent, and you will be two percent better." The reality is that the percentage they are right is probably much higher than two percent.

When we are in a conflict situation as leaders, we are often quick to want to show people how they were wrong. What we need to realize is that while the *facts* may have been wrong, their *perception* is what is important. So even if they are one hundred percent wrong, you still need to be asking yourself as you listen, "How did they get this perception?" *You have a learning opportunity here.*

- Your goal is not to win the conversation. It is to learn and to gain back their trust and confidence.

- Your goal is not to change minds. It is to learn. Listen and then thank them. This will surprise and disarm them.

Yes, you can explain your thinking and reasons, but do not be defensive. This is critical. At the end, they will be wondering if they have damaged their relationship with you. Conclude by asking them if you can seek their advice again in the future.

Indirect Criticism

When you have heard criticism indirectly, it is more difficult to deal with. Like a weed, it must be pulled or it will spread. If you don't know the source, deal with it publicly at your leadership or volunteer meetings. Don't hesitate to say, "I've heard there is some concern with this decision. I'd like to hear your thoughts. I'm open to ideas as we address this challenge."

If you do know the source, be brave and graciously approach them. However, do not accuse by saying, "I heard you said . . ." Simply ask their opinion on the matter and give them an opportunity to express their thoughts. They may wonder if you heard their complaints, but regardless, they will have had an opportunity to express their opinion directly to you. At the end, thank them and assure them, "You can always bring your concerns directly to me. I want to know your thoughts. I value them."

Love Your Critics

"Keep your friends close and your enemies closer" applies in ministry, too. We might not consider people in our ministry enemies, but unaddressed criticism is an enemy, even from the nicest person.

"Even if they are ninety-eight-percent wrong and only two-percent right, learn the two percent, and you will be two percent better."

Conflict can't be avoided in ministry. We must be proactive and seek to stamp out vague uncertainties in ministry wherever they may be. Be bold and talk through conflicts. As respect and understanding grow, conflict will be minimized.

Surprisingly, some of your biggest critics will become some of your biggest supporters as they will come to see that you value their input. They will marvel at how you are constantly coming to them for advice. Your best advisers are those who disagree with you most often. They are the ones you can trust to be the most honest with you. If you only ask for input from friends and fans, you might be missing out on some valuable perspectives when you are making important decisions.

We don't enjoy personal criticism, but the reality is we need it. And smart leaders seek it!

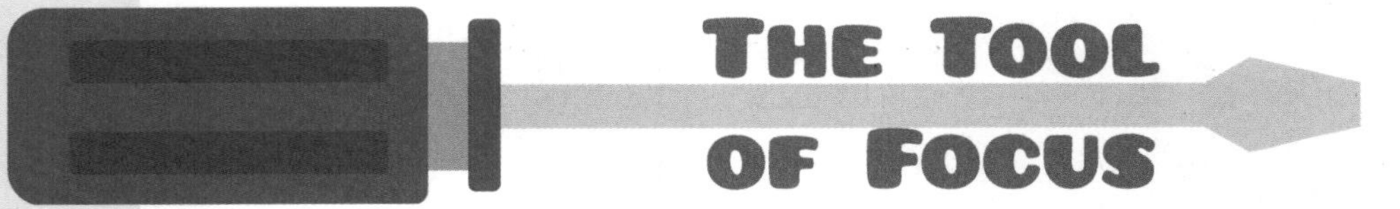

Writing Your Own Job Description

Without looking ahead, take a few moments and jot down the first things that come to mind when you think about why you went into children's ministry:

____

____

____

____

____

Now, jot down, honestly, what fills most of your time as a leader in children's ministry:

____

____

____

____

____

Let me guess—these lists are very different, aren't they?

Most children's ministry leaders go into ministry because they love children. They are great teachers, enjoy organizing events, or have a passion for evangelism. However, they soon find themselves buried in administration, organization, communication, marketing, endless meetings, and lots of other ministry minutia.

There is a reason many children's ministry leaders don't last. Some return to being volunteers because they miss just being able to be with the kids. While that is an option, it isn't the only way to keep doing what you love. What is needed is the tool of focus. (As well as the Tools of Teamwork and Delegation which we will get into later in this book.)

One of the most powerful tools in your ministry toolbox is the tool of focus. You could even call it the "No" Tool, but I prefer to use positive terminology.

You have incredible power over your daily routine and ministry priorities. And you have incredible power of choice over where you focus your time and energy. You can't do everything. If you try, you'll end up only getting done what others ask of you. You will never get to do the things that you enjoy most and that God has called you do.

Perhaps you have heard the classic story of the big rocks. If not, you are going to love it. And if you have, it is worth hearing again. It is something you will struggle to apply the rest of your life, or else you will live your entire life with regret.

There once was a professor who wanted to teach his class a lesson on time management. He brought out in front of the class a large, clear, plastic box, approximately four feet square. He then brought out a wheel barrow loaded with giant rocks and asked a volunteer to put as many as he could into the clear box until the volunteer felt it was full. Once the student declared it was full, the professor brought out a wheel barrow filled with stones and had another student add those until she thought it was full.

Once she decided the box was now filled completely, the professor wheeled out a wheel barrow filled with gravel. Another student worked to pour the gravel into the box, filling all the extra space until he declared the box was finally full. But the professor just responded by bringing in several bags of sand. When a volunteer was done pouring bag after bag of sand into the box, the students thought the box was finally full, but the professor had one more surprise.

He pulled in a garden hose from outside and turned it on, pouring an amazing amount of water into the box until finally the top started to overflow. Then he turned it off, declaring that only now was the box finally full. Then he announced that the topic of the day was time management and asked what this object lesson demonstrated.

An eager student raised his hand and declared, "There is always room for more!" The professor frowned and replied, "No. What it illustrates is that if we don't put the large rocks in first, we'll never be able to fit them later."

The point is obvious. The challenge is identifying the giant rocks in our life and ministry and then placing them first.

Let me challenge you to consider what the giant rocks are in your life. Don't just think about ministry, think about your personal life too. What are the things that must be placed first? Write some of them here:

____

____

____

____

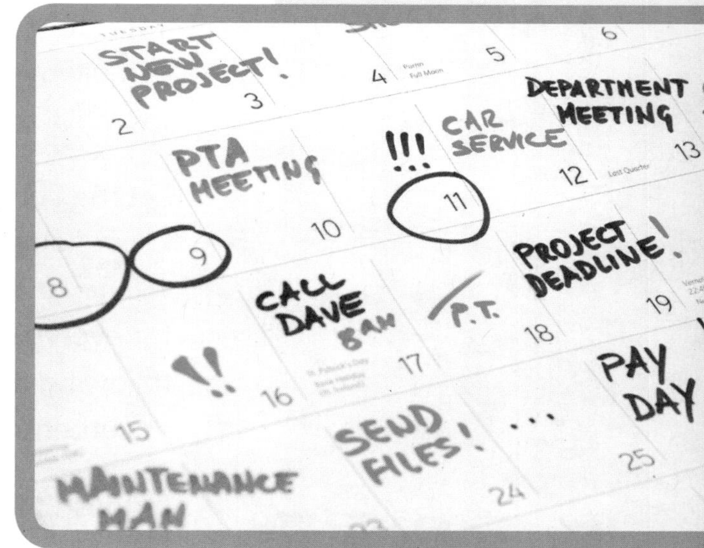

Next, is the hard part. **Schedule them into your life.** Years ago, I heard a pastor say, "If you want to know what is important to someone, you don't ask them, you look at their checkbook and their calendar." In other words, it isn't what we say that counts, it is where we spend our time and money that reflect what is truly important to us.

At the end of the day, we can't blame our church, our pastor, our volunteers, our job, or anyone else if we are missing out on what matters most. We will have only ourselves to blame. In Andy Stanley's book *Choosing to Cheat*, he emphasizes that in life we have to cheat *someone.* It is just a matter of deciding who we are going to cheat. Unfortunately, we tend to cheat our families and ourselves the most in order to avoid cheating the church.

KEEPING SHARP

"If you want to know what is important to someone, you don't ask them, you look at their checkbook and their calendar."

When doing workshops at conferences, I will often ask a room full of children's ministry leaders, "How many of you have said no to your family for the sake of the church?"

Every hand will go up. When I reverse it and ask, "How many of you have said no to the church for the sake of your family?" very few hands go up.

Why are we so quick to sacrifice our families and so slow to sacrifice the church?

- Are we concerned with job security?
- Will we really get fired if we miss a meeting or cancel an event?
- Perhaps we are more concerned with how we will be perceived?
- And yet we are less concerned with how our family perceives us?

It is time to sharpen your tool of focus! Choose what is most important in your job. Do that first. What you don't get to can always be done next week. And the things you never get to? Well, they probably weren't that important anyway.

Let me challenge you to write your own job description. I know you got one when you were hired, but most likely, it will never be looked at again. Granted, you are responsible for everything in there—and you should make sure you are following it. But what I'm referring to is a functioning, living document that determines how you actually spend your time.

It doesn't have to be long. In fact, it should be short. But it should list, in priority order, what is important to you and how you will spend your limited and valuable time.

- Things that aren't on your list, you should delegate
- Things you aren't good at, recruit others to do for you
- Things that aren't that important, postpone until later, or even indefinitely

Above all, make sure your big rocks are at the top of the list.

Write Your Own Job Description

What are the TOP 3 THINGS that are the most important for you to accomplish each week:

1.

2.

3.

What are the NEXT 3 PRIORITIES you need to focus on each week?

1.

2.

3.

What are the NEXT 3 THINGS you should look at every other week?

1.

2.

3.

What important tasks should you delegate to someone else to oversee?

1.

2.

3.

What should be given annual attention?

1. ____

During what month(s)? ____________

2. ____

During what month(s)? ____________

3. ____

During what month(s)? ____________

What areas of responsibility need help?

1.

2.

3.

Self-Evaluation Form

Today's Date: ____________

Don't wait for the boss. Give yourself an honest performance review.

In each of the categories below, rate yourself on a scale of 1 through 10 (1 being the lowest and 10 the highest). Be honest; this is for your eyes only. There is an optional space for comments if you want to add explanation for future reference. Consider doing this annually to compare progress.

Spiritual Life

Time in the Word	1 – 2 – 3 – 4 – 5 – 6 – 7 – 8 – 9 – 10
Time in Prayer	1 – 2 – 3 – 4 – 5 – 6 – 7 – 8 – 9 – 10
Time in Worship (not job related)	1 – 2 – 3 – 4 – 5 – 6 – 7 – 8 – 9 – 10
Time in Service (not job related)	1 – 2 – 3 – 4 – 5 – 6 – 7 – 8 – 9 – 10
Time in Rest/Solitude	1 – 2 – 3 – 4 – 5 – 6 – 7 – 8 – 9 – 10

Comments: ____

____

Self-Discipline

Exercise	1 – 2 – 3 – 4 – 5 – 6 – 7 – 8 – 9 – 10
Diet	1 – 2 – 3 – 4 – 5 – 6 – 7 – 8 – 9 – 10
Personal Hobbies	1 – 2 – 3 – 4 – 5 – 6 – 7 – 8 – 9 – 10
Family Time	1 – 2 – 3 – 4 – 5 – 6 – 7 – 8 – 9 – 10
Promptness/Office Time	1 – 2 – 3 – 4 – 5 – 6 – 7 – 8 – 9 – 10
Personal Organization	1 – 2 – 3 – 4 – 5 – 6 – 7 – 8 – 9 – 10

Comments: ____

____

ADMINISTRATION/ORGANIZATION

Office Work Environment	1 – 2 – 3 – 4 – 5 – 6 – 7 – 8 – 9 – 10
Electronic/File Management	1 – 2 – 3 – 4 – 5 – 6 – 7 – 8 – 9 – 10
Volunteer Processing	1 – 2 – 3 – 4 – 5 – 6 – 7 – 8 – 9 – 10
Visitor Follow-Up	1 – 2 – 3 – 4 – 5 – 6 – 7 – 8 – 9 – 10
Team Management	1 – 2 – 3 – 4 – 5 – 6 – 7 – 8 – 9 – 10
Curriculum/Volunteer Needs	1 – 2 – 3 – 4 – 5 – 6 – 7 – 8 – 9 – 10
Resources/Supplies	1 – 2 – 3 – 4 – 5 – 6 – 7 – 8 – 9 – 10
Special Events/Planning	1 – 2 – 3 – 4 – 5 – 6 – 7 – 8 – 9 – 10

Comments: ______________________________

____

COMMUNICATION

Family	1 – 2 – 3 – 4 – 5 – 6 – 7 – 8 – 9 – 10
Friends	1 – 2 – 3 – 4 – 5 – 6 – 7 – 8 – 9 – 10
Work Office	1 – 2 – 3 – 4 – 5 – 6 – 7 – 8 – 9 – 10
Leaders/Volunteers	1 – 2 – 3 – 4 – 5 – 6 – 7 – 8 – 9 – 10
Parents/Children	1 – 2 – 3 – 4 – 5 – 6 – 7 – 8 – 9 – 10

Comments: ______________________________

____

RECRUITING, TRAINING, AND RETAINING LEADERS & VOLUNTEERS

Recruiting Leaders and Volunteers	1 – 2 – 3 – 4 – 5 – 6 – 7 – 8 – 9 – 10
Retaining Leaders and Volunteers	1 – 2 – 3 – 4 – 5 – 6 – 7 – 8 – 9 – 10
Training Leaders and Volunteers	1 – 2 – 3 – 4 – 5 – 6 – 7 – 8 – 9 – 10
Leaders/Volunteers	1 – 2 – 3 – 4 – 5 – 6 – 7 – 8 – 9 – 10
Parents/Children	1 – 2 – 3 – 4 – 5 – 6 – 7 – 8 – 9 – 10

Comments: ______________________________

____

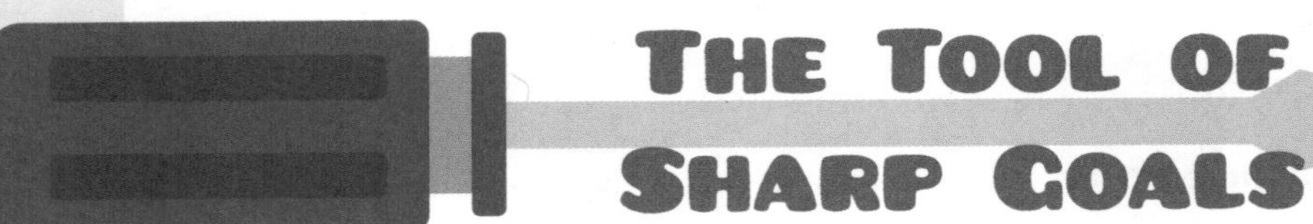

The Tool of Sharp Goals

Keeping Your Goals SHARP

I'm sure you've heard the saying, "If you aim at nothing, you are sure to hit it." Most people agree that goals are essential to success, yet the majority of people don't make goals. Why is this? Perhaps it is fear of failure or simply not wanting accountability. But if we want to see our ministry grow—if we want to build something that will last—we must make goals!

If you fail to plan, you plan to fail.

Vision and mission are critical to a ministry's success, and we will discuss the Tools of Vision and Mission later. But know now that without goals, both vision and mission are difficult to bring into reality. Evaluating your progress also becomes nearly impossible. Goals break down a grand vision into attainable action steps.

If big decisions are made of lots of little decisions, then big visions are made up of lots of little goals. Many leaders try to take the express elevator straight to the top floor of their vision, but they leave their team behind. Or perhaps they try to take the escalator, thinking they can take one bold step and it will carry them all the way up.

TAKE NOTE

Goals break down a grand vision into attainable action steps.

The reality is, a ministry vision will not become reality without taking the stairs one at a time. No building was ever built by building the upper floors first. The foundation may not be the most attractive part, and it may be invisible later, but you have to start at the bottom and work your way up. Goals enable steady progress forward and upward.

Goals vs. Good Intentions

Too often, people *think* they have set goals when, in reality, they have only stated direction or good intentions.

Imagine if I said my goal was to love my wife more. Doesn't that sound like a wonderful goal? My wife might even agree! However, that is not a goal. Why not? Well, how will I (or my wife) ever know whether I accomplished that goal?

Suppose I asked her after a month, "Do you feel more loved than you used to?" She would probably answer, "Uh, I think so." And I would be thinking, "I hope so." The problem is that while loving my wife more is a noble thing to attempt, there is no way to know whether I have succeeded. I can only trust that she appreciates my good intentions. Loving my wife more is not specific enough.

A goal is not a goal if it is not specific

Let's suppose I decide I want to love my wife more, so I am going to buy her a present. Then she will know that she is loved. Is that specific enough? Well, let's test it.

How will I know when I have accomplished my goal of buying her a present? What happens when someone asks me in a month, "Have you bought your wife a present yet?" If I have, then I have met my goal! But if I haven't, I can always say, "No, but I am going to!" So while I had a specific goal, it was not measurable—I could always claim that it is coming soon. (Much to my wife's disappointment!)

It may have been specific, but with no end in sight, you'll never know if I succeeded or not. Therefore,

A goal is not a goal unless it is both specific AND measurable

The best goals go even farther than just being specific and measurable. There are a few more factors that ensure they actually help you achieve what you are trying to accomplish.

You can buy a tool at a store where everything costs one dollar, or you can get one at a hardware store that is made by a trusted brand. What is the difference? You'll get one that might work poorly just once, or you'll get one with proven strength, experience, materials, and durability. Let's look at what makes goals that will last and get the job done right.

The Best Tools Are Sharp Tools

So I like to make **S.H.A.R.P.** goals!

Keeping Sharp

S.H.A.R.P. Goals Are:

Specific: They aren't vague generalities.

Healthy: They don't cost more than they are worth.

Adventurous: They aren't easy; they are a challenge!

Realistic: They aren't pipe dreams. They are actually possible.

Perceptual: They can be measured. You know when they are accomplished.

Specific

They aren't vague generalities.

Set goals that state clearly what you are going to accomplish and why. Don't make lofty generalities that either describe what you are already doing or leave you never quite sure if you are done. For example, "Reaching boys and girls for Christ" is not a goal. You are hopefully already doing that. "Until every child knows Jesus" isn't a goal either. Not sure you can really do that. But you may be able to "Share the Good News with one hundred kids who have never been to our church in the next twelve months."

Healthy

They don't cost more than they are worth.

It is wonderful to set great goals, but not wonderful if they negatively impact your personal walk with God, your marriage, your family, or even your ministry. Of course, you want to reach as many kids as possible with the Good News of Jesus. But setting a goal to share the gospel with so many children that you no longer have time for your own family will negate an otherwise noble ambition. Healthy goals don't cost more than they are worth. Your family will rejoice in them. You'll grow closer to God as a result of the pursuit rather than end up feeling strained in your relationships.

Adventurous

They aren't easy; they are a challenge!

While we all want to feel the joy of success, that doesn't mean we make our goals so easy that success is a sure thing. They ought to be a challenge. Start with what you know you can do, then add what you can do with God's help. You might even consider doing what you could accomplish with some faith. You want God-sized goals that will require trust in him. At the same time, you aren't trying to back God into a corner where he must perform a miracle to bail you out. I like to call these stretch goals. Not only do they stretch our expectations, they also stretch our faith.

Realistic

They aren't pipe dreams. They are actually possible.

Realistic goals are the balance to adventurous goals. If everyone thinks you can accomplish the goal, it likely isn't adventurous. If nobody thinks you can, it may not be realistic. A good goal lies somewhere in the middle. Only you can determine where that is. The answer lies with a plurality of wise counsel, prayer, and then making a decision. If you don't make a goal, that isn't a crisis. You adapt and adjust when you make your next goal based on what you learned. Rest assured, if you've set an adventurous yet realistic goal, you will have accomplished far more than if you made no goal at all.

Perceptual

They can be measured. You know when they are accomplished.

The final requirement for a sharp goal is to answer the question, "How will I know if I accomplished my goal?" Usually, this is based on time. There is a deadline when you will know whether or not you accomplished your goal. If it is an event (such as, "before the new senior pastor is hired"), rather than a calendar date, set some adjustable target dates. This way you aren't caught by surprise when something happens earlier than expected.

Be Flexible!

Yes! It is OK to adjust goals and deadlines as you go. Perhaps new information surfaces, and your goal isn't realistic. Adjust it. Perhaps you accomplish it so far ahead of schedule that it is clear it wasn't adventurous enough. Celebrate your success and make a new goal!

Adjusting goals means you are aware of progress or lack of progress. Without goals, you are just moving forward without any idea of whether you are behind or getting ahead! Remember, not hitting a goal is not failure. It is a tool to measure progress, and it is a valuable learning experience. Without goals, you have no way of knowing your progress.

Let's Practice

Making Some Goals!

I'm sure you've heard the saying, "If you aim at nothing, you are sure to hit it." Most people agree.

Goals for Your Ministry

Today's Date: ____________

Let's determine some goals for your ministry. This is just for practice, so don't stress over it. You can do this for real later—ideally with some other leaders.

1. Take several sheets of paper, and at the top of each, write in big, block letters an area of ministry. (Examples: Nursery, Sunday School, Children's Church, Club, Visitors, Facilities, etc.)

   Example: Visitors

2. Write a one paragraph description of what you wish that area of ministry looked like. (This is vision, which we will get into later in more detail.)

   Example: We want every visitor to be positively impressed when they enter the building, to quickly find where their children go, and to feel comfortable leaving their children. We want them to be able to find the worship center easily and relax during the service, knowing that we can find them if they are needed. We'd also like them to be pleasantly surprised when they pick up their child and to feel welcome and encouraged to come again.

3. Look through your description and underline key phrases that need action steps to become a reality. Break that description in sections as subpoints based upon key words you see in the vision. Leave a blank space between those.

EXAMPLE: We want every visitor to be positively impressed when they enter the building, to quickly find where their children go, and to feel comfortable leaving their children. We want them to be able to find the worship center easily and relax during the service, knowing that we can find them if they are needed. We'd also like them to be pleasantly surprised when they pick up their child and to feel welcome and encouraged to come again.

4. Under each subpoint, write some specific things that need to happen to bring that into reality. Afterward, add a due date, the resources needed, and the person assigned to the duty.

EXAMPLE: Resources and due date are not included in example, but they are needed in yours!

- positively impressed
  Banner in entrance; balloons?; greeter
- quickly find
  Maps of children's ministry area; host to take them to room(s); good signage
- feel comfortable
  Staff with name badges; smiles (training)
- find the worship center
  Good signage; worship center on map; host to take them there
- relax
  Beepers in nursery or number display in sanctuary; statement in bulletin about loving and trained staff.
- pleasantly surprised
  Take-home paper, pictures of happy kids on bulletin board / TV monitors; happy child (training)
- encouraged to come again
  Welcome packet; brochure about children's ministry; letter in mail; packet to child in mail with coupon for prize upon return

5. Write three goals that would bring some of these ideas into reality. Don't try to do everything at once. The point of goals is to pace yourself.

EXAMPLE:

- By the beginning of the next quarter, I will have someone take pictures of children in the classrooms laughing, smiling, or playing. Then they'll create three collage posters to display in the registration area so that visiting parents can get a glimpse of the fun experience their children are going to have in the children's ministry.
- I am going to put together a survey with ten questions centered around a new parent's experience visiting our church. I am going to give it to three couples who have attended the church for over five years, three couples who have been coming for less than a year, and to three families who visit and return. The survey will ask several perspectives on how we can do a better job on greeting them, registering their children, making them feel welcome and comfortable dropping off their kids, and how we can better communicate with them both on Sundays and during the week. The results should be collected and compiled within three months and submitted to the leadership team for discussion.
- Recruit someone to improve the overall appearance of the welcome and registration area for the children's ministry. The area needs to be cleaned up; unneeded and unused items removed, signs updated, and decorations improved to be bright, fun, and inviting. This is critical so we need this done in the next month.

In these sample goals:

- Can you identify the **S.H.A.R.P.** elements in each of these goals?
- Are any of the elements missing?
- What would you change, if anything?

KEEPING SHARP

S.H.A.R.P. Goals Are:

SPECIFIC: They aren't vague generalities.

HEALTHY: They don't cost more than they are worth.

ADVENTUROUS: They aren't easy; they are a challenge!

REALISTIC: They aren't pipe dreams. They are actually possible.

PERCEPTUAL: They can be measured. You know when they are accomplished.

Goals Worksheet

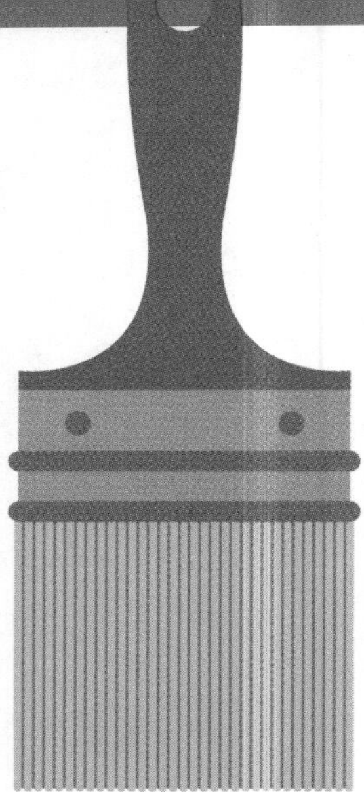

Area of ministry:

Description of how you would like your ministry to be:

Underline key words above, and then list them here:

Key Word or Phrase	Notes/Thoughts/Goals:

Make Three Goals:

Remember, this is just practice for now, though you are welcome to take it seriously!

1.

2.

3.

A New Tool Box

Cleaning Out Old Tools

Are you ready to get started? Many times, when I move into a new house, I go to the hardware supercenter and buy a shiny new tool box. It somehow helps me feel ready for the challenges this new home will present. I get out all my tools, remove duplicates, get rid of some old ones, and decide which ones need to be replaced. I might even buy a few new ones as I looked at the projects ahead. Nothing beats a cleaned-out tool box that's free of clutter and some brand new tools just itching to be used!

The tools we consider for building our children's ministry are conceptual rather than physical, and we store our tools in our minds and hearts. You have a ministry toolbox, and just like the one out in your garage, it likely needs a little attention before you begin this new adventure. It's time to sharpen some tools, toss some, and perhaps pick up a few new ones.

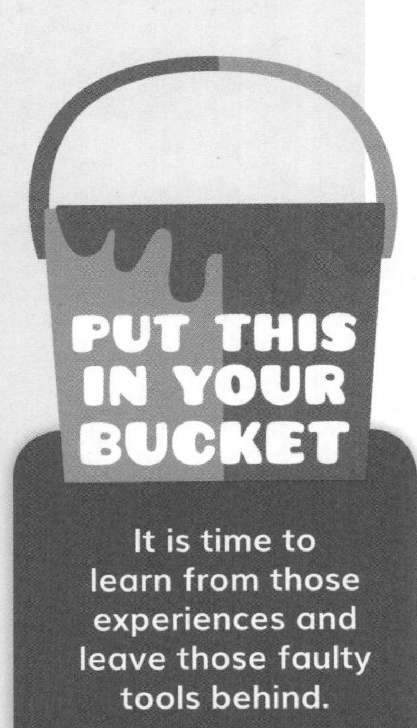

Perhaps there are some old tools that need to be discarded. You may have some past mistakes. It is time to learn from those experiences and leave those faulty tools behind. You'll want to operate much sharper going forward.

Many times over the years, I have coached leaders who shared with me that they face the same problems in every ministry. I have had to gently help them see that they were the common denominator in each situation. Often, we blame others for our problems, when the issue is a tool in our own hand.

Outdated Tools

You likely have some tools that are outdated. They did a great job in the past, but there are updated requirements to the building codes of today, and you'll need to step up the quality.

Timeless Tools

This isn't to say you should automatically toss any tool just because it is old. Some of the old tools are still the best and will always be essential. Just as there will always be hammers, screw drivers, and pliers, there are ministry tools that are timeless. Some are obvious, others will surprise you as we explore more tools in this book.

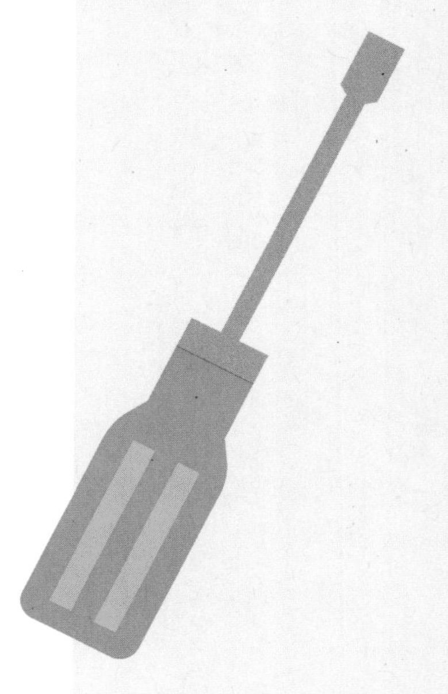

Super Do-Everything Tools

We also need to toss any of those "Super Do-Everything" tools we may have bought from an infomercial. Real work requires real tools. There are no shortcuts when it comes to quality work. While it may be tempting to keep the duct tape around, our objective isn't to make quick fixes. It is to repair things correctly and in a way that will last a long time.

Ministry Memory Tools

There may be a few tools that you hang onto because sentimentally they are attached to great ministry memories. But as time and methods change, some of those tools need to be tossed as well. We want our toolbox to be filled with current, practical, well-made, and sharp tools.

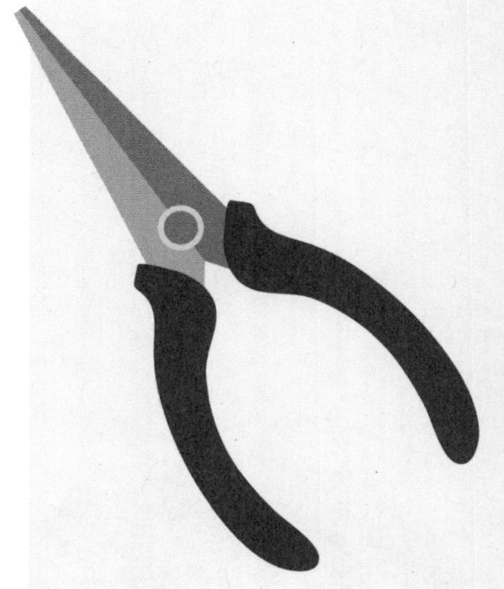

Human Nature Tools

Some of the tools we need to eliminate are simply the result of our fallible nature. Are we allowing tools, such as pride, to keep us from asking for help? Is the tool of self doubt keeping us from attempting bold things? For some, the tool of insecurity causes us to be unable to make decisions. Some of these old, rusty, negative tools have been in our toolbox for so long that we fail to recognize their presence. Some we grab instinctively as our go-to tool and fail to recognize how they are hindering our process.

Assess Your Tools

It is time to take a hard, honest assessment of our personal tools. We need to acknowledge, confess and get rid of the negative tools. They will often mysteriously reappear back in our toolbox, and we will need to toss them out again and again.

Let's make an assessment of your personal toolbox. There are three categories below.

TOOLS TO KEEP:

List the character traits, leadership skills, and talents that come to you naturally. These are the sharp tools that you already own. They don't require a lot of work to keep sharp. These are your strengths and what people already expect from you. While you can always improve, these skills take the least effort.

TOOLS TO TOSS:

These are the character traits, habits, or even sin issues that are threats to your building project. This is only for yourself, so an honest assessment is the best way to acknowledge and then keep an eye out for the things that are going to hinder your work.

TOOLS TO GET:

These tools are skills and character traits that you know you need to either add or improve for the sake of your ministry. They may either be nonexistent or be areas that need improvement.

Go to any giant bookstore or search online in the self-help section, and you'll find endless books telling you how to identify your strengths and talents. I have always marveled that there are not more books that help you discover your weaknesses. It is in discovering our weaknesses that we grow the most. Then we have a clear understanding of where we need to grow and the type of people we need to surround ourselves with.

The Tool of Prayer

Demonstrating Our Dependence on God

I could write an entire chapter on prayer, but I'm pretty sure you already have several books on your bookshelf about prayer. So let me just state one simple truth: Prayer is not only asking for help, it is a tangible demonstration of our dependence on God. If we do not pray, we tell God that we do not need him.

Begin this process of building or remodeling your children's ministry by asking God for his help and demonstrating to him that you actually do want his help.

Take Note

Hear this: God doesn't anoint plans, he anoints people. We don't submit our plans to God for approval. We submit to God to get his plan for our ministry.

Finishing Touches

Write out your prayer here, and then let's get started!

2: Leadership Tools

Introduction

Becoming a Proactive Leader

If you are the one placed in charge of a children's ministry, you are a leader. It doesn't matter whether you hold a paid or volunteer role, you have been entrusted to build the children's ministry and take it to the next level. What an honor!

You have an important choice: Are you going to be a fireman, responding to and putting out fires, or are you going to be a construction foreman who not only responds to needs but is building something?

There is a difference between a leader who reacts and one who advances the ministry. I sum this up in the charge to be a proactive leader. Proactive leaders are leaders with the initiative to see positive change happen.

Unless you are intentional, the weekly demands of ministry programs and needy volunteers can quickly push you into a role of being a *reactive leader*—constantly reacting to the needs that are presented to you via email, voicemail, and in person. You will be doing a lot of good, but you'll soon feel like the ministry isn't going anywhere—and you'll be right. It will be treading water, and it will be all you can do just to keep your nose above the surface.

Take Note

Proactive leaders are leaders with the initiative to see positive change happen.

You may be a servant leader, and that is a *good thing*—but if you want your ministry to improve, you must seek to become a *proactive leader*—one that is driving and determining their actions more than being driven by the endless demands that are constantly pouring in.

What does it mean to be a proactive leader?

It means you *lean into* the challenging situations that face you. A proactive leader returns that phone call on Monday rather than putting it off until Thursday hoping for an answering machine. They meet in person with someone when a phone call would be the easier way out of a tough conflict. They are the ones who choose to bring up the awkward topic in a meeting knowing it needs to be addressed.

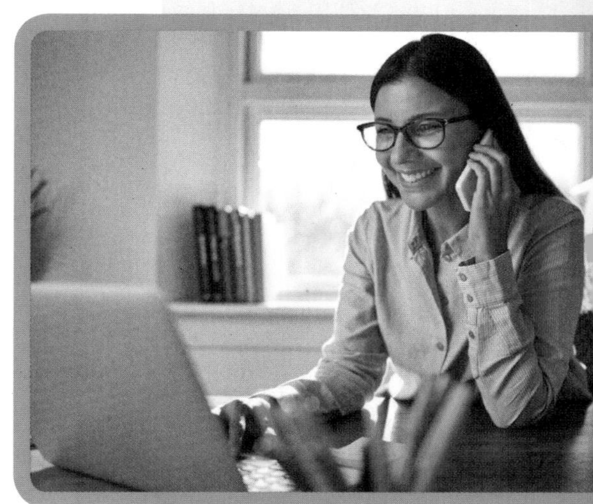

The proactive leader keeps short accounts by resolving conflicts quickly so that friendships are preserved and relationships are strengthened. They ask questions first and listen. They process without being defensive because they are more concerned with growing than they are with being right. They seek feedback and constructive criticism even when they think they are doing a great job. They are learners as much as they are doers.

Proactive leaders avoid the easy path and shortcuts because they have learned that neither are worth it.

When proactive leaders make a mistake, they point it out. They want others to learn from it and allow it to serve as an example the ministry can benefit from. If they have had a conflict or made a mistake to a degree that could be reported to their boss, they will be the first to give a heads up.

Take this as an example: "Pastor, just wanted you to know, today during children's church, we removed Mrs. Smith's child for hitting, and she was upset that we did so without finding her first. We made an effort, but felt due to the repeated offense and for the safety of the other children we needed to do so. When she came and didn't see her son, she was upset. You may be hearing from Mrs. Smith this week. Please let her know we are sorry for the confusion and the scare that gave her."

By telling the boss before Mrs. Smith does, you accomplish two things. First, if she calls, he is prepared to comfort and minister to her because he is aware of what she went through and can defend you because he already knows the situation. If she doesn't call, you've built credibility and trust with your pastor because you aren't waiting until things go wrong.

The proactive leader is a visionary.

Proactive leaders are not just looking at what needs to get done; they are looking ahead at what *could* be done. The proactive leader asks, "How could that be done better?"

- They are constantly trying to see the ministry through fresh eyes.
- They energize and excite volunteers by painting a clear picture of what the ministry could be.
- They react to the needs of now in the context of where they are going in the future.
- They exude energy and momentum.

Being a proactive leader isn't only more effective—it's more fun. Being reactive gets wearisome. Being proactive is energizing!

If you want to be a more proactive leader, start your day by praying, "Lord, who would you have me minister to this week? What would you have me move forward this week? What needs to be improved?" Then, make a short list of a few things you think need some proactive leadership. Jot down a few action steps to get them in motion.

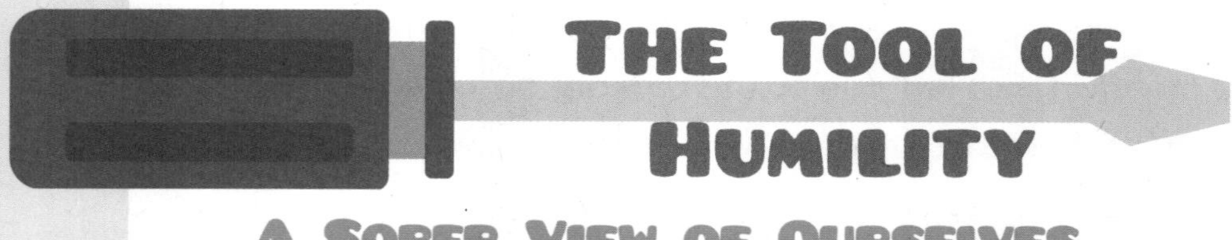

The Tool of Humility

A Sober View of Ourselves

It may surprise you that the first tool in the section on leadership appears to be more of a personal character trait. In fact, you may wonder if this chapter belongs in the previous section on personal tools. However, it is here quite strategically. While humility is certainly a personal character trait, it is the very first tool that a leader should have and one he or she should wield frequently.

Because of the privilege and authority God has given me, I give each of you this warning: Don't think you are better than you really are. Be honest in your evaluation of yourselves, measuring yourselves by the faith God has given us.

Romans 12:3

Humility happens to be one of the most misunderstood character traits of the Christian. When people picture a humble person, what often comes to mind is a quiet, unassuming Clark Kent type person who speaks softly and is full of self-doubt. Meekness and humility are often confused. Even meekness is often seen as weakness, when it is actually a great strength retrained for the sake of another.

On the other hand, someone who is bold, full of action, and confident can often be accused of being prideful. These misperceptions come from a lack of understanding of what biblical humility truly is. Humility is not the opposite of pride. Did you know that a humble person can be proud of their ministry?

Be Proud!

Before I tell you to be more humble, let me start by encouraging you to be proud! This may come as a surprise to many of you, but a healthy understanding of pride is critical to developing a biblical sense of humility, which is critical for a Christian leader.

I know. This isn't what you were expecting. You expect me to tell you to be humble. Yes, be humble. But be proud, too. How can I say that? There is a significant difference between pride that is sinful, which is arrogance, and pride that is an honest, positive measurement of oneself.

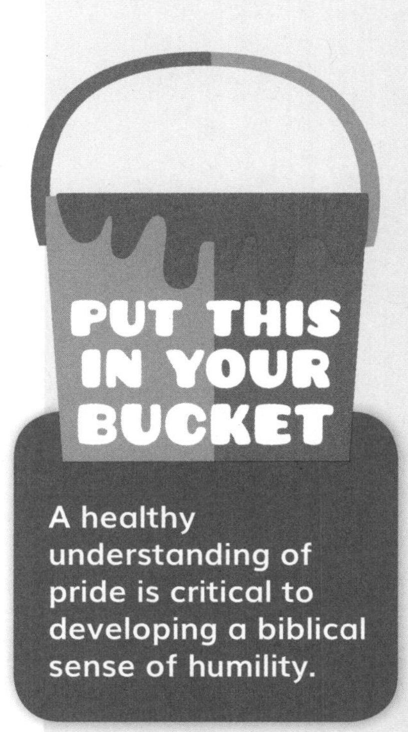

A healthy understanding of pride is critical to developing a biblical sense of humility.

The key to the difference depends on whether you are measuring yourself in comparison to others. Consider what Galatians 6:4 says:

Each one should test their own actions. Then they can take pride in themselves alone, without comparing themselves to someone else.

You see? As leaders, we *ought* to be considering whether we are doing a good job. When we test our own actions and know in our heart, "I hit that one out of the park," we can feel proud about it!

The bad kind of pride, which we are commanded to avoid, comes when we start thinking too highly of ourselves. The Bible warns about that to when it says in Romans 12:3,

If you are good at something, it's O.K. to be proud about it. It's when you start comparing yourself to others that arrogance sets in.

Because of the privilege and authority God has given me, I give each of you this warning: Don't think you are better than you really are. Be honest in your evaluation of yourselves, measuring yourselves by the faith God has given us.

You see, if you are good at something, it's OK to be proud about it. It's when you start comparing yourself to others that arrogance sets in, and the Bible has plenty to say about that, including the well-known verse from Proverbs 16:18,

Pride goes before destruction, and haughtiness before a fall.

This is especially important as leaders. Too often we start comparing our ministry to others and our ministry accomplishments to other churches. That is when we start moving into sinful territory. But we can and should be proud of the good work we do for the Lord. Need proof? Look what the Apostle Paul writes in 2 Corinthians 1:14,

Then on the day when the Lord Jesus returns, you will be proud of us in the same way we are proud of you.

So, until then, be proud of your hard work, the great events you pull off, and the impact your ministry has on kids, volunteers, leaders, and families. But be proud with a humble heart, understanding that:

- Every good and perfect gift is from God (James 1:17)
- And that everything we have we received from God (1 Corinthians 4:7)
- So when we boast, we are truly boasting in the Lord! (1 Corinthians 1:31)

Signs of a Humble Leader

So, with a healthy understanding of pride in our ministry, what does a humble leader look like if that doesn't mean they have to be self-effacing, quiet, and unassuming?

They lead as one under authority.

While they may be in charge, they acknowledge respectfully the leadership they serve under. They speak respectfully of the leadership above them. They follow the guidelines and policies they are subject to, even when they may not entirely agree with them in all aspects. Outside of matters of doctrine or personal moral conviction, in which case resignation may be more appropriate, they enthusiastically promote and support the leadership of the church.

They ask for help.

Humble leaders recognize their limitations, are comfortable admitting them, and ask for help in their areas of weakness rather than attempt to hide them. They are more concerned with the ministry looking good than themselves looking good.

They share the spotlight.

Even in areas where they shine, humble leaders are willing to step aside and let someone else shine. They know they could easily get the attention and applause, but they prefer to allow others to enjoy using their gifts, too. They are as comfortable in the audience as they are on the stage. What is important to them is not whether they are seen, but whether God is seen working through a plurality of leaders.

They redirect the spotlight.

When a humble leader receives praise, they graciously accept it with gratitude but are quick to point out the others who also deserve credit and thanks for the accomplishment that is being acknowledged. Their understanding and appreciation for those who helped them is not kept a secret; it is frequently shared.

They ask for feedback.

Leaders who are humble want to know how they can improve. They want feedback on programs, events, and the ministry overall. Even when things are fantastic, they will ask how it could have been better. More importantly, they ask what *they* could have done better.

They own the results, regardless of blame.

President Harry S. Truman, who popularized the phrase, "The buck stops here," kept a sign with that phrase on his desk in the Oval Office. The president has to make the decisions and accept the ultimate responsibility for those decisions.

It isn't a question of whether things go wrong. They will. When they do, the humble leaders accept responsibility. They aren't quick to make excuses or blame others. While there may have been factors beyond their control or even failures by leaders on their team, they own the situation and instead of deflecting blame or making excuses, they choose to learn from the incident.

So, be proud of the gifts and talents God has given you for the ministry, give the glory to him, and lead humbly!

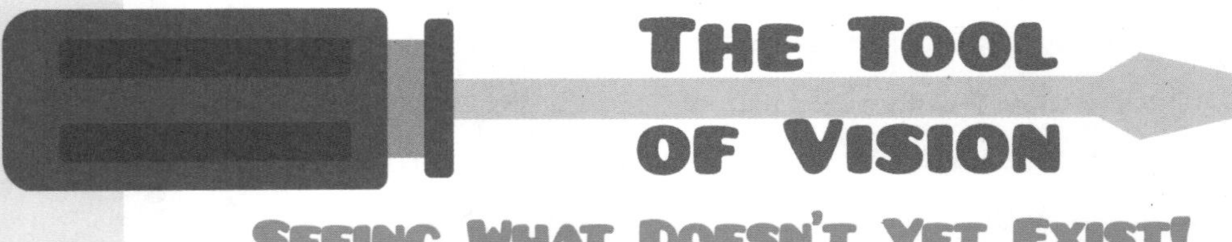

The Tool of Vision

Seeing What Doesn't Yet Exist!

You may have been hired to *maintain* a children's ministry, but God invites you to a higher calling—to *build* a children's ministry! There is a significant difference. Maintaining is important, and I'm thankful for those who keep a watchful eye on maintaining the things we take for granted every day. But when it comes to ministry, you have an opportunity to be a builder instead of a maintainer.

What is the difference? One just keeps things going (maintaining), while the other focuses on *building* the ministry to make it bigger, better, and broader in its impact on kids and families.

Before any building exists, someone saw it in their mind. Through a lot of effort and team work, eventually the real building came into existence. That is the purpose of the Tool of Vision—to see what can be, or more importantly, what ought to be, long before anyone else sees it. But without vision, there will never be the result. The vision comes first!

Write the vision; make it plain on tablets, so that a runner may read it.

Habakkuk 2:2 (NRSV)

THE IMPORTANCE OF YOUR OWN VISION!

Too often, children's ministry leaders look at other ministries that they deem as successful and try to copy what that church is doing. Their vision is simply what someone else is doing.

What they fail to realize is that these well known churches are not successful because of what they do but because they sought a vision from God for their ministry and faithfully pursued it. What we see are the results of them following a God-given vision!

When you emulate other ministries without understanding the reasons behind why they are doing the things they are doing, you risk ending up with completely different results and then wondering why it didn't work. You may end up blaming their methods instead of realizing that their vision did not fit your ministry.

Honestly, you don't need to copy other ministries to see amazing success. The end result is that your ministry will be one of a kind, custom made, personally tailored, and unique to your ministry.

You have an amazing God who is as able and willing to give you a vision for your ministry that is exactly what your church, your kids, and your leaders need.

Are you ready to sharpen your Tool of Vision and apply it to your ministry? Let's get started!

What is VISION?

Vision is the ability to see what isn't there. It is a leader's ability to create a mental image of the ministry they are building.

When you have vision, you see what others cannot. When your ministry has vision, your volunteers see more clearly why they do what they do and where you are heading as a ministry.

- A rough Sunday without vision is depressing.
- A rough Sunday with vision is still progress.

Vision brings hope. Volunteers without hope are merely doing a job or fulfilling a duty. Volunteers who have caught a vision will go above and beyond because their focus is clearer. They are part of something much bigger and grander than just the area they are serving.

Perhaps you've read Proverbs 29:19,

Where there is no vision, the people perish (KJV).

Look closely at any vibrant ministry, and you will discover a clear vision. Even if they have not stated it anywhere in print, if the ministry is alive and thriving, one interview with its leader will reveal the vision. They will have a clear sense of what they are doing, why they are doing it, and where they are headed. When a leader lacks this passion focused on a clear objective, the ministry perishes. It meanders aimlessly, losing all direction, focus, and energy.

Vision is essential because it is how you know if you are accomplishing anything. It is a description of the ministry you are building. It provides the targets you aim for. Vision provides a horizon to set your heart on and a task to set your hands to.

KEEPING SHARP

Perhaps you have heard the story of the man who was driving through the country and saw on the side of a barn several dozen targets with a single arrow sticking out of the very center of each target!.

He was so impressed with the marksmanship of this local archer that he pulled into the farm one day to ask for a demonstration. The farmer was more than happy to oblige.

He grabbed his bow and arrow and a can of paint. When they got around the back of the barn the farmer quickly shot yet another arrow at the barn.

Then to the visitor's amazement, the farmer proceeded to paint a target around the empty spot where the arrow had landed.

His secret was shoot first and paint the target second. While it made him look good to those who drove by his farm, the reality was he never actually hit a target.

Vision enables you to say no to good things that won't bring the vision into reality. If your vision describes what already exists, it's time for a bigger vision—or it may be time to move on. Your vision needs to be created and owned by your entire leadership team and key leaders. It must be bought into and agreed upon by everyone who will be a part of making it happen. There are even times to remove a good worker if they have a different vision than the leadership.

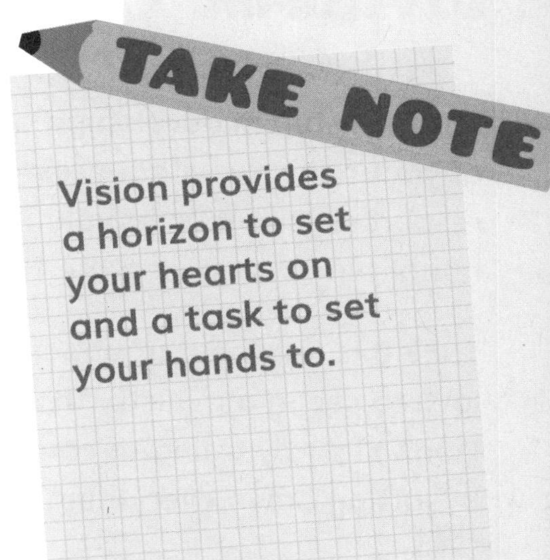

We can disagree on some of the methods of ministry, but everyone's got to be working toward the same vision. Different areas of ministry may work on different aspects of the vision, or get there in different ways, but the whole group needs to be building toward the same outcome.

Don't let your vision be a secret

Develop it. Hone it. Wordsmith it. Then, boldly share it and promote it every chance you get. Paint a verbal picture of the ministry you are trying to build. Often, when you walk past a construction site, you will see a beautiful rendering of the building that will soon be standing there. The builders are already presenting their vision. They want folks in the neighborhood to know that the mess and noise of construction is all for good reason, and soon there will be something exciting in that spot.

Be bold, and don't limit your vision to present staff or resources. Trust God, and watch what he will do! If the vision comes from him, he will be faithful to bring it to pass!

Let's try some visionary exercises! Take some time now to prayerfully begin to envision what God may be wanting to show you!

Developing a Vision—Exercise One

The first step in developing a vision for your ministry is to prayerfully imagine the potential of your ministry without restraint or restriction. Don't focus on the limitations of facilities, resources, budgets, or volunteers. If we truly believe God can do anything, we must honor him by allowing the Holy Spirit to enable us to see beyond our present situation.

Take this full sheet of paper, use extra if you need to, and begin to write out what you'd love to see in a ministry that is fully accomplishing what you believe would please God. Don't start by trying to come up with a pithy or catchy short vision statement. Start by jotting down everything that comes to mind. Run-on sentences are acceptable!

Some people call this a brain-dump. I'd prefer to call it a heart-deposit. Just put down everything that is on your heart for your ministry. Take as much time and space as you need, and try to cover as much as possible. Narrow it down later, but for now just put it all down. There may be a hidden nugget.

While you can also do this exercise on computer, I recommend writing by hand. The pace of writing can at times be in better sync with your thoughts than typing. This can help you better capture your thoughts. The next page can be reproduced as many times as needed for capturing your visionary thoughts.

Ready? Take time to pray, and then start dreaming and writing. Go!

____

____

____

____

____

____

____

____

____

____

Developing a Vision—Exercise Two

Once you have put your many thoughts and ideas and dreams down on paper, you are ready to move on to the next step. It's time to start marking it up!

Get a highlighter or colored pen and go back through what you wrote. Read it several times and circle or highlight key phrases or words that stand out.

- Perhaps there are words that reoccur in different contexts.
- Perhaps there is a sentence that resonates with you.
- Look for words that are unique to your ministry, location, demographic, or culture.

Below, jot down the key words, phrases, themes, or ideas that you highlighted. These will form the structure of your vision. Before many tall buildings go up, you'll see that steel frame begin to form, and it gives you a good idea of the type of building that will soon stand there. Like that steel frame, your vision's structure will soon support the entire ministry.

____

____

____

____

____

Developing a Vision—Exercise Three

Take all those heart-felt prayers, ideas, dreams, and creative thoughts that you narrowed down to key ideas and concepts. Then, translate them into a stated vision that you can champion to the volunteers and families at your church. Be sure to share your drafts with some friends who are good at editing. What may make perfect sense to you could be confusing to someone else. You are painting with broad strokes, so you don't need to include everything, but you don't want to be so broad that your vision would describe any ministry. It needs to describe your ministry at your church.

Write three completely different vision statements, then choose your favorite, perhaps borrowing parts of the others, and start to finalize what the end result will be.

Draft One

Draft Two

Draft Three

Now Put it All Together

The Tool of Teamwork

Together, Everyone Accomplishes More!

TAKE NOTE

If you don't have a leadership team, it isn't because of a lack of people willing to serve. It is only because you have chosen not to.

It is impossible to overemphasize the importance of the Tool of Teamwork. The absence of this tool in a leader's toolbox will most certainly lead to failure or even injury. Not just injury to the ministry, but perhaps to the leader and his or her family.

When I mention the importance of team, I am not merely referring to all the volunteers in the ministry in a generic sense. Of course, every leader and volunteer is part of the children's ministry team. What I am talking about is the leader sharing the *leadership* of the ministry with a leadership team. Far too many ministries have one leader, and everyone else reports to the leader. This is a perfect blueprint for chaos and collapse of a ministry.

I have met thousands of children's ministry leaders over the years. Whenever I have met one who is weary, stressed, and on the verge of quitting, my first question is, "Do you have a leadership team?" Nearly every time the answer is no. Next, I start to hear all the reasons why they don't have a leadership team.

I've heard all the reasons, and they aren't reasons. They are excuses. Hear me on this: If you don't have a leadership team, it isn't because of a lack of people willing to serve. It is only because you have chosen not to.

Sharing leadership is a choice. It is an essential choice.

PUT THIS IN YOUR BUCKET

When you build a leadership team, you . . . are building up the body of Christ and enabling others to use their gifts to serve God as well.

WHY IS SHARING LEADERSHIP SO IMPORTANT?

You simply can't do it yourself.

I don't care how small your ministry is. You need a team. Even in the smallest church, what happens if you

- Get sick?
- Move?
- Become ill?
- Die?

A ministry built on one person will not last.

You are doing more than just getting help.

You are building up the body of Christ and enabling others to use their gifts to serve God as well. Don't hog up all the opportunity to serve and the resulting blessings for yourself!

I remember my first full-time ministry fondly. I was so excited to be a full-time pastor after my first stint as a part-time pastor at my previous church. I was newly married and entrusted with both the children and youth ministries at a small church. I had so much fun! I taught children's church, created my own midweek program, hosted special events constantly, directed Vacation Bible School, and was active in outreach and pastoral visitation.

Then, suddenly, life took some unexpected turns, and God led me into a new ministry. A few years later, when I visited my former church, the folks enthusiastically greeted me. They complimented me, told me how wonderful it was when I was there, and described their current struggles to get things back to how I had left it. They heaped praise on me, saying they missed how things were when I was there.

While I appreciated their compliments, and understood that they were trying to describe a successful ministry season, I knew the hard reality was I had failed them. When I left that ministry, everything left with me. They had to start all over. As I said farewell to their smiles, feeling heavy in my heart for their struggles, I vowed privately that I would never allow that to happen again.

When I got back to my new church, I immediately began to form a leadership team. Since then, even during the hiring process of any new ministry, I have made it clear that if they think they are hiring me to run the kids' ministry, they are mistaken. They are hiring me to build a team that will build the children's ministry.

Of course, that early ministry has since recovered from my rookie ministry skills, but more telling is that several of my volunteer leadership team members have gone on to become full-time professional children's ministry directors. One of them even replaced me after the Lord called me on to a new assignment.

How can we "equip God's people to do his work" (Ephesians 4:12) if we are doing everything ourselves? Building teams builds the Kingdom of God and allows others to share in the responsibility.

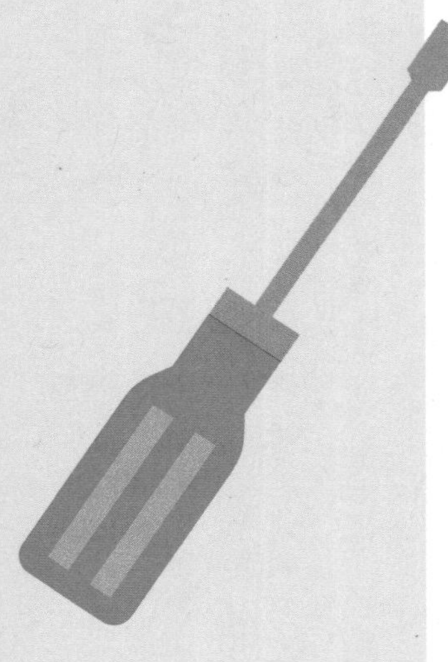

How Do You Build a Leadership Team?

Step One: Acknowledge that you need a team and won't run the ministry without one.

Stop the excuses. Whatever your current reasons or perceived obstacles to forming a leadership team, write them down, and then ask God to help you overcome them. Some of the excuses are internal and you simply need to buck up and be willing to work hard at this. Other obstacles may need to be addressed positively but boldly.

Step Two: Get buy-in from the leadership you serve under.

KEEPING SHARP

Secret: Top-quality people rarely volunteer. They wait to be asked.

If you are already at a church, discuss your ministry vision with your pastor or leader. I have never once heard of a pastor telling a children's ministry director they couldn't build a team to help them. Often, they are surprised there isn't a team or pleased to see their director taking initiative.

Step Three: Start sharing the vision.

Please note, I did NOT say you should start sharing the need. People don't respond to needs. They respond to vision.

In over twenty years of ministry, I've never had a single opening in the children's ministry. But I've certainly had many opportunities available! People don't volunteer to fill openings. They love seizing opportunities.

Start asking people to join you in praying that God would raise up leaders for the children's ministry as you will be forming a leadership team. As people pray, they will sense if God is calling them to step up. Others will flat out ask you, "How can I get on that team?"

Step Four: Invite people to join you.

Please, don't use bulletin announcements. A leadership team is a critical team. You want the best people on the team. Here's a well-guarded secret: **top-quality people don't volunteer. They wait to be asked.** You don't want just anyone on this team. You want passionate, gifted, dedicated, hard-working, reliable, godly people on this team. At the very first children's pastors conference I attended, Roger Fields challenged the attendees in the workshop, "Go home and announce that you are no longer accepting volunteers for the children's ministry. State that serving in the children's ministry is by invitation only." I thought he was nuts, as I had just started my first paid ministry and had lots of volunteer needs. But I was young and foolish and inexperienced and perhaps desperate enough to try exactly what he said. The result was incredible. It raised the bar of the children's ministry. Instead of the culture being one of desperation and taking any warm body that would volunteer, it became known that we only accepted the best.

Step Five: Meet regularly with your team.

Let them pray with you. Plan events together. Delegate responsibilities. Make decisions as a team when it comes to policies, events, and outreach ideas. I may not be the sharpest tool in the toolbox, but when I'm on a team with a bunch of other sharp tools, the end result is amazing.

A leadership team will not only make your life much less stressful, you'll also have more time to live, laugh, and learn as you do ministry with a team.

Meeting Agenda

When planning a meeting with the leadership team, it is helpful to have a template of things to discuss. Over the years, I have developed a simple outline using seven words that begin with the letter *P*. This ensures that I address every area of ministry. It also allows each team member to contribute and feel that their area of ministry is addressed and considered.

On the next page is an overview of what I put on the agenda.

Meeting Agenda

Date	Date of the meeting
Invited	Who was invited?
Present	Who actually attended?
Prayer	Team members share personal prayer requests for their area of ministry.
Praise	Team members share something positive that happened or is happening in their area of ministry.
Problems	Team members briefly share a problem they are experiencing. This isn't the time to solve it but to make it known. The leader can determine whether it is something the team should address together or something the leader can work out with the individual member.
Projects	Members give updates on existing projects and discuss as needed. They also discuss possible projects for the future.
Planning	Members schedule ministry events on a calendar and designate roles for event planning.
Prospects	The team discusses possible leaders and/or volunteers for the ministry. Names are brought up, confidential insight is shared, and there is approval to invite them to serve.
Parents	The team discusses issues with parents, better ways to communicate, and improvements to better serve and partner with parents.

Practice: Meeting Agenda Form

Fill out this agenda as you think about who you would invite and what you might discuss at a team meeting.

TOPIC	NOTES	ASSIGNMENTS
PRAYER		
PRAISE		
PROBLEMS		

PROJECTS

PLANNING

PROSPECTS

PARENTS

The Tool of Delegation

Helping Others Help You Help Others!

The Tool of Delegation is kept right next to the Tool of Teamwork in your toolbox. While I've never met a leader who would deny the importance of delegation, many wrestle with it. It is easier to recommend than to use.

KEEPING SHARP

What's the point of having a team if you don't delegate some responsibility to your team?

If you struggle to delegate, you aren't alone. Even Moses struggled with sharing leadership and needed his father-in-law to set him straight (Exodus 18:14-23).

There are many reasons we fail to delegate. Here are a few of the top reasons. Add some of your own to the list:

1. No one to delegate a particular task to
2. Lack of trust that the person will follow through
3. Nervousness over the quality of the work that will be done
4. Would rather do it myself to know it's done the way I want
5. ______________________________
6. ______________________________
7. ______________________________

8. ____________________

9. ____________________

10. ____________________

While they may never say it out loud, many leaders secretly cling to the conviction, "If you want it done right, you have to do it yourself." What they are really saying is, "The only way to ensure it's done my way is to do it myself."

Delegation requires releasing control, and that's not easy for leaders. Leaders tend to be good at what they do—it's how they ended up in leadership. As a result, they know how they want things done. But to build a ministry, we must delegate, and that means accepting that some things will be done differently, and, yes, perhaps not as well at times.

It all goes back to what our larger objective is. Are we building a ministry, or are we building people? I hope you recognize that our goal is to build people. And we can't build people if we never put tools into their hands and let them swing them around and bang on some things.

Even if you are able to do something better than other leaders, allowing them to take the lead builds more than the ministry. It builds them. As a humble leader who is learning to recognize your own weaknesses, you will start to discover who can do things better than you.

KEEPING SHARP

Delegation is powerful if we give away everything we can.

How Do You Choose What to Delegate?

Here are some questions to ask yourself to discover what you probably should or could delegate to someone else.

What *Could* I Give Away?

There are some things you shouldn't be doing and ought to be delegated as quickly as possible. They don't require a lot of skill, but they do eat up a lot of time. Take an honest assessment of the tasks that fill your time and consider:

- What could you give away?
- What duties take up valuable time that anyone could do?

You may be surprised the amount of time that is wasted on tasks that don't take advantage of your strongest skills and talents. Every hour spent on those tasks is taking you away from building in your strengths.

I had a team leader for our midweek club who was always in the building for hours after club putting everything away. This leader's spouse and kids were helping and waiting until they could finally all go home. Noticing this trend, I asked him to make a list of everything he had to do after club in order to go home.

He made a list, and it was several pages. Then I asked, "What can only you do on this list? Which of these tasks require a skill that only you possess?" The answer, of course, was none.

Then I gently challenged, "Within a few weeks, I want you doing nothing on this list. Delegate all of it. Your job will simply be to make sure everything on the list gets done."

He delegated the tasks to a variety of people based on their physical strength, the room they served in, and what tasks could be done together. Soon, everyone was heading home within thirty minutes of club being over.

If you build it they will come.
Field of Dreams

Try This: If you write the job description, the leaders will come!

What *Would* I Give Away?

The next category of things to delegate is tasks that require some skill. When you consider delegating, there is an "if" in the consideration.

- "If" I had someone with this skill.
- "If" there was a person who enjoyed this.
- "If" someone was willing to dedicate time to this.

These are things you don't need to be doing, but you are doing them because there is no one else.

For years I pecked away on my computer doing data entry because I couldn't imagine that anyone in the entire world would want to help me. It had to be done, but who would I ask? How could I ask someone else to do what I hate?

It took me far too long to make the startling discovery that God wired some people to love doing what I hated. In fact, these same people hate doing what I love. Imagine that! Sounds almost like the body of Christ with each designed for a different task.

It is time to define what your "If only" is.

- If only I had a bookkeeper.
- If only I knew someone who could do graphic design.
- If only I had an administrative assistant.

TAKE NOTE

Too often leaders use "there isn't anybody" as an excuse for why they don't delegate, when the reality is they really haven't made much effort to find anyone.

What are some of your "If onlys?" List them here:

IF ONLY ______________________________

IF ONLY ______________________________

IF ONLY ______________________________

IF ONLY ______________________________

IF ONLY ______________________________

The secret to getting your "If only" positions filled is to first state them and then create a job description. Start to pray about it and talk about it. I've been amazed by the ministry leaders I've gotten after first creating a job description for a position that didn't exist.

You will be surprised at the leaders you'll get if you start to envision them, describe them, pray for them, and prepare for them. **Don't allow "If only" to be an excuse. Make it a strategy!**

What *Should* I Give Away?

This next stage of delegating could come first, but unfortunately, it takes leaders time to get here. Let's face it, you stink at it.

- If your promo materials are lame, someone else should be doing it.
- If your bulletin boards look like they were done in the seventies, it's time to delegate.
- If your videos or media presentations are weak, someone likely could do better.

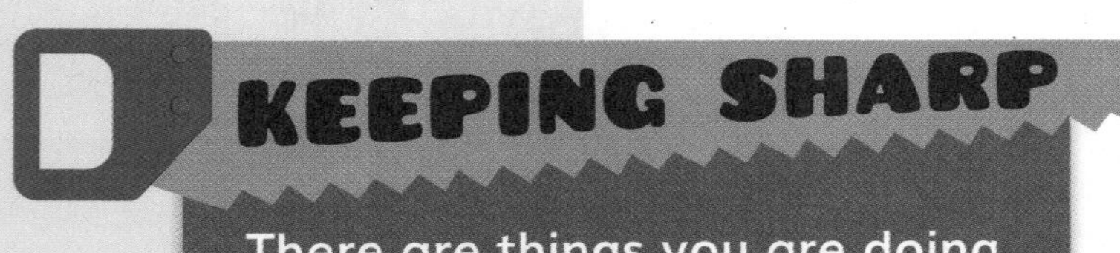

There are things you are doing that others are better at.

If you want to know what you *should* be delegating, ask some people who love you and are brave enough to tell you what you may not want to hear. If you are married, start with your spouse.

Your volunteers will tell you if you can gain their trust. Listen to your boss. If you are getting criticism constantly in an area of your ministry, you may need to delegate and oversee rather than lead that area.

Here is a hard question to ask yourself that may reveal some things to delegate or even discontinue. If you were to suddenly leave your ministry, what are you currently doing that the leadership above would say, "We've got to keep that going"?

There are likely things you are doing—good things—that would be quickly forgotten. If no one is asking you to do these good things and they wouldn't be missed, how important are they?

What *Shouldn't* I Give Away?

Lastly, there are some things you shouldn't delegate. These are the things that only you can do. You've got some God-given gifts and talents. While you can share these skills and allow others an opportunity to also use the same gifts, be sure that the majority of your time is spent doing the things that only you can do.

- If you are a gifted teacher, prioritize teaching in your ministry.

WHAT SHOULD YOU DELEGATE TO NOBODY?

Take a hard look at

- What fills our time and
- Who should be doing what

If we are honest, we will discover some things that

- We should not waste our time doing and
- Nobody should be doing

Eliminate time wasters!

AN EXPERT OPINION

Now these are the gifts Christ gave to the church: the apostles, the prophets, the evangelists, and the pastors and teachers. Their responsibility is to equip God's people to do his work and build up the church, the body of Christ.

Ephesians. 4:11–12

- If you are an encourager, make time for investing in others and building them up.

You know what your strongest skills are—likely they are what you enjoy the most. Don't completely delegate areas of ministry, or your joy in ministry will be diminished.

I left one ministry because a new leader wanted me to delegate the things that were my greatest strengths and joys. The ministry was growing, I loved the church, the kids and parents loved me. But I knew that if I had to delegate away my strongest gifts, the entire ministry would suffer.

Again, this doesn't mean you hog all the fun stuff. You need to model your strengths and train others and provide opportunities for others to learn from you, but never completely give up the things that only you can do. The uniqueness of your ministry will reflect the unique strengths you bring to it.

Before moving on, take some time to reflect on the Tool of Delegation, and make some notes.

What *Could* You Give Away?

List some things you are doing that someone else could do. Note who that someone else might be.

____

____

____

What *Would* You Give Away?

List some things you could delegate to the right person.

What *Should* You Give Away?

List some things that would be better if someone else were doing them.

What *Shouldn't* You Give Away?

List the things that only you can do and that you should prioritize.

Hopefully, you are getting excited about sharpening your Tool of Delegation! For many leaders, this tool is rusty, but as you start to use it, it gets sharper, and your ministry will improve dramatically as you share the load and the joy of serving God and building the ministry.

Few things in ministry are as fulfilling as seeing leaders grow and develop as we delegate to them. The true fruit of our ministry will not be the number of people that attended events or the size of the programs we established. It will be the number of leaders we developed, and leadership development begins with delegation.

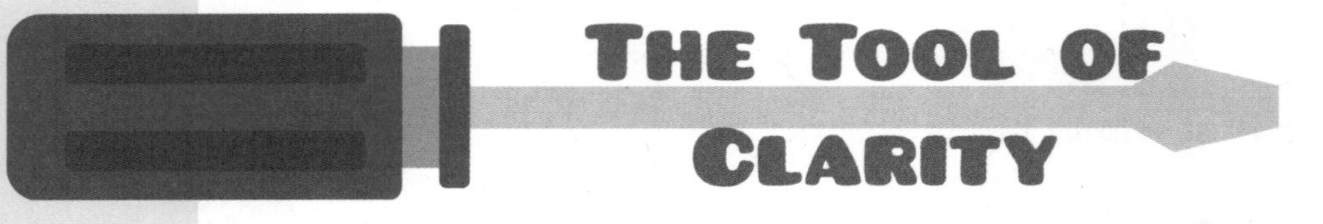

The Tool of Clarity

The Essential Job Description

Your toolbox is growing! You've added the Tools of Teamwork and Delegation, but your team members need to know exactly what is being expected of them. Clarity is essential for leaders to succeed. Nothing is more frustrating to volunteers than ambiguity in what is expected of them. Providing what is expected, in writing, gives people a clear blueprint and sets them up for success. Clarity can be provided in flow charts, job descriptions, and good signage.

Organizational Chart

One of the first things you should do is create an organizational flow chart of your ministry. This helps to clarify the structure of the ministry, the team members, and the team organization. Unfortunately, if not thought through ahead of time, many ministry flow charts will show every single leader and volunteer reporting directly to the children's pastor or director. This is a plan for frustration and failure.

No one person can be responsible for everything, or everything won't be done well. Instead, at the center of the flow chart should be the ministry team. Each volunteer should report to a certain leader within that team. Only ministry or program leaders should report to the children's pastor or director.

Job Descriptions

Every position should have a short but clear job description. Included should be:

- Title
- Qualifications
- Description of role
- When and how they serve
- Specific duties and responsibilities
- Term of service
- Task descriptions

TAKE NOTE

Nothing is more frustrating to volunteers than ambiguity in what is expected of them.

Title

Give every position a clear title. No one should simply be a volunteer. They should be:

- Grade-level leader
- Teacher
- Assistant
- Helper
- Greeter
- Host
- Worship leader
- Media technician

If someone asks a volunteer about their role, they should be able to answer with a clear response rather than just, "I help out in the children's ministry."

Qualifications

Be sure to include qualifications. It is always best to address this up front rather than waiting to react when something goes wrong. If a person is placed in a position they aren't qualified for, they are being set up for failure. Anything that goes wrong is on the leader, not on the volunteer.

Include things that may seem obvious or assumed, such as being a Christian, regular in attendance, etc. Prevent future awkwardness by stating up front what is needed and expected.

Online Resource: "Does your CM have an Org Chart?" Visit Kidology.org/toolbox

Description of Role

This is where you not only give a basic description of the role, but also where they fit within your overall vision. Let volunteers know what they are doing as well as the higher purpose of the position they fill.

For example, if someone is being recruited to help with check-in on Sundays:

- Instead of telling volunteers they are "Helping families check their kids in when they arrive at church."
- Tell them "They will provide a positive first impression to families as they arrive. Without worrying about the safety and security of their children, parents can get the most out of their church experience."

Manning a computer or tablet check-in doesn't sound very appealing or fulfilling. Helping families get the most out of their Sunday experience is far more inviting. Link their role to your vision, and you'll see increased commitment and dedication to their role.

When and How They Serve

Be specific about when and where a volunteer is committing to serve. Volunteering for the children's ministry shouldn't mean "Anywhere at any time you are called upon." Volunteers should be assigned a specific area and time to serve. Even a super volunteer who serves in more than one role should know what is expected in each role.

Specific Duties and Responsibilities

Clearly define what is expected during the time of service. You can't be too detailed. Often leaders get frustrated because later they are putting things away or wishing volunteers had done something differently. Remember what James 4:2 tells us,

You don't have what you want because you don't ask God for it.

The same applies to asking your volunteers for what you want from them.

Term of Service

There is a completely avoidable reason some people do not volunteer for the children's ministry. It can be perceived as a life appointment. Last I checked, the terms of a Supreme Court Justice did not apply to a children's ministry volunteer. Yet, so many times when recruiting, I've heard people say, "Oh, I used to serve in kids' ministry, but I finally escaped."

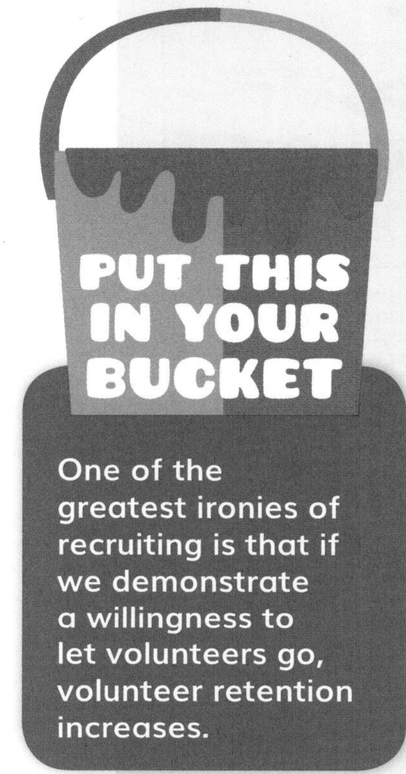

One of the greatest ironies of recruiting is that if we demonstrate a willingness to let volunteers go, volunteer retention increases.

While these may be jokes about the challenging time they had, hidden in the jest is the reality that in our ever-present need for volunteers, we are reluctant, if not completely unwilling, to let any go. One of the greatest ironies of recruiting is that if we demonstrate a willingness to let volunteers go, volunteer retention increases. People are more receptive to being asked to serve for a season.

Include in the job description when the term of service concludes. Remember, people can always volunteer again, but when we hold them with an open hand, we not only allow them the flexibility to do something different and perhaps find a better fit, but we also show that we are as concerned for them and their needs as we are for the needs of the ministry.

Task Descriptions

In addition to job descriptions, it is important to provide details on how things ought to be done. If you have a sound room or media center and are frustrated by volunteers messing things up, it may be as simple as providing some-step-by step instructions on how to turn on, run, and shut down the equipment.

Provide instructions anywhere they could be helpful, especially where multiple people are doing the same task, in order to provide consistency. Of course, you'll always have people who don't follow the instructions, but at least you'll have something to help them improve.

DON'T TOUCH!

DON'T MOVE.

DON'T USE!

DON'T EVEN THINK ABOUT IT.

Other Clarifiers

Signage

Signage is important. Signs can

- Help guide
- Help instruct
- Warn
- Even inspire!

Avoid signs that are negative.

I once had a leader that posted negative signs all over her area of ministry. Signs that instruct what not to do are negative.

Negative signs are the result of negative emotions. It is frustrating when people use supplies we were counting on, leave things out, don't clean up, or neglect to think of others. But negative signs are restrictive. They communicate, "We aren't here to serve you, we are here to make your job difficult."

Even when you need to post a sign that restricts, think of how you can state it in the positive.

Instead of...	Consider...
DO NOT USE	These supplies are for Sunday morning classes. If you need snack or paper supplies, please look in the cabinet next to the sink.
DO NOT MOVE	Please return this white board clean and ready, so the next group will be able to easily find and use it.
DON'T LEAVE THE MARKERS OUT!	Help prevent little hands from marking up our walls or themselves by placing the markers back in the box in the supply cabinet. Thanks!

When Things Go Wrong

- Volunteers will frustrate you.
- They will disappoint you.
- They will do things incorrectly.

When a volunteer lets us down, our first impulse (even before correcting them) ought to be, "did I make this clear ahead of time so they were set up for success?" If not, the appropriate response is to apologize because the error is no longer theirs.

When things go wrong:

- A strong leader's goal isn't to assign blame but to see how they can improve clarity to prevent the same thing from happening again.
- A good leader handles mistakes with grace and patience.
- A great leader loves when things go wrong because they see it as an opportunity to improve the ministry.
- A leader who is building will be thankful that a weakness was exposed and will work to correct it.
- A powerful leader is always working to sharpen the Tool of Clarity.

Let's Make an Org Chart!

Use this page to create a rough draft of an organizational chart. Start by listing your leaders, programs, and ministry positions. Then, place them in a chart that illustrates how the ministry is organized or how you think it should or could be organized.

List of Programs	List of Key Leaders

Draft Your Children's Ministry Organizational Chart

At the beginning, draw your organizational chart by hand as you think it though. Once you have a plan, switch to using an application designed for creating flow charts. This kind of application makes creating, labeling, and moving the boxes around a lot faster and easier.

Practice Job Description

Choose one volunteer position in your ministry and create a job description. Once you have a template, creating the rest will get a lot easier.

Title of the Position:

Duration of Service:

Qualifications for the Role:

- ______________________________
- ______________________________
- ______________________________
- ______________________________
- ______________________________

Description of Role:

When and Where this Role Serves:

____

Specific Tasks and Duties:

____

____

____

____

____

____

____

____

Signage and Instructions Needed

- Take a walk around your ministry facility.
- Think through the various areas of the ministry.
- Ask yourself where clarity would be helpful.
- Ask some leaders and volunteers what they think needs more clarity.

Make a list of areas where you could improve clarity.

Needed Signage:

____

____

____

____

____

____

____

Instructions Needed:

____

____

____

____

____

____

____

The Tool of Organization

A Place for Everything—And Everything in Its Place

Children's ministry is extremely stuff intensive. I don't think any other ministry in the church has as much stuff as the children's ministry.

We've got

- Curriculum
- Books
- Bibles
- Games
- Toys
- Diapers
- Glue sticks
- Puppets
- Costumes
- Decorations
- Props
- Candy
- Hats
- Hula hoops
- Construction paper
- Crayons
- Scissors
- Parachutes
- Balloons
- Stickers
- Slime
- Rubber ducks
- Beads
- Pipe cleaners
- Popsicle sticks
- Stacking cups
- Cardboard tubes
- Wet wipes
- Plastic eggs
- Flags of every country
- First-aid kits
- Cups and napkins
- Goldfish crackers

And so much more!

Organization is far more than just keeping all that stuff in order—but that's a great place to start! We have to maintain a tricky balance in children's ministry. We keep some things because we'll reuse them again, but we also hang on to stuff that we *might* need again. While you will have saved money if you actually *do* use the item again in five years, there is a cost to storage and clutter that can't always be measured in dollars.

Take Note

If you want an organized ministry, it begins with getting yourself organized.

The Apostle Paul encourages us in 1 Corinthians 14:40,

Be sure that everything is done properly and in order.

One the best things a leader can do for a ministry is to bring a sense of order and organization.

Let's take a quick look at how you can sharpen your Tool of Organization and bring a sense of order to your ministry.

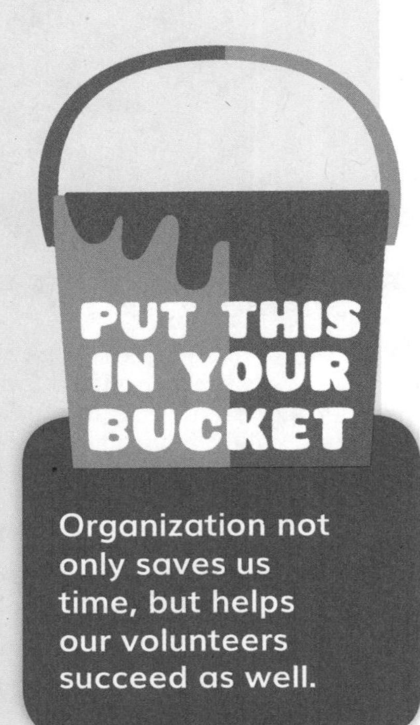

Organization not only saves us time, but helps our volunteers succeed as well.

An Explosion of Order!

You've likely got a messy closet filled with miscellaneous props, assorted supplies, old curriculum, musty costumes, ancient VBS kits, and countless broken crayons. I'm not going to tell you to start by cleaning out that closet. For now, you can close that door and pretend it doesn't exist.

You'll get to it, but don't start there. Effective organization starts from the center and works its way outward. Just as an explosion will have an epicenter and send ripples of destruction outward in concentric rings, order can have the same explosive impact if it begins at the center.

What Is at the Center?

If you said, "Me," you guessed correctly! Order and organization begins and ends with you. If you want an organized ministry, it begins with you getting organized. Children's pastors are known for their messy offices. For many, a chaotic office is considered a badge of honor. When ministry props and supplies are stacked all over, mixed with artifacts from the world of kids, it just screams children's ministry, doesn't it?

To outsiders, what it really says is, "My leadership and my ministry is a mess." Is that really the message you want to send?

Available ministry space is different for every church. However, you can decide that your office will be neat and professional, and that doesn't mean it won't be kid-friendly. Yes, you can display ministry props and toys, but display them tastefully and invitingly.

Beyond the basic neatness of your office, organize your space to function. As much as possible, don't use your office for storage. Except for decorations, it should be filled only with things that you actually use. Anything that won't be touched in a year should go somewhere else. Create a storage room or resource room, or (gasp!) get rid of things that aren't really needed.

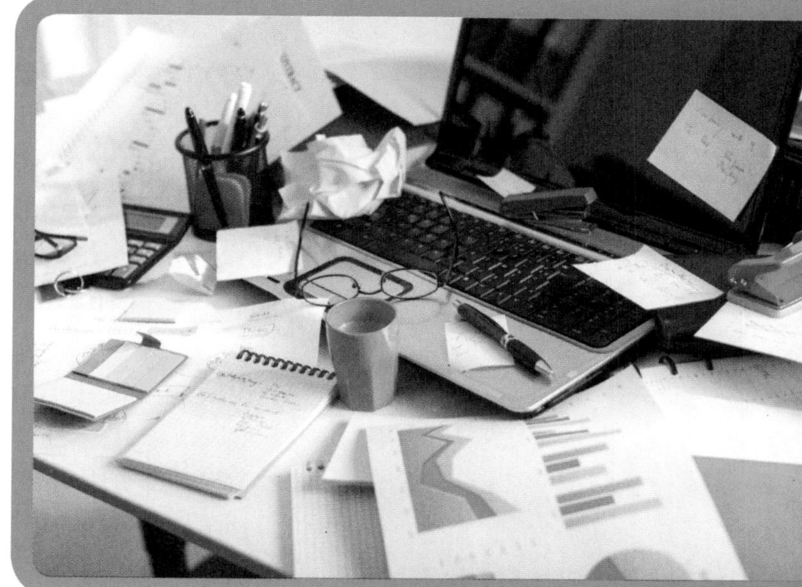

Tips to Organize Your Epicenter

When you decide to get your ministry organized, make your first priority to get your office and daily schedule organized. You'll be amazed how other things will fall into place once the epicenter has order.

- Start with your computer, files, calendar, and paperwork. Choose a system that you'll use for organizing your files, both physical and digital.
- Organize your week. Determine what tasks you do on each day of the week. Schedule your big tasks early in the week.
- Make each of your desk drawers have a defined purpose besides deep, long term storage. If your desk gets quickly cluttered, have a defined place you can stack it all at the end of the day so you can go home with your desk clear. You can dive into that stack the next day.
- Keep your trash can close, and use it often!
- Work from a to-do list every day. It doesn't matter whether you use a smart phone app

or paper index cards. Determine what your daily goals are at the beginning of the day, and let your to-do list guide your day.

- Don't work from email. Schedule when you will check email, and close it at all other times so you can focus on what you need to get done.

Tips to Organize Other Spaces

Once you've centered your epicenter by organizing your office and daily schedule, widen the circle. Organize classrooms, closets, media rooms, and anywhere else you find chaos. Cleaning out may be what is most needed initially. However, these spaces won't stay neat if the role of each space isn't clearly defined.

- Determine what goes where, and make your label maker your new best friend.
- Use signage and personal communication to explain the purpose of each space.
- If donations are cluttering up your rooms and closets, make it known that the children's ministry will not accept any donations. You may clarify that to say only donations in new or in like-new condition will be accepted. Make sure people understand their donation might end up at a local thrift store. Remember that you are under no obligation to accept donations.
- Defend order fiercely! Defend it kindly, but with resilience.

Storage vs. Resource Room

OK. Now it's time to get to that closet that I said you didn't have to begin with. Every children's ministry ought to have both a storage area and a resource room.

Ideally, these should be separate areas. If not, then designate what is storage and what is resources. If you have to work to claim some space, do so. It will be well worth it.

Storage

Is it worth it?

Make sure you are storing things that are worth storing. Often children's ministries keep everything because, well, they spent money on it. It is OK to toss out or give away things after an event.

When you go out to eat or to a movie, you spend money on the experience and enjoy it. However, afterward, there is nothing to show for it or to store. The same is true of church events. Many of the props and supplies we buy are for the experience alone. If the event was a success, the people had a great experience. The investment made in props, supplies, and decorations was well worth the expense.

You do not need to keep everything that is leftover!

- Send things home with people.
- Donate items.
- Simply throw some things away!

Only keep items if you know for certain *when* they will be used again. It makes sense to save things for annual events. Each year you can make the event better by using your budget to invest in new things reusing things from previous years.

The point is to evaluate each thing wisely. It is OK to buy some things again if it means freeing up limited storage space all year long.

- Categorize your storage.
- Label things.
- Make sure you have a list of what is available.

What is the point of storing something if later people end up spending money because no one even knows what is in storage?

Most ministries have limited storage and need to use it wisely. However, if you have plenty of storage, it becomes even more important to organize it or no one will ever be able to actually use anything.

Resource Room

Whereas storage is long-term collection of ministry tools, the resource room is where volunteers can get the supplies they need on a regular basis. As with long-term storage, resource rooms quickly fill up with supplies that aren't needed. Leftover materials, odd donated items, miscellaneous craft supplies, and other tidbits can quickly make it hard to find the most basic items that are needed quickly.

Never start organizing a resource room by looking at what is currently in there.

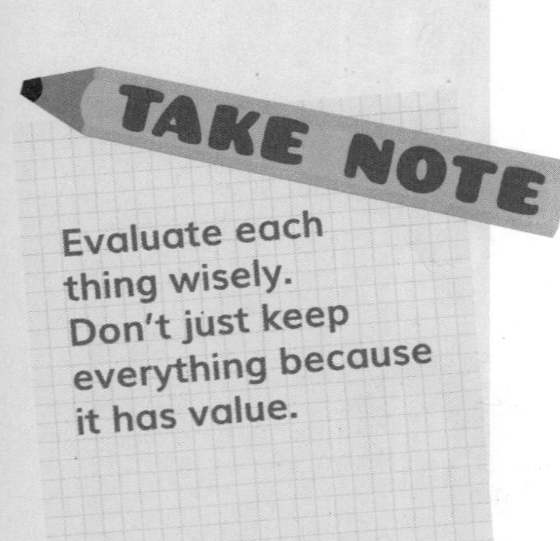

Start by making a list of basic supplies that *ought* to be in there. Next, ask your leaders and volunteers what items they would appreciate being on hand when they minister to kids.

Find out what they may be purchasing with their own money. You may find that some volunteers are personally equipping the ministry with needed supplies. Ideally, the church should be providing needed supplies, and volunteers should be directing their giving toward the church. You can't get an accurate report on what ministry costs if people are donating supplies directly. What happens when that volunteer moves away or is no longer able to provide that resource? Suddenly, you are asking for new funds for the children's ministry.

Of course, volunteers can always do extra things for the kids they are ministering to, but basic supplies ought to be provided. While volunteers will rarely complain, it can impact general church giving and even be a reason volunteers quit—though they may never tell you this. Avoid this awkwardness by providing what they need for success!

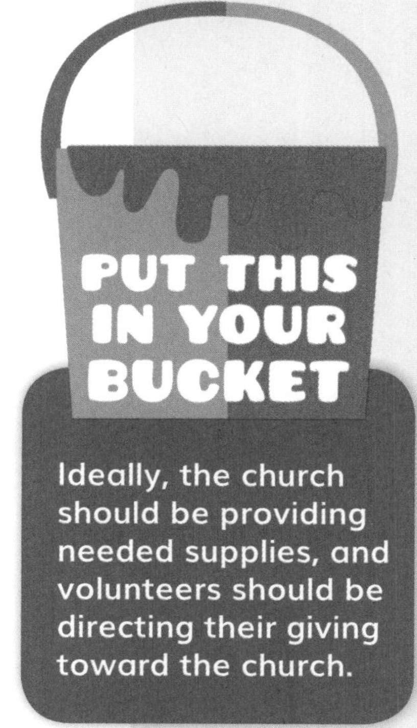

Ideally, the church should be providing needed supplies, and volunteers should be directing their giving toward the church.

Once you have made a list of the resources that ought to be in the resource room, clear it out and organize it. If this isn't in your skill set, there are certainly organizers in your ministry who enjoy this. Recruit them to help or do it for you.

- Get totes and drawers and label them.
- Sort things by holidays as well as age group.

If you have never done this, you'll be amazed at how encouraging it is to volunteers to have a neatly organized and well supplied resource room. It communicates to them that they are important and that you desire to equip them for success!

Out with the Old!

If your church is like most churches, there is a collection of old curriculum taking up valuable space. If it isn't going to be reused, get rid of it. You may be able to donate it to another ministry, but in most cases, it is trash.

Many leaders hate to toss out curriculum because of the money that was spent on it, but you have to look at it a different way. The investment of money was for the experience when it was used. It was well spent, but it is past. There is nothing wrong with dispensing of the material after it has been used.

Yes, you can save money reusing curriculum, but only keep it if it truly is going to be reused. In most cases, you are going to want newer material in the future, and the used material often is incomplete and can't be used due to missing items, used items, and the inability to replace what is missing. Toss it out guilt free. Make your ministry space count.

Check Lists and Instructions

Another way to bring order to your ministry is to make sure that your volunteers have clear instructions on how to do the tasks assigned to them. People don't like to ask when they've already been told, so they will guess. If you find yourself frustrated by people doing things incorrectly or inconsistently, perhaps it is because you haven't provided clear instruction.

Check lists and point-by-point instructions are welcome by volunteers who want to do things correctly. Of course, you need to have grace for those who will ignore instructions and still make mistakes, but at least you are setting people up for success. Whether it is copy machine instructions, sound board, die-cut machine, or simply the helium tank, instructions help people feel like they can succeed without bothering you for little details.

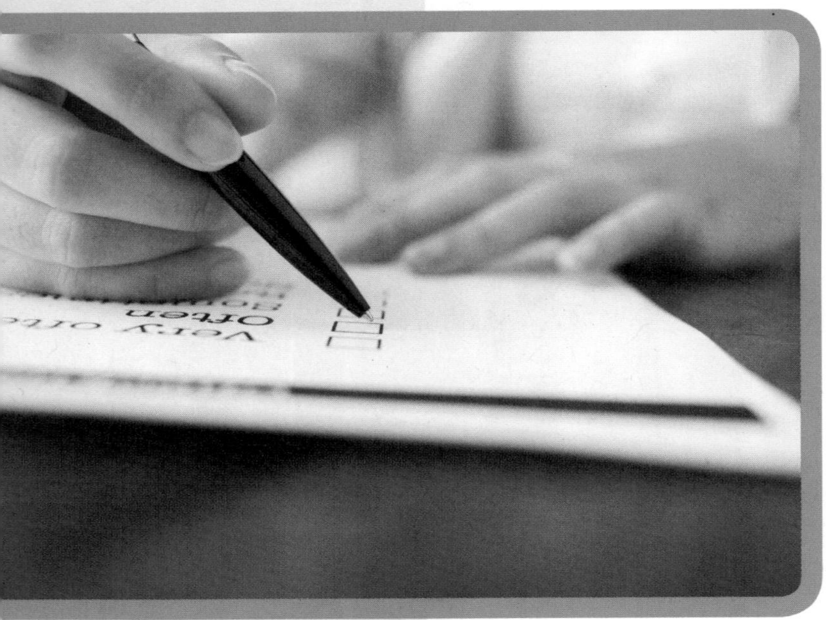

If I find myself explaining something more than once, or to more than two people, I know it is time to type out those instructions. Not only will it help others, but it will save me time as well.

Be sure to let people know they are always welcome to ask for help. The instructions are to help, not to prevent them from asking for help or clarification. Often what is clear to us may be confusing to someone else, so be sure to get feedback on your instructions.

Ask people if the instructions were helpful or how they could be improved. Better yet, ask someone who is already trained to create the instructions for you. They may do a better job!

Ask for Input

Ask often, "What can we do to help you succeed?" Find out what would make people's jobs easier. Create an atmosphere where feedback is welcome and encouraged. As people see that you are approachable and teachable, they will make suggestions that will make things better for newer volunteers. After a new volunteer is up and going, ask, "How could we have better trained you or got you to where you are today?" They'll help you identify things you might never see.

Operation Organization

Take a tour around the church building, starting at your own desk. In the chart below, make notes of the space and of what could be done to improve that area. If you have multiple storage areas, consider if each could have a defined purpose rather than being general storage. After you make an assessment, share it with your pastor or key leaders for additional input. Then make a plan to get more organized.

Ministry Space	Observations/ Descriptions	Possibilities

The Tool of Recruiting

Secrets to Building a Ministry Team!

Did you skip ahead to this chapter? While I'll never know your answer, I do want you to realize that there is a reason this isn't Chapter 1! In fact, I was tempted to make it the last chapter in this section. Why? Because if you start recruiting without addressing the overall vision, health, and organization of your ministry, you'll have a much harder time getting people to join you.

Stage One: Blueprints

Cast the vision for the ministry and document not only your current needs, but more importantly, the desired volunteer structure of your ministry. Current staffing and needs are irrelevant at this stage!

Vision is the ability to see what doesn't exist. Too often, children's ministry leaders only see immediate needs. It can seem silly to think about the positions you'd *like* to have when you haven't filled your current positions. It's important to realize that everything that currently exists was once just a thought and most likely seemed impossible.

Take some time to think about where you would like to be, and start drafting what that would look like. It is worth taking a full day to focus on the future. Don't worry, your current needs will still be there tomorrow. Give yourself the time to think beyond your current needs.

A seasoned leader once told me, "How did I organize a bus ministry with eighty buses? I planned for eighty when I only had one." This leader didn't just figure out how to run a single bus, he

Keeping Sharp

If you start recruiting without addressing the overall vision, health, and organization of your ministry, you'll have a much harder time getting people to join you.

organized his bus ministry to continue adding more buses in the future. He planned for more, and he was prepared.

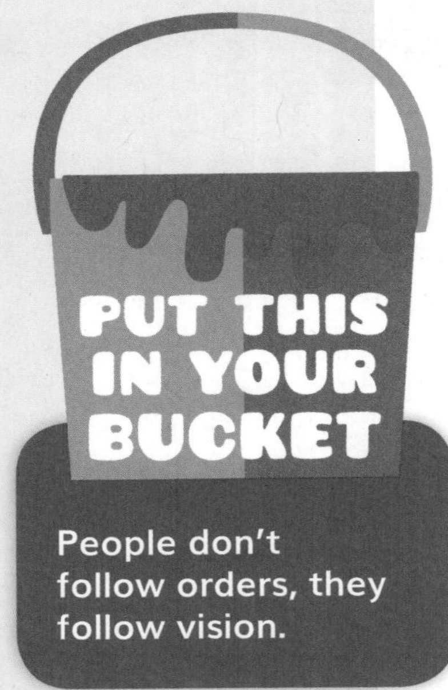

People don't follow orders, they follow vision.

- Take time to prayerfully dream about what God wants to do with this ministry. What could it look like in a few years?
- Dare your volunteers to dream. As you form a leadership team, challenge them to envision what *could be* rather than focusing on the current needs.
- Drop visionary hints. When you hear of something amazing that another church does, it's OK to show it to your leaders and volunteers. Say, "Wouldn't it be amazing if we could do something like this someday?"

People don't follow orders, they follow vision. As you talk about an exciting future, people will get excited. They begin to feel like they are part of something purposeful and exciting. They might begin to invite others as well.

Frame your needs as opportunities with amazing potential, and you'll see dramatic results.

Here is a list of the documents you may want to prepare for your blueprints:

- Organization chart
- Job descriptions for every role, present and future
- A brochure that describes the ministry's vision, programs, and purpose

Stage Two: Foundation

Create the implementation plan that addresses what to do after volunteers are hired.

Ask yourself, "If one hundred people signed up to serve in the kids' ministry, would I be prepared?" When I was first asked this question by a veteran leader, I said, "It would be wonderful if one hundred people signed up to serve!" Then, I realized I wasn't ready for one hundred new volunteers. In fact, I wasn't ready for ten people to sign up to serve.

- If someone calls or emails to join the ministry as a volunteer, how much work is required to get them screened, trained, and placed into ministry?
- Are you writing an email or letter to thank them?
- Are you trying to figure out how to get them oriented and answer their questions?
- Are you running the background check yourself?

If one new volunteer generates lots of work, you've got to speed up the process! Start planning for one hundred new volunteers.

- What would you need?
- Whose help could you enlist?
- How can they all be screened, trained, provided orientation, and placed into ministry?

Here are some things you may want to consider to be ready for the next volunteer:

- A form that provides their basic contact information, areas of interest, and availability
- An automated response email that welcomes them, briefly explains the process, and expresses your excitement to have them on the team
- A letter that explains the full process in more detail

KEEPING SHARP

As your vision begins to solidify, start documenting it. It is powerful to develop an organization chart that reflects your goals. As you create job descriptions—both for existing roles and potential new roles—excitement grows. Many times, I have created a job description for a dream position, and within weeks that person appeared, seemingly from nowhere.

This happens for a variety of reasons. People with unique skills respond to ideas that will enable them to use their God-given gifts. Also, once you've written down the dream job, you'll start to look at people with these qualities in mind. You'll hear things in regular conversations that you otherwise might have missed. These will lead you to invite someone to fulfill a unique role. Don't underestimate God's role in this. Likely, the Holy Spirit guided you to thinking of a unique role because he already has someone in mind that would excel at that very task!

- The form or application required to process a background check with a letter that explains why you do this
- A children's ministry policy document or handbook

Sample of an Invitation Email to a Potential Volunteer

Send after a potential volunteer has expressed some interest in serving. Be sure to edit for your ministry specifics.

Dear (Name),

Thank you for your interest in serving in the children's ministry at (Name of Church)!

Our goal at (children's ministry name) is to make Sunday the best day of our kids' week. Why? Because when kids are having fun, they keep returning and learning!

We want every child who comes through our doors to feel loved, come to know Jesus, and find a place where they can grow through fun and life-changing experiences.*

A big key to our success is having volunteers who love God and enjoy serving with children. We are always seeking people who are faithful, teachable, and take their role seriously—even as we have a ton of fun ministering to kids!

If that is you, please complete the ministry application and return it to me (your name). We also ask that all volunteers read, sign, and understand the Child Protection Policies. (Just return the final page signed.) After you pass your background check, we'll ask you to watch some training videos, schedule you to observe the ministry in action, and then schedule you to serve.

Thank you for your patience in this application process. We assure parents that every volunteer is both screened and trained to ensure a safe environment and a great experience for their kids.

I'm eager to see you as a part of the children's ministry team. If you have any questions, please do not hesitate to ask. I'm here to serve you as you serve our kids.

(Leader's Signature), (Leader's Position)

* This sentence is our ministry's vision statement. While you are welcome to adopt it, consider creating your own mission or vision statement that summarizes what your goals are for the ministry.

Online Resource: For a download of a Volunteer Interest Form from Karl's church, visit Kidology.org/toolbox

Sample of a Welcome Email to a New Volunteer

Be sure to edit for your ministry specifics. This email is worded informally to make it sound friendly and less corporate. You'll want to use whatever style of writing best suits your church's culture.

Dear (Name),

I'm so excited you are joining the children's ministry team at (name of church) and serving in (area of ministry).

We have so much fun ministering to the kids each week! Our goal is to make learning about Jesus and God's Word fun and life changing for our kids.

Attached is a bunch of important stuff. Please start by reading the attached letter, and then thoughtfully go through all the rest of the material included. There are some hoops to get set up initially, but let me tell you, it's all worth it!

I want you to know that I'm here for you as well as the kiddos. If you have any questions about your own faith journey or have questions or needs, I'm your pastor, too. Please don't hesitate to talk to me or let me know.

Also, serving kids isn't a reason to skip "Big Church" (as we call it kids' ministry). We expect you to attend the adult service even on Sundays when you serve with kids. As we like to say, "attend one, serve one." So, if you serve first service, attend second service, or vise-versa! That's why everyone can join us for the volunteer huddle at 8:40 a.m., where we pray together, get updates, see who is here, and get ready for another awesome Sunday right before kids start to arrive! Then you can hustle off to first service or just start greeting the kids if you serve first service.

We start off with connection time for the first 15 minutes, then worship, followed by the large group lesson time, which I typically lead. There will still be ways to help during that with games and other activities. So be alert and ready to help.

I'm excited you are joining the team!

You'll be getting some emails and texts from our church scheduling system, so you can accept or decline in that system, but you can also text me if you need help.

If you have any questions, let me know!

WELCOME!

(Leader's Signature), (Leader's Position)

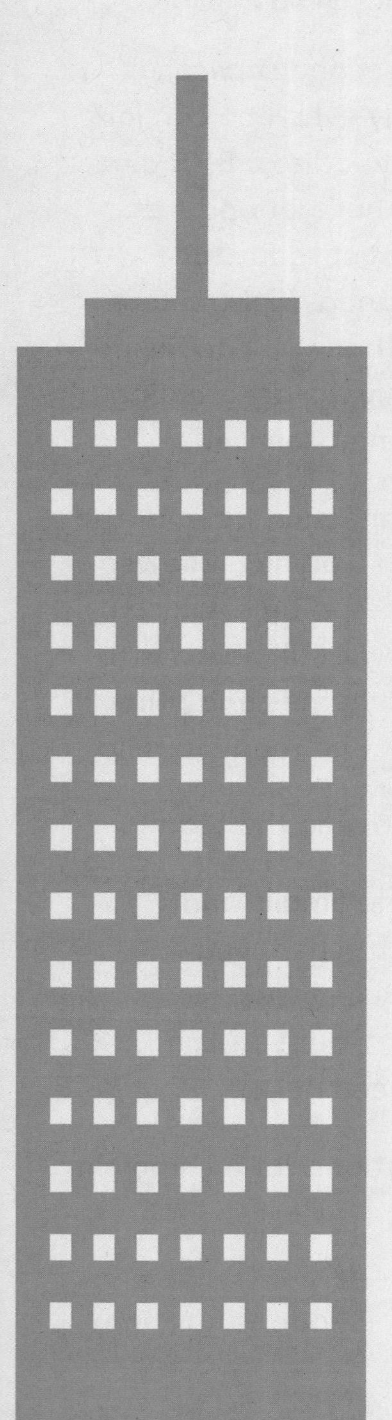

Stage Three: The Framework

Focus on building a hierarchy of leaders or a chain of command within your ministry. Everyone will build off of this to delegate work and complete projects efficiently. A ministry will not grow if the primary leader does not release authority to other leaders.

Before you can build a beautiful children's ministry, you have to establish the frame. We've all seen the frame of a skyscraper. You know a beautiful building is in the works, and soon that frame will never be seen again. On the outside, it will be hidden behind glass, steel, and creative architectural design. On the inside, it will be hidden by walls, paintings, desks, and practical furniture.

Like a building, the ministry's frame will determine the ultimate size and reach of your program. Additions and expansions can happen later, but it is the initial framework that determines the ministry scope for the next season.

Many ministries are structured to have one leader and then a host of volunteers. That structure will not allow for growth. It may be successful for a Sunday morning with a limited amount of kids and families, but to build a ministry, you must build the team. To build the volunteer team, you must add leaders.

As leadership expands, the number of volunteers expands naturally. This is because the primary leader is no longer doing all the recruiting. Recruiting a team of recruiters is far more effective than trying to add volunteers.

As discussed earlier, developing an organizational chart helps you envision the framework that is needed for a solid and healthy ministry. Your organization chart can include leadership positions that you do not currently have. The vision of that structure will inspire people. Leaders will emerge as they see what you are building. Remember, people don't respond to needs, they respond to vision.

Determine the framework for your ministry, and look for key leaders to head up each area. In smaller churches, these will be volunteer roles. As the church grows, you will naturally need to add part-time paid positions, and eventually you may need some paid support staff. Regardless of ministry size, don't make the mistake of thinking, "I'll add leaders when we get bigger." You don't add leaders after you grow, you add leaders *in order to grow*.

Successful leaders see themselves not as the leader of the ministry, but as a leader of leaders. They are builders, not just of a ministry, but also of leaders who build the ministry. This is true regardless of the size of your ministry. I don't care if you have ten kids. You start adding leaders if you want to double your kids. Doubling a ministry of ten kids takes the same strategy as doubling a ministry of one hundred or one thousand. Growth in children starts with growth in leadership every time.

TAKE NOTE

To build a ministry, you must build the team.

+ + +

If you are in need of more volunteers, start by adding more leaders.

STAGE FOUR: INVITATIONS

Invite others to join the children's ministry. How this is done will vary by ministry, but it must be relational and personal in every ministry.

This is where it gets exciting! Now it is time to start inviting people to join the children's ministry! So how do you ask?

There are three levels of appeal, and you must use all of them. If you compare recruiting to fishing, you can cast a wide net and hope to draw some in. You can use a fishing pole with bait and hope to lure a specific type of fish, or you can spear a specific fish you want. No, I'm not suggesting you spear any potential volunteers! But you do want to use all three methods of appeals: general, focused, and personal appeals.

You don't add leaders after you grow, you add leaders in order to grow.

General Appeals

You must make the vision of the ministry known to the entire church. Notice that I didn't say the needs of the ministry. Use whatever means you have available to you.

- Print it in your church newsletter or bulletin.
- Post it on your church website under the children's ministry area.
- Use the management database or email list. However, don't send out e-blasts asking for worker—share what God is doing.
- Create slideshows and highlight videos showing what happens in the children's ministry. Get your church media team to show the slides and videos before and after worship services. Or better yet, play them as the pastor makes an announcement about all the exciting stuff going on in the children's ministry.

Your goal with general appeals is to make the children's ministry attractive to church attendees at large. You can add a line such as, "Find out how you can become a part of the children's ministry by contacting so-and-so."

Negative promotion will undercut the next two levels, so keep it positive, celebratory, and inviting. You are sowing seeds of positivity and making people feel like they are missing out on the best area of ministry in the church. You are casting the net wide, and you just might catch some volunteers. More likely, you are creating curiosity and general interest that will help you in the next stage.

In general appeals, you will only snag people who already have a giftedness and calling to minister to kids.

Focused Appeals

Similar to general appeals, these are wide appeals that are focused to a specific group.

- **Parents**—Because you'd like to see every parent serving in some capacity in the children's ministry
- **Seniors**—Because they make wonderful helpers in the early childhood department and can help rock babies or read Bible stories
- **College students**—Because they need to do something while they are home for summer
- **Teenagers**—Because younger kids look up to them, and teens need a sense of responsibility
- **Men**—Because kids need to see men in the classrooms as much as women

Choose your target and send a more direct invitation explaining why you are inviting them. It's not a general appeal to everyone under the sun; it is uniquely suited to them. A targeted appeal says, "We need you, and here is why."

Focused appeals can be sent in a variety of ways.

- **Email** is easy and fast, but it is just as easy to miss, delete, or ignore. You may need to send an email appeal several times just to be noticed in our email-saturated age. And then you risk being annoying!
- **A letter** in the mail takes more time and has more cost associated with it, but it also causes attention. You took the time to write. A hand-written note in the mail is incredibly powerful because "nobody does that anymore." They may know you wrote to more than one person, but you certainly didn't write to hundreds. You chose them.

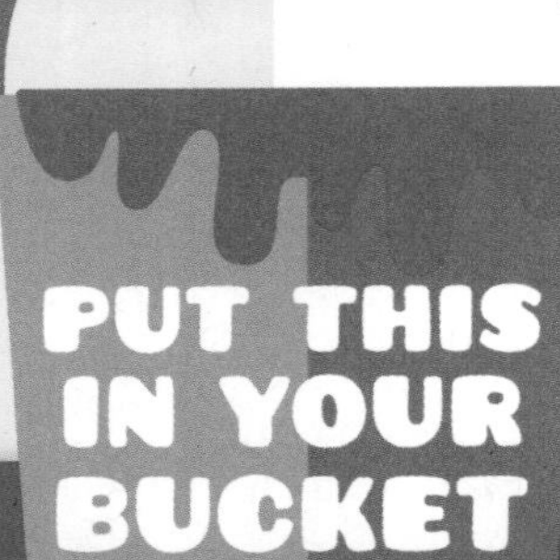

PUT THIS IN YOUR BUCKET

The Personal Appointment

The most powerful invitation is a personal appointment. You can meet at church if your location is conducive to a warm meeting, but meeting at a coffee shop or restaurant can be much better. Don't jump right in to recruiting. Learn about their family and interests. Discover how they came to know Christ and what led them to your church. How have they volunteered in the past? What do they do for work professionally? Ask what they would do if they could do anything they wanted.

Your goal isn't just to gain a volunteer, it is to get to know them and help them get into a ministry position that is a perfect fit for them. There will be times you end up recommending them to another area of ministry in the church. That's OK; we are building the kingdom of God, not just the children's ministry. As you build friendships with volunteers, they will end up working with you for a lot longer than if they had just responded to a general or focused invitation to help out.

Off-Site Meetings

When meeting off-site with potential volunteers, be wise with gender guidelines. In general, men should meet with men and women with women. Whether you are single or married, it is best not to meet alone off-site with a member of the opposite sex. Not only do you want to prevent the seeds of any relationship growing where it shouldn't, but you also want to avoid any negative appearance of impropriety as you are seen in a public place. Invite a spouse or another leader to join you. Meetings of three are often more enjoyable, and conversation often flows more easily.

- **Flyers, posters,** and **monitor screens** provide a means for a focused invitation.

General appeals make the children's ministry attractive. Focused appeals say to a select group, "Join us!"

Personal Appeals

What is the single most effective recruiting tool? The personal invitation. Nothing beats a leader asking an individual one on one. You can tell why you think they are a perfect fit for the ministry. You have seen how:

- They interact well with children.
- They are a positive person who is always smiling.
- They are an encourager or faithful in attendance.
- They are quick to help out at church events.
- They simply have a servant's heart.

Build them up by letting them know why you want them on your team. Personal invitation nearly always results in a new volunteer.

I recommend you put together a folder of helpful information to give to prospective volunteers. You can include a personal letter, children's ministry brochure, policy manual or handbook, ministry application, and other helpful information unique to your church. I include a hand-written sticky note inside that says, "I hope you'll join our team!"

Managing Prospective Volunteers

Keep track of your contacts and interactions with potential volunteers. There are many online tools today for managing to-do lists. You can also simply document on your computer or a giant white board in your office.

1. Begin with a list of potential volunteers and the ways you will appeal to them. General appeals go to everyone, so there is no need to track those, but note your focused appeals. If you send out an email to every dad in the ministry, make a list of who received it by name.

2. Next, follow up. Start with phone calls. Keep track the messages you've left. When you call, say, "I'm just following up to see if you got my email. We want to increase the number of dads in our classrooms, and I think you'd be awesome!" If you talk to someone who wants more information, note that, and send them a follow-up letter and application!

3. If they decline, note that so that you don't reach out to them again for a while. Leave them off any follow-up email that you send out. Note whether this is a permanent decline because there is a reason they will never serve, aren't qualified, or whether it is just a season.

Online Resource: Download the Meet Our Newest Volunteer poster. Go to Kidology.org/toolbox

4. If someone says, "I can't right now due to my job being a little crazy." Respond, "Sorry to hear that, what if I called you about helping over the summer for a few months?" Then note their response. If they say yes, be sure to follow up later. Take some time on the phone to encourage them and ask if you can pray for them. When you reach out to a potential volunteer, show that you care about them and that you don't just see them as a potential worker.

Work the List

Make your list, work the list, and follow up on the notes and leads you get. Ask people who they think would be great volunteers and add them to the list. It is wonderful to be able to call and say, "I'm calling because Greg Johnson recommended I reach out to you about serving in our children's ministry. He thinks you'd be great." That is a much stronger opening than a straight cold call.

If you have team leaders making calls, share your lists to collaborate on your calls, emails, and appointments. Many online tools make sharing and collaborating easy. Some are even free! A little research (even contacting this author) will allow you to find a tool that works for you.

When you get new volunteers, celebrate them! Introduce them to the current volunteers with cheers and applause! Post them on social media—this adds to your general appeal. Show pictures of them serving to parents. Every new volunteer is a win, so celebrate each and every one of them as win!

Stage Five: Décor and Upkeep

Continually seek to make the ministry attractive to your volunteers. Volunteer retention is as important as recruiting. Upkeep is where you start to adjust and respond to feedback so the ministry continually improves and becomes more attractive to new volunteers.

Every volunteer that doesn't quit is one less position you need to recruit!

Once the building is buzzing with volunteers, you might think your job is done, but it isn't! Almost more important than getting new volunteers is keeping them. If you visited the grand opening of a new building and inside you discovered it was bland and boring—no one greeting you, nothing special about it, and no one even said thank you for visiting—there is a good chance you'd never return. Not out of any sense of revenge or strong negativity, just simply because there is no positive reason to make you want to return.

Getting volunteers is a huge task, but getting them in the door is only half the task. Keeping them is what counts!

You must think of volunteer appreciation as part of your volunteer-recruiting strategy. Every volunteer that doesn't quit is one less position you need to recruit. You must honestly address why volunteers quit and what you can do to keep them both equipped and encouraged.

The Room

Start with the room in which they serve.

- It is clean?
- Attractive?
- Safe?
- Well equipped?
- If you served in there, how would the room make you feel?

If there are issues with the room itself, address them right away.

I had a volunteer tell me that, at her church, everyone in the nursery complained about an issue with the changing table. Interestingly, no one told the leader. This volunteer fixed the issue on her own time. While she did a great thing, the leader should have seen this issue and addressed it long before a volunteer had to.

Leaders should:

- Examine the rooms
- Ask for feedback
- Be approachable and never defensive when people raise concerns

Of course, not every suggestion or idea can be acted on, but every idea can be listened to and responded to. If volunteers feel heard, even if an issue can't be addressed as they would like, they will know they have a voice and that the ministry they serve in is valued.

Appreciation

Never underestimate the power of words. A simple thank you to volunteers may not seem like a big deal, but the absence of those words is. People will never say, "Wow, the leader came into my room today and said thanks." But they will say, "Wow, I've been serving in there for six weeks, and not once has anyone said thank you."

Appreciation can be expressed in so many ways. Verbal appreciation is important, but look for creative ways to express your gratitude to your volunteers.

- Small appreciation gifts are wonderful. You can even have on your leadership team a Director of Encouragement, someone whose entire role is to focus on ways to encourage volunteers.
- Drop notes in the mail to thank them. Be specific, and mention noteworthy things they have done.
- Get a postcard app on your phone. Take a picture on your phone, add text, and mail it as a postcard to your volunteer by pulling their address right from your contacts list.
- Host an appreciation dinner for your volunteers to feed them and encourage them. You can do some training, too, but it may be more effective to provide some fun entertainment.

Feedback

Volunteer Feedback

Our ministry will grow as we learn and make strategic improvements. The best people to ask are the volunteers. Make sure you have a system for volunteers to provide feedback on the ministry. Seek to discover:

- What do they enjoy?
- What would be helpful?
- What would make their job easier?

Included on the next page is a feedback form that volunteers can use.

Help Us Improve!

Based on your experience as a volunteer, do you have any suggestions to improve our ministry for other volunteers, parents, and/or children? Please provide your name. Anonymous notes are discarded. We want to be able to follow up with you. Thanks!

Comments:

Date:

Name:

Volunteer Feedback

Help Us Improve!

Based on your experience as a volunteer, do you have any suggestions to improve our ministry for other volunteers, parents, and/or children? Please provide your name. Anonymous notes are discarded. We want to be able to follow up with you. Thanks!

Comments:

Date:

Name:

The harvest is plentiful, but the workers are few. Ask the Lord of the harvest, therefore, to send out workers into his harvest field.

Matthew 9:37–38 and Luke 10:2 (NIV)

Parent Feedback

Getting input from parents is important as well. Surveys can be helpful, but talking to parents is best. As you meet their needs, the ministry will improve. Included on the next page is a Parent or Guardian Survey. Please modify it for your own ministry, but keep it short for the best results.

In Closing

Recruiting is never easy, but it is much easier if you develop a strategy before you start. No building appears without advanced planning. Remember, it's God's ministry. He will provide the workers, but we need to prepare the field.

Jesus said in both Matthew 9:37–38 and Luke 10:2 (NIV),

The harvest is plentiful, but the workers are few. Ask the Lord of the harvest, therefore, to send out workers into his harvest field.

My dad used to say, "When God puts something in his word twice, he's trying to make sure you don't miss it." Twice, God acknowledges that the workers are few.

It's normal to need help, but God also reminds us that he is in charge. We are admonished to pray and ask for workers. He knows what we need and who we need. And he is quite capable of moving minds and hearts to serve in the children's ministry.

Talk about encouraging—we have God on our recruiting team!

Perhaps you need to stop reading for a moment. Right now, lift up your ministry to God in prayer. He is ready and waiting to respond.

Parent or Guardian Survey

How Are We Doing?

Parent/Guardian Name(s): ______________________________

Parent/Guardian Email(s): ______________________________

Parent/Guardian Phone(s): ______________________________

How long have you been attending our church?

How did you hear about our church?

What were your first impressions of the children's ministry?

What do your kids like best about their experience at church?

What keeps you coming back to our church?

Is there something we could be doing to better serve or minister to your family?

How can we pray for you?

These questions serve as a guide to help us continually improve our ministry. If there is something you'd like to share that isn't covered here, please let us know. You are welcome to use additional space, send an email, or make an appointment if you'd like to discuss anything further. We are here to serve you, and your feedback is important to us!

The Tool of Communication

Say It Often; Say It Well!

Communication is one of the biggest challenges in ministry. So many issues rise or fall based on communication between our families, leaders, and volunteers:

- Ministry growth
- Recruiting
- Special events
- Planning
- Child security

Everyone is bombarded by hundreds of marketing messages every day on radio, television, print, email, web ads, and even text messages. How can we cut through the clutter and get *our* important information noticed?

There is no one way to cut through the noise and effectively communicate with everyone you hope to reach. This is not an area where you can just wing it—you need to be intentional and strategic. A communication strategy will cover:

- Who are you trying to reach?
- What communication tools will you use?
- How often will you push out communication?
- When will you try to reach them?

Make a plan, and then work the plan!

Step One: Cover the Basics

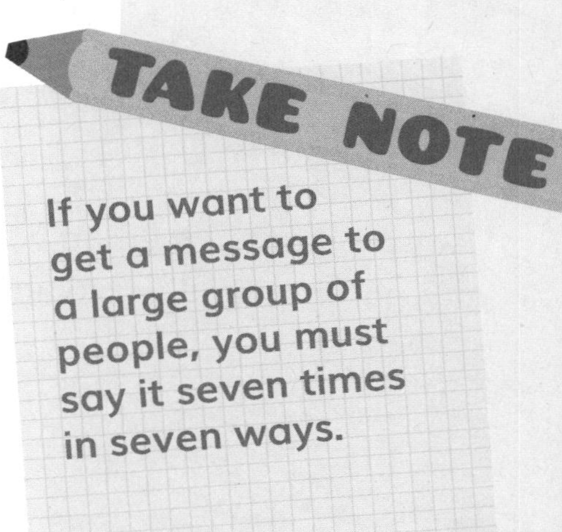

Get the information out to the right people on a regular basis.

There is a marketing principle that says if you want to get a message to a large group of people, you must say it seven times in seven ways. People are busy, and often they miss a message and need a reminder. We need to deliver messages in formats that will produce the most responses.

Before we get into some ways to communicate, take a few minutes to fill out the form on the next page. If you have a staff or leadership team, this is an excellent activity to do together.

Communication Methods

Tools We Are Using

List every tool or method you are using to communicate with your parents, leaders, volunteers, and community.

Tools We Could Use

List new ways you could communicate. Disregard any obstacles or challenges that prevent them from being used. Those can be addressed later. For now, you are just listing ideas.

Crazy Ideas!

Just for fun, list some crazy ideas you likely could never do but think would be awesome. You might end up using one!

Methods of Ministry Communication

Here are some of the basic methods of communication that you should use in your ministry, if you aren't already.

The Church Bulletin

While often decried as an ineffective mode of communication, it is still critical to use it for minimal ministry details. Think of church bulletin announcements as press releases. While they do not generate many direct leads, they are a direct source for people looking for information. If people want to get the basic date, time, and other general information about something, they will look here. Later, they may try more creative means for discovering the event.

Church bulletins are a waste of time and effort if they are the *only* method used. Many churches limit bulletin announcements to events that are church-wide this may not always be an option for children's ministry.

The Church Newsletter

If your church publishes a print newsletter, make sure the children's ministry has a presence in it. While this isn't the most effective means for younger families, it can be a great tool for communicating with the older generation that prefers a print newsletter over emails. Use this tool to communicate your bigger needs or even dreams. The newsletter audience is one that can support your ministry prayerfully and financially.

Email Blasts

We live in an electronic age, and email is a part of everyone's day. You can reach people today on their smartphones, tablets, and computers with email. Here are some tips to make email effective.

- **Use a consistent subject line and email address.** When people want information, they can easily find your email and get the details they need.

Humor is helpful! 😄

- **Create a consistent header image.** Readers will know at a glance that this is from you and that it contains important children's ministry information.
- **Keep your messages short.** Format the email with easily accessible details, perhaps with bullet points.
- **Provide links for more information.** Links could be to a webpage, blog, social media post, or downloadable file.
- **Use engaging images.** These catch the eye and draw the reader in. Humor is helpful, too!
- **Know your audience.** If you are combining audiences, such as parents and volunteers, make it clear which section is for whom. Otherwise, people will stop reading as soon as they think it isn't for them.
- **Include a summary.** People delete emails frequently, knowing they will get another one. At the bottom of each email, include a summary of upcoming events, dates, and links.
- **Choose strategically when to send.** Marketing experts say that Tuesdays and Wednesdays are the best day to email. Friday is the worst. Choose your strategy, and then stick with it.
- **Be consistent.** People will start to count on your messages if you are consistent. It's OK to skip a message if there is no pressing need. However, you may choose these times to share an encouraging story or report that will keep the ministry on their mind.
- **Be focused.** Don't promote everything in every email. There may be times you promote only one thing. People tend to delete long emails or decide to read them later. And we know that later rarely comes.

Text Message

We live in an era where we can reach people instantly. This can be a good thing, but it can be abused as well. Texting suggests urgency. Therefore, use it for reminders and alerts. Texts are ideal when people are unlikely to see an email. You can remind volunteers of commitments the day before they serve, of openings that spring up on Saturday, or of event registration that is about to close.

Many volunteer applications ask, "How do you prefer to be contacted with ministry updates?" Text is usually an option. Preferences do not necessarily mean that you don't contact everyone via that route, but it's helpful to know the most effective way to communicate.

Flyers

In a digital world, a flyer is something tangible. It may be true that half the flyers end up in the trash, but as a mass mail marketer once quipped, "I know half the mail I send is never opened. But until they figure out how to tell me which half, I'll keep mailing all of them."

- **Tell it all.** Flyers allow you to provide a lot more detail than other mediums.
- **Make it fun.** The front can be bright and bold. The reverse side can have smaller text that provides more complete details.
- **Be creative.** Choose different sizes to capture attention: business cards, bookmarks, etc.

Knowing that kids often turn flyers into paper airplanes, I once sent home paper airplanes that said "Open Me" on the wings. I hoped that a curious parent might wonder what was inside. Go ahead, file that under "Crazy Ideas" on your Communication Methods worksheet (p. 132).

Brochures

The target audience for a ministry brochure is new people at your church. Every ministry ought to have a sharp looking brochure that provides an overview of the entire children's ministry.

- It also needs to answer the question, "Why should we bring our children to this church and not the one down the street?"
- Address potential concerns parents may have about child safety and security. Are your volunteers screened and trained? Do you use a secure check-in system?
- Be sure to provide short and succinct information.

If possible, enlist the help of someone who is skilled in creating marketing pieces. Remember, your brochure is often the first impression you give to guests. It is also something you can drop in the mail to guests after their first visit.

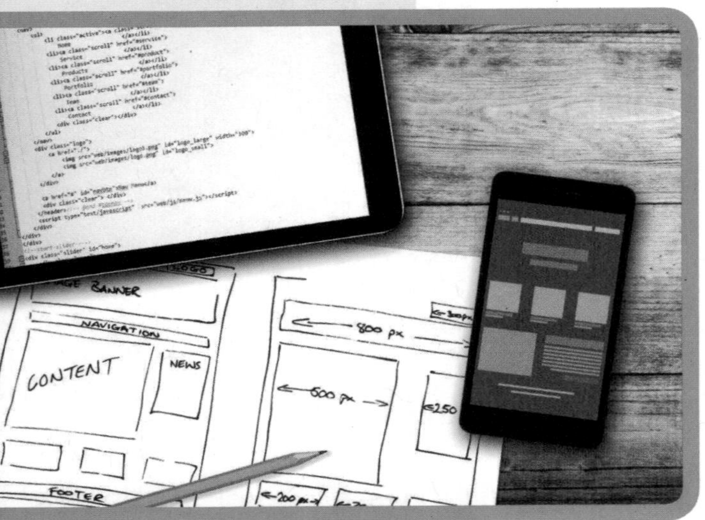

Website

Your website needs to be mobile friendly because half of your content will be read on smart phones and tablets. Take some time to visit your church's website. Focus on the children's ministry area. Is the information up to date? Is the information helpful to prospective visitors to your church?

Most families today will check out a church's website before visiting the church. An outdated or confusing website may mean they never even arrive at your church. Not every children's ministry leader is skilled in creating webpages or updating them. That's OK. Just find someone who is and oversee what they do.

If your church website is static or you are unable to edit it, consider creating a separate site for the children's ministry.

A blog can be fairly easy to set up and used as a communication portal for parents, volunteers, and event promotion.

Social Media

Many ministries today use social media as a primary means of ministry communication and promotion.

- A **social media page** can be a simple way to make your ministry discoverable. It is open to the public and should only be used for public announcements and promotion.

- A **social media group** can be far more effective in day-to-day communication. If you use a closed group and only admit parents and volunteers, you also make it safer for people to post pictures of children.

KEEPING SHARP

Use pictures and videos to promote events beforehand and to celebrate them afterward. You can post to social media about:

- Recruiting needs
- Reminders of events
- Encouraging notes
- Helpful information for parents and volunteers

Social media can also be a powerful tool in keeping up with what's going on in the lives of your families and volunteers so you can minister to them appropriately.

Signs and Posters

- Consider signs and posters as a method for creating awareness.

- Make them attractive, and present key information in bold, easy-to-read fonts.

- Don't clutter them with too many details.

- Most people will look for more information in other mediums.

- Remember, an inquiring person is an engaged person!

Think creatively about where to place the posters. Any place people pause is a good place for a poster.

Place them above drinking fountains, near the coffee machine, and where parents wait to pick up kids. Some churches are bold enough to post them inside restroom stall doors and even above urinals! I know a youth pastor who placed posters on the ceiling because he noticed the youth were often laying on the floor during the message.

Walk around your building and think about where you could place some strategic signage.

Monitors

Televisions aren't just for shows any more. Most monitors today have USB or HDMI ports. If connected to a USB or computer, images will scroll on the screen via slideshow. Some churches even hang the monitors vertically to catch the people's attention and display rotating images. Short videos can be used as well. Notice how monitors are used in restaurants, stores, and malls.

Try Something New

We can wring our hands and complain about how people don't read, aren't responsive, or ignore our efforts. Or we can look for new and creative ways to capture their attention.

I've seen inflatables, wind socks, giant balloons, puppets, or costumed characters used to capture people's attention.

First get a laugh, then engagement, and then the message is delivered. Look back at some of the crazy ideas you listed. Pick one and try it! You might just be amazed at the results!

Step Two: Message Evaluation

I know some leaders will read the previous ideas and think, "I'm doing all of that, and no one reads any of it." Perhaps it is time to change the question from "How can I better promote?" to "Why aren't they listening?"

The hard reality? Those you are trying to reach:

- Know exactly when and where their favorite sports teams are playing
- Remember where to drop off their kids for activities
- Are capable of remembering important things

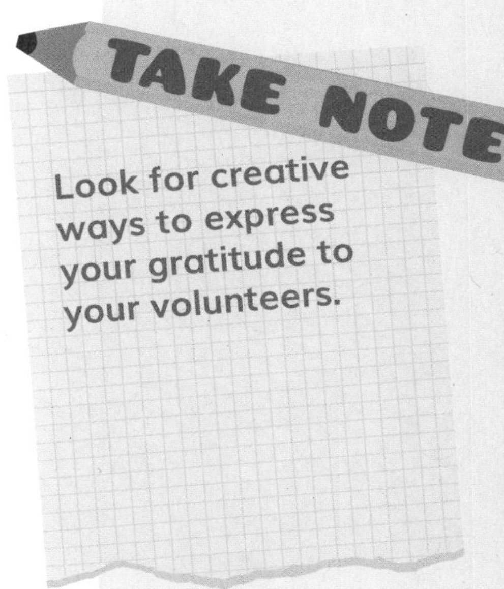

Before you get upset about how the church is such a low priority to Christians, breathe. Take a more positive approach. Ask some honest questions of yourself as a leader.

If what you do at church is truly valuable and important, then *people will look for the communication!* Your job isn't just to get the information out, it is to raise the bar. Make church activities something they won't want to miss!

Let's take a hard look at some of the communication problems that plague the church. Maybe others are as frustrated with us as we are with them. Instead of blaming the audience, let's take a look at our message.

Consider the questions below. Some of these may be tough to answer. If you are willing to make an honest assessment—and make changes as a result—you will see improved communication.

1. **Is your information easy to find?** If you were new to the church, and wanted to be instantly involved in everything, how easy (or difficult) would it be to find the information you needed? Don't make people work so hard.
2. **Where is your information?** Do you have a centralized location at the church where people can get information on anything related to children's ministry? Or is information scattered all over the church on various tables and bulletin boards? Perhaps people are trying to get information, but you've made it into a game of hide-and-seek.
3. **Is your website accessible?** Can people get the information they need in a timely manner? Is it linked well on the main site?

4. **How's your lingo?** Do you use recognizable names for your programs and events? Or is your ministry like an exclusive club where only insiders can understand the lingo? Cool names can be confusing. It's fun to brand our ministry programs and rooms, but they need to be labeled so newcomers can figure out where to go.

5. **How regular is your communication?** Do people know what is going on, or are they always wondering how and when they will find out? Consider asking some volunteers and parents if they ever have such questions.

6. **Who are your messengers?** Do you primarily count on children to communicate or deliver important information to their parents? I hope not. Kids are adorable, but they are lousy at transferring information to parents.

7. **Are you using ALL your resources?** Do you think your work is done after you post a bulletin announcement? Be creative and consider more ways to reach people. Do you utilize:
   - Bulletin announcements
   - Bulletin boards
   - Church website
   - Parent mailings
   - Pulpit announcements
   - Email lists
   - Phone calls
   - Voicemail
   - Postcards
   - Calendars
   - Take-home flyers
   - Banners
   - Posters
   - Bathroom signs
   - Drinking-fountain signs
   - Windshield flyers?

   Great! That's a good start. Now think up some more!

8. **Are you doing too much and overwhelming families with lots of activities?** You've heard it said, "too much of a good thing is not a good thing." Less can be more.

9. Is it worth it? Is the quality of your ministry worth attending? Seriously. If you weren't paid to come to your church, would you bring your family?

Bottom line: The challenge is not to get your families and volunteers to read. The challenge is to make your message valuable to them. It's a high calling, but it's the highest calling there is.

STEP THREE: GOING RELATIONAL

This is the secret weapon in your communication toolbox. At the end of the day, people respond to people. People come to an event (or volunteer to work an event) because of relationships. They either have a relationship with you or another leader, or they desire to have relationship.

In a world of mass marketing, personal communication stands out.

No technological advance will ever replace the power of the personal invitation. It is effective precisely because it is less expected today. When you call someone on the phone, stop them in the foyer, or send them a personal note. It makes a dramatic difference. In a world of mass marketing, personal communication stands out. When people scan their inboxes, what are they primarily looking for? Personal notes. When people screen phone calls, what is the criteria for answering? A familiar voice.

- Use the phone.
- Write personal emails.
- Handwrite notes. (This will truly shock people today!)
- Stop them at church and invite them.

Change your message from, "We hope to have a great turn out," to, "I'm hoping you'll be there!"

If you have a larger ministry, you may not be able to invite every single person personally, but others can. Assign your leaders to make personal calls. Use leadership meeting time to write handwritten notes. Take people out to lunch or coffee, and let them know how important they are to you, not just to the ministry.

Despite the time and effort I've spent on making amazing posters, in twenty years of ministry, I've never received a compliment. Rather, people thank me for personally inviting them. You still need all the marketing tools, but it will always be the personal invite that is the most effective. Use it often. Use it well.

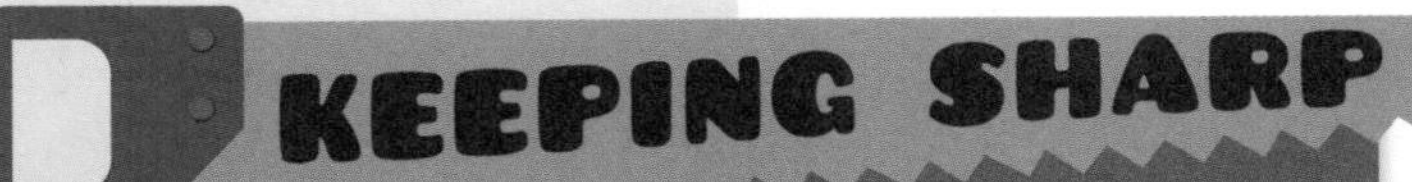

The challenge is not to get your families and volunteers to read. The challenge is to make your message valuable to them.

Sample Communication Plan

Audience	Method	When	Frequency	Notes
Everyone	Website	Updated Monthly	Continual	Website reviewed monthly to make sure nothing outdated is live.
Everyone	Flyers/ Posters/TV Monitors	Updated Weekly	Continual	Flyers with details, poster to announce, and TV monitors to promote, updated weekly.
Children's Ministry Leadership	Email with PDF Report	Wednesday	First Wednesday of the Month	Create a ministry report with attendance, highlights, and upcoming events with info leaders need to know.
Parents	Email Blast	Wednesday	Weekly	We'll use an email service and encourage all parents to sign up for weekly ministry updates.
All Children's Ministry Volunteers	Email Blast (Same one as parents)	Wednesday	Weekly	Same email parents get, but with section for volunteers, might encourage some parents to volunteer
Children's Ministry Volunteers	Email Blast	Thursday	Weekly	Send small group guide and ministry updates
Children's Ministry Volunteers	Video	In Thursday Email	Monthly	Update on upcoming series and any program changes and special events
Special Needs Ministry	Email Blast	Friday	Bimonthly	Contains updates on the ministry, needs, and encouraging articles
Church Wide	Newsletter	December	Annual	Children's Ministry News created to report on the year. Event highlights, attendance report, significant needs, spotlight on volunteers, etc.

Use the form on the following page to make a plan of how you will communicate with your various audiences. Note that some can be combined. You need to be intentional in who you are reaching, when you are reaching them, and how often you are reaching out.

Review and update your communication strategy regularly. Consider if you are missing an audience or if another method could be used.

Communication Plan Worksheet

Audience	Method	When	Frequency	Notes

The Tool of Encouragement

Don't Forget It's a Ministry

It is critical that we never lose sight of the *ministry* we are leading. Our time gets filled with recruiting, program planning, marketing, organizing, and communicating. All of this is important—and is a part of ministry—but it isn't the ministry itself. When it comes to church work, these tasks are all a means to a higher end.

Our mission is to bring people to Christ, build them up, and equip them for a life of serving God. Constantly look for ways that you can encourage your families, leaders, and volunteers. I'll give some examples, but allow the Holy Spirit to prompt some of your own ideas.

TAKE NOTE

The number one reason volunteers leave church positions is that they didn't feel like anyone cared about them. Make sure this isn't true in your ministry.

Pause after asking, "How are you?"

Often, we ask this question as a friendly greeting instead of as a sincere question. When people answer with a generic, "fine," you can follow up with a sincere question. This lets them know that you weren't just greeting them. You really do want to know how they are doing. Sometimes, people will answer honestly but vaguely because the time or setting isn't ideal for a deep conversation.

Answers like, "It's been a tough week," or, "I'm just glad the week is over," or, "Let's hope next week is better," are honest hints that life has been tough. If church is about to start, you may not be able to delve too deeply at the moment. But you can say, "I'm so sorry to hear that, later I'd like to hear how I can pray for you." Talk to them as soon as you can. If you miss them after church, a call the next day—or even a text—lets them know you actually heard them and that you care.

The number one reason volunteers leave church positions is that they didn't feel like anyone cared about them. Make sure this isn't true in your ministry.

Revive the written word.

A handwritten note or postcard stands out like a shining beacon declaring, "You are worth my time." If you send birthday cards, add a personal touch. Out-of-the-blue notes are even better. They tell someone that you thought of them and wanted to let them know how important they are to you and the ministry.

When you notice a volunteer doing something amazing, write to them. How often do we think that no one even notices the things we do? Make sure your volunteers know that you notice them.

Reach out and touch someone.

A jingle from a 1980s phone company ad sings, "Reach out, reach and touch someone." The principle is true in ministry. Relationships are strengthened when we talk. Utilize downtime to reach out. Perhaps you have time in your car or while doing mindless tasks. Work through a list of volunteers or simply ask the Holy Spirit to bring to mind those who need a personal touch from you today.

Break bread together.

We often joke about food being a necessary ingredient for fellowship, but that's a good thing. Meals are relaxed. Conversation flows naturally. Invite people out to eat who are valuable to you.

- Find out how they are doing.
- Ask how you can pray for them.
- Get to know them and their interests.

I heard a pastor once say that our close friends are those who have been into our home. Prayerfully consider your home as a ministry location.

When you invite people to your home, they get to know you beyond just your leadership role at church. They see your hobbies and your interests, and your relationship will deepen. While you shouldn't invite yourself into someone else's home, never turn down an invitation to visit someone.

There are smartphone apps that allow you to take a picture, write a note, and send a printed postcard. You can have the entire thing done and sent before you even leave church!

"I've learned that people will forget what you said, people will forget what you did, but people will never forget how you made them feel."

Maya Angelou

Hospitality is a spiritual gift that, when used wisely, can reap great benefits for the ministry.

Strive to be known for caring more about people than about amazing programming. If the Apostle Paul were writing 1 Corinthians 13 today, he might have written,

> *If I build amazing ministry programs, but do not have love, I am only a resounding gong or a clanging cymbal. If I have the gift of leadership and vision, can organize the supply closet, or execute a special event flawlessly, but do not have love, I am nothing. If I can recruit more than enough workers and sacrifice my body working long hours (even doing all the clean up myself) but do not have love, I gain nothing.*

Encourage because people need it. Your leaders and volunteers are helping at church on top of many personal struggles and challenges. You have the power to make their work at church uplift and strengthen them, not only in their ministry work, but also as individuals in whom God is working.

Keep your Tool of Encouragement sharp and handy. Use it daily!

Use the form on the next page to make a list of the people you need to encourage on a regular basis. Use additional copies of this page if necessary.

While verbal encouragement is fantastic, make sure you make efforts demonstrating that you took time out of your busy life to build into theirs. Set a goal for when you will contact every person with a word of encouragement.

Make no mistake. Encouraging others can be exhausting work. But the benefits you will reap from your efforts will make it all worthwhile. Think of the time and energy you'll save by having ready, willing, able, and *encouraged* volunteers by your side at all times!

Operation Encouragement Checklist

GOAL: Complete this page by: _______________

Name	Method of Contact (Circle)	Date Done	Notes
	Call Email Text Note Other:		
	Call Email Text Note Other:		
	Call Email Text Note Other:		
	Call Email Text Note Other:		
	Call Email Text Note Other:		
	Call Email Text Note Other:		
	Call Email Text Note Other:		
	Call Email Text Note Other:		
	Call Email Text Note Other:		
	Call Email Text Note Other:		
	Call Email Text Note Other:		

3: Teaching Tools

Introduction

What Makes Great Teaching?

One of the highest honors of a children's ministry leader is being entrusted to teach children. Not every children's pastor or director teaches as a regular part of their ministry. Because their giftedness lies in other areas, some leaders recruit teachers. If you do not teach children directly, that is fine. You still need to read this chapter.

In fact, as the leader of the ministry, you must understand what makes great teaching so you can properly oversee the effectiveness of your teachers. Once you've read this chapter, share it with your teachers.

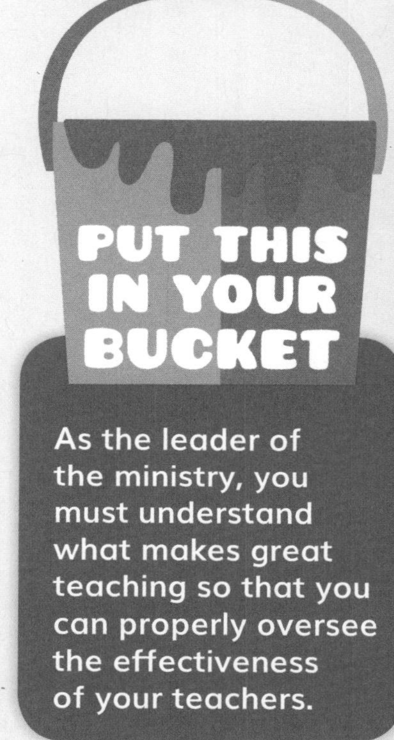

PUT THIS IN YOUR BUCKET

As the leader of the ministry, you must understand what makes great teaching so that you can properly oversee the effectiveness of your teachers.

If quality teaching is not a high priority, I would challenge you to raise the bar. Ineffective teaching makes everything else in your ministry a waste of time. Imagine going to a fancy restaurant with an amazing atmosphere, friendly staff, and impressive menu. If the food is terrible, you'll never go there again. In fact, you'll likely warn others to avoid it as well. It's the food that matters.

The same is true with your children's ministry. It doesn't matter how amazing everything else may be. If the teaching is boring or ineffective, the rest doesn't matter.

WATCH THIS VIDEO:
The High Calling to Teach
Visit Kidology.org/toolbox

Building great lessons requires sharp teaching tools. The effective teacher has a toolbox filled with a variety of tools that, if used correctly, can make their teaching fun and effective. Let's look at some tools that will make your teaching terrific.

Teaching Tool 1: Curriculum

While purchasing a curriculum isn't necessary, it is extremely helpful. Curricula save a lot of time in lesson preparation. They also have an overall strategy, called a scope and sequence, to what is being covered by the teaching.

Scope and Sequence

Some churches will skip purchasing curricula in order to save money. If you do this, know that some intentional effort needs to be put into planning what will be taught. You don't want teachers simply to teach whatever they want on a weekly basis. Without an overall strategy, some topics are repeated more often than necessary, and other important topics can be missed completely. Writing your own lessons can be rewarding, but if you do, plan out the entire year (or more) so that you have an intentional strategy for what will be covered. Consider putting a team together to determine the scope and sequence of the lessons you plan to write.

If you are going to use a published curriculum, take a close look at its scope and sequence so you'll know what the lessons' goals are. Remember, you can modify a curriculum's scope and sequence in any way you want so it better fits your own goals

KEEPING SHARP

The scope and sequence is your blueprint for what kids are going to learn by attending your programs. It describes both what will be taught and the order in which it will be taught. When reviewing curriculum for purchase, request the publisher send you the scope and sequence. Carefully review it to determine if you like the objectives of the material. If you are writing your own curriculum, develop your scope and sequence even before you write the first lesson.

and objectives. The key is to develop a well-rounded education. You don't want your ministry to have any critical gaps in what the kids should learn and know.

Selection Process

The market is filled with many different options. It can be overwhelming! Avoid the tendency to look at a lot of curriculum websites and drown yourself in marketing materials.

First, make a list of what is important to you.

- Do you want your kids to study through the Bible?
- How long do you want that to take? One year? Two? Three?
- Do you want the gospel included?
- What about a missions emphasis?
- How will you group the classes? Large? Small? By age?
- Do you want a lot of media or very little?
- Are crafts important?
- What engages parents?

Once you've listed all the objectives you'd like, rank them in order of importance. A curriculum doesn't need to have everything you want, but you do need to determine what is most important to you.

Something's Missing

Look at the curricula you're considering, and see which best fits your objectives. Even if a curriculum is missing something you want, it's worth considering if it's strong in meeting other important objectives. You can always find another source or create your own material.

Stick with It

Choosing a curriculum is important, but once you do, it is important to stick with it for a few years. If you change curricula too often, you'll run into repeating some lessons and missing out on other content.

Make It Your Own

Finally, keep in mind that the curriculum exists to serve you. It is a helpful tool, but you are still the teacher. While it's good to stick to the main theme to accomplish the overall goals of the lesson, use your own ideas to better communicate concepts or build on the material. God appointed you as the teacher—not the curriculum. It is your guide, not your master. Prayerfully consider the main objectives and suggestions as you plan. But in the end, make the lessons your own.

Teaching Tool 2: The Anatomy of a Lesson

The Opener

You've heard it said, "You don't get a second chance to make a first impression." How you start your lesson will greatly determine how engaged and interested your audience is for the rest of your limited time with them. Don't start like a locomotive that slowly picks up speed.

God has appointed you as the teacher—not the curriculum. It is your guide, not your master.

Start like a horse race. Right out of the gate, have something interesting and engaging. Immediately engage both the eyes and minds of your group.

How?

- Games
- Object lessons
- Visual aids and videos
- Puppets
- Music

Many teachers start by saying, "Today we are going to be learning about such and such." When you do this, you are asking your audience to decide whether or not the topic is of interest to them. Don't give them that choice.

The only worse opener is to lecture the kids to sit still and be quiet because the lesson is about to start. Unfortunately, I've seen this approach far too often. Imagine if the adult service started out with a lecture on how the adults need to sit down, face the front, put their phones away, and give their pastor the attention he deserves. If that would be a disastrous start to an adult service, why would we do that with children?

Never command the attention of children. Instead, capture it. Put intentional thought into how you will begin your lesson. A strong opener will have the kids' attention for the rest of the lesson.

The Closer

Closing strong is as important as starting strong. The goal of the closer is to make sure the children leave knowing the purpose of the lesson. While an opener can be several minutes long, a solid closer is short, sweet, and to the point. It is memorable and practical.

Some teachers find it helpful to script their closer and memorize it. It really is that important. You don't want to ramble on and on. You aren't trying to give them every possible application to the lesson, but *one thing* you want kids to walk away with.

If done well, when parents ask their children what they learned, your closer will be what they repeat to their parents. It is the main point, the big idea, the ultimate reason you taught your lesson today.

Most lessons include a main point, big idea, lesson goal—whatever it's called, in a good curriculum, it will be there. This is your closer. If you aren't given this statement, determine it for yourself. It can be repeated multiple times throughout the lesson, but in your closer, bring it home.

Application

Also called life application, application is what your kids are expected to do as a result of the lesson. It answers the question, "So what?" Why was this lesson important? Make it both practical and realistic, but it's OK to be challenging.

Most often, application is included in the closer. It could also be part of small-group activities. Regardless of where it is written into a lesson, it should be incorporated into everything kids do, see, and hear. The best curricula will write it into every activity the kids do.

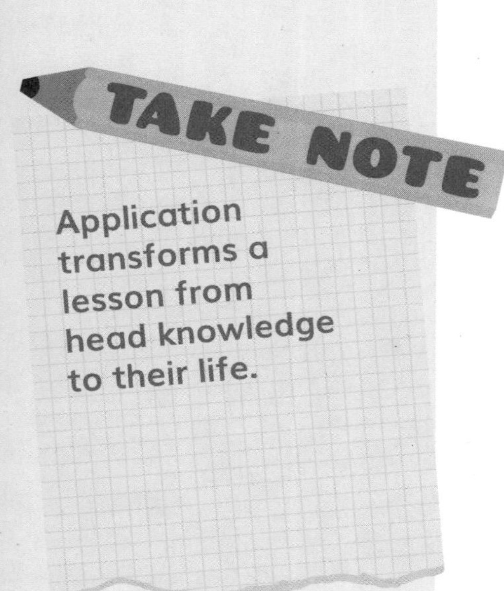

Some of the best stories you'll hear are the ones parents tell you about their kids applying an application challenge to their lives. Most of these amazing stories would never have happened if the kids had not been intentionally and specifically challenged to do something with what they learned. Application transforms a lesson from head knowledge to their life. It translates knowledge into action.

As you pray, plan, and prepare your lesson, ask yourself, "If challenged, what might a child be able to do as a result of this lesson?"

Teaching Tool 3: Tricks of the Trade

Show and Tell

One of the most important methodologies of teaching children is to be visual. While there are different learning styles, everyone learns better with visual reinforcement. Direct instruction—talking at kids—is one of the most common and least effective teaching methods. When we talk at kids, they usually zone out.

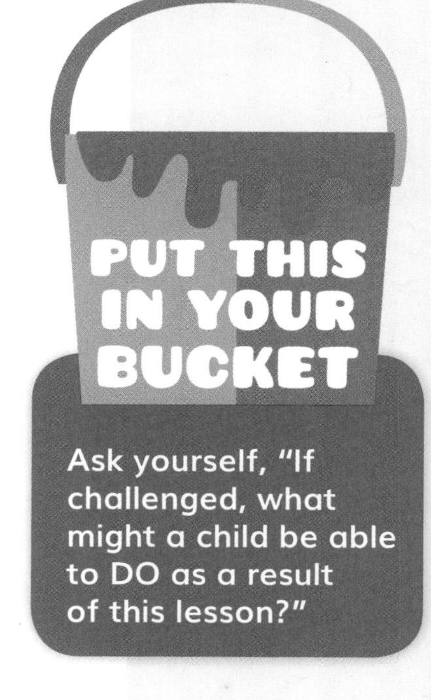

Ask yourself, "If challenged, what might a child be able to DO as a result of this lesson?"

Instead, think of your lesson as a show-and-tell presentation. Give children something to look at while you are talking.

Use:

- Props
- Costumes
- Image displays
- Puppets
- Object lessons
- Magic tricks

You can:

- Draw on a white board
- Have kids hold objects
- Have kids hold letters to spell out a word

Your kids' retention of the lesson will dramatically increase when you are a visual teacher.

When you are planning your lesson, continually ask yourself, "How can I show this?" Understanding and retention will dramatically increase when you are a visual teacher.

Pace

The key with teaching is to keep things moving.

Remember screensavers? If we use one today, it's just for fun, but there was a time when a screensaver actually did save your screen. But they still kick in the same way. If there is a lack of engagement with the computer, the screensaver kicks on, and it stays on until there is motion. A tap of the keyboard or a bump of the mouse will wake the computer up. However, if the screensaver is on long enough, the computer completely shuts down.

Kids have their own internal screensavers. Unless we keep them engaged, their internal screensaver kicks in. Instead of a flying toaster or coastal view of Hawaii, they start to think about what they are going to do after church, a video game they enjoy playing, or who knows what else. The crazy thing is you can't tell the screensaver is on by looking at them. They may appear to be looking at you, but their mind is somewhere else. The only way to bring them back is to bump their attention somehow.

This internal screensaver is why pace is so important when you are teaching. Keep things moving. You want your kids on the edge of their seats. You want them wondering what will be next.

One of the best tips I ever got was to stop while they like it. It sounds counterintuitive: If you have an activity the kids like, the tendency is to stretch it out as long as possible. Ironically, this can completely backfire.

If you stop an activity once the kids are weary of it, the next time you want to use it, the kids won't remember the twenty minutes that they loved it. Instead, they remember getting bored, restless, or exhausted and won't want to do it again.

But, stop an activity while the kids are loving it—despite their cries of despair—and the next time you bring it out, they will remember the last associated emotion, and it will be completely positive.

Movement

God wired kids to move! While pace is about what you are doing, movement is about the children. Grown-ups may be able to sit still during a sermon, but to expect kids to sit still during a long lesson is not only unrealistic, it may be cruel.

Consider implementing a five-minute rule. If the kids haven't had an opportunity to stand or move in five minutes, they need one!

Have them:

- Jump up to answer a question
- Do hand motions that go with the lesson
- Repeat rhymes
- Compete against the other side of the room for the loudest cheers
- Come on stage to participate
- Hold props
- Represent geographical locations as you tell a story
- Play hangman to guess a word

As you plan your lesson, ask yourself, "When do the kids get to move?" Bottom line: keep the kids and your lesson moving.

Participation

If I had to give only one piece of advice to those who teach children, it likely would be to **turn spectators into participants.** As already mentioned, God wired kids to move. But this point is less about honoring their energy and more about how children learn. Kids don't learn by listening alone, they learn by doing. We all do! When we are a part of the learning, our retention is increased.

Don't miss out on opportunities to include kids in your lessons. The more your students are engaged in the lesson itself, rather than just sitting and watching, the more they are going to learn and retain.

As we plan our lessons, we need to constantly consider, "How can I include the children?" When first looking at a lesson, consider how much opportunity there is for the children to participate. Train your parents to ask their kids, not "What did you *learn* today?" but "What did you *do* today?" As kids describe what they did, they will reveal what they learned.

Print out the one-page poster on the following page and post it where you will see it when you are planning your lessons.

Preparation

It should go without saying: Good teachers prepare. Anyone who says, "I only teach kids," is in the wrong line of work. Teaching children is an honor and a privilege and incredibly important. Church researcher George Barna noted,

More often than not, what a person decides about truth, sin, forgiveness, and eternal consequences during their pre-teen years is the same perspective they carry with them to their grave—and beyond, wherever that may take them (*Transforming Children into Spiritual Champions*, page 63).

Take your teaching role seriously. Plan your lesson. Gather your supplies. Have your lesson plan written out, and dare I add, practice the most important aspects of your lesson. We reap results based upon our preparation. Minimal prep will result in minimal results. Prepare as though your lesson truly matters. Because it does!

Live Teaching

It's no secret we live in a highly sophisticated technical world. Many of the children we teach are already carrying smartphones and tablets. Technology is a part of their world and it's important to utilize it to reach this digital generation. But technology will never replace the effectiveness of live teaching.

TURN
SPECTATORS
INTO
PARTICIPANTS

In an age when kids spend countless hours looking at screens from phones, tablets, computers, televisions, and game systems, we can make the mistake of over-utilizing this technology in our teaching.

- A screen can't love a child.
- A screen can't care.
- A screen can't see when a child is sad or hurting.
- A screen can't relate or empathize.

We must never let screens replace relationship. There is an abundance of video-based curriculum today, and while many of them are incredibly well-produced, video can be overused. It is helpful to understand where video teaching originated and where it is best used.

A screen can't love a child. We must never let screens replace relationship.

The whole concept of video teaching was created when large churches were unable to provide enough quality teachers for their many classrooms and campuses and from the desire to have a uniform experience across all classrooms and campuses.

For a very large church or multi-campus ministry, a video-based curriculum can help to bring consistency across the experience for all the children. But even they will tell you, the videos should never replace the personal and relational interaction between children and those who are ministering to them.

It is a bit ironic and perhaps tragic that small churches, where these challenges do not exist, have allowed video teaching to take the place of real, live people communicating God's Word to the children. Even if the videos are a better quality than what a live person can offer, a real person is preferred *any time*.

Technology

Much of today's technology is fairly easy to use. Technology has made our lessons more visual, made our ministries more secure, increased the speed of communication, and so much more. Technology is constantly evolving and improving. It can be fun, but it can also be overwhelming. Just when you get something working, something newer, faster, or easier pops up.

As a child, one of my first ministry positions was serving as the overhead transparency flipper. Every worship song was printed on an overhead transparency sheet, so I had to flip them in perfect timing with the musicians. In addition, teachers used them to illustrate their lessons—and many preachers in the adult service did as well.

Then came video projectors, and the overhead projector got relegated to a distant storage closet as it was replaced by PowerPoint presentations. I once spent hours a week making PowerPoints filled with sound effects, animated words, and slide transitions. Now, I edit videos. Perhaps in a few years we'll be using augmented reality to bring the Bible to life!

The great evangelist D.L. Moody illustrated the importance of teaching children by comparing a tall candle to a short one. He asked which represented the adult and which the child. Usually, it is assumed that the tall candle represented an adult and the short one a child. Moody explained that the tall candle signifies a child because it has its entire life ahead of it. In contrast, the short candle represented a life that is nearly spent.

Don't become too dependent on it.

No matter how up-to-date our technology is, we need to make sure that it is serving us. Otherwise, we become dependent on it. I stopped spending hours on PowerPoints and finally realized that though they were effective, the value didn't measure up to the time invested in creating them.

I now set a time limit when editing a video, realizing that the audience rarely notices the difference between a video I spent thirty minutes on and one I tweaked for hours. In fact, in order to save time, I often use software or websites that will generate a highlight video automatically for me.

Ways you can use technology.

It's fun to experiment with how technology can enhance our lessons. Any time you see a new technology, ask yourself, "How can I use this to teach kids?"

- At Christmas time, the stores carry small gadgets to turn on Christmas lights. Those gadgets also allow you to turn on just about anything you want from a button in your pocket. I recently used a floor button to make items turn on with a tap of my foot. Meanwhile, I pretended the items were voice-activated. I'd tap the floor button as I said key words.

- Don't assume the newest technology is the best in every situation. I have used flannelgraphs and overhead projectors to engage today's kids. What may seem outdated to us is new to kids who haven't been around as long as we have. When I have introduced an overhead projector to today's kids, they have always been fascinated by how it works.

- Some pretty amazing technology is in everyone's pocket. A smartphone today is more powerful than all the computers used to send man to the moon. Tap into all that power with apps for communication with your teachers, parents, and community. Editing photos and videos is easy, improving our ability to market our ministry and show what God is doing.

- GIFs are super popular today. Download an app that lets you make your own!
- Take advantage of the fact that every leader now carries a camera as part of their phone. Leaders can use their phones to take pictures or video of the kids doing assignments.
- I know a pastor of pre-teens who has the kids text him questions during the lesson. He reads the questions anonymously and then answers them.

Never stop thinking of ways you can use technology to enhance your ministry. Just never give into the idea that you need technology to succeed. Remember, Jesus lived in an era with no electricity, yet he was able to minister.

Technology is valuable, but it can never replace the power of relational teaching. Many churches overuse technology at the expense of solid relational teaching. Bottom line—make sure your use of technology merits the time invested and is the most effective way to accomplish your goal. A Bible story video may be professionally produced and impressive, but a well-taught story by a live teacher can be more effective.

Games

Kids love to play! It's a huge part of how kids learn.

- As they roleplay, kids explore their identity and dreams.
- As they play organized games, kids develop social skills as well as enhance their physical and mental well-being.

Games are an essential part of effective teaching—but don't miss that they are for teaching, not filling time. Games ought to have a plan and purpose, even if that purpose is simply relationship building and social interaction.

The best games illustrate the point of a lesson.

Kidology.org is loaded with games that have a teaching application. For an example of a fun game with a message, look for the candy game on Kidology.org/toolbox.

You can incorporate games into your program in many ways:

- Have games out for children to play as they arrive.
- Do group games where everyone participates or choose contestants to compete as the rest watch.
- Have ongoing games, such as raising funds for charity or bringing friends to church.

TAKE NOTE

Have a fun game you made up that has a teaching point? Be sure to share it on Kidology so other kids can enjoy it too! Just submit at Kidology.org/submit

Kids love to play and enjoy competition. Don't feel you always have to give prizes. Sometimes just winning is enough of a reward. If you do give prizes, give something to everyone for participating and doing their best. This helps remove the sting or embarrassment of not winning.

The point is having fun. Silly prizes are the best. I've even awarded an official pat on the back delivered with great fanfare so that even the other team just gets a laugh and realizes they didn't really miss out on a great prize.

Learning Styles

We all learn differently. Some kids are visual learners, while others are auditory learners. As you may have noticed, many kids need to move. The term for that is *kinesthetic learners*.

We need to make sure we are hitting as many learning styles as we can as we teach. While you can't include every style in each lesson, you can try to hit as many as possible. If you use several styles in a lesson, you're likely to hit on at least one style that works for each person, since everyone learns through a combination of styles.

There are seven learning styles. It is important to be familiar with each of them. Review the information in the table about each learning style.

VISUAL (SPATIAL)	Learn through visual reinforcement: acting it out, gestures, pictures, images, videos, etc.
AURAL (AUDITORY-MUSICAL)	Learn through what they hear: sound, music, etc.
VERBAL (LINGUISTIC)	Respond best to the use of words, both in speech and writing.
PHYSICAL (KINESTHETIC)	Learn by using their bodies, hands, and sense of touch.
LOGICAL (MATHEMATICAL)	Prefer using logic, reasoning, and systems to understand.
SOCIAL (INTERPERSONAL)	Learn best in groups or with other people.
SOLITARY (INTRAPERSONAL)	Prefer to work alone and use self-study.

How do you plan your lessons and make sure you are effective with all the learning styles in your audience? Focus on the three main styles: visual, auditory, and kinesthetic.

Visual Learners

Tips for visual learners:

- Use PowerPoint presentations or videos.
- Use posters, signs, or banners to display information.
- Object lessons help kids connect physical objects to abstract concepts.
- Use skits, costumes, props.
- Draw on a white board.

Auditory Learners

To connect with your auditory learners, you have to be a little more creative. Tips for auditory learners:

- Have kids repeat key phrases.
- Teach kids to say the same response any time they hear a key word. For example, if the teacher says, "God is good," they respond, "All the time!"

A response phrase not only involves your auditory learners, but it helps all the kids pay attention. This will pull in your verbal learners as well, who learn best by repeating what they hear.

Kinesthetic Learners

We already discussed how to engage your kinesthetic learners when we discussed keeping it moving. But to summarize:

- Keep kids moving around, doing motions, or responding by standing up, sitting back down, etc.
- Play games to keep kinesthetic learners focused on the lesson.

Environment

When it comes to our teaching, we need to put attention into the environment. Environment not only has a huge impact on learning, but also influences mood and enjoyment of a situation.

Whether it is a fun-themed restaurant like the Rainforest Café or a dimly lit Italian restaurant, our environment can draw us in or turn us off. The finest food served in a dirty dive will likely end in a bad review. But serve average food in a clean restaurant with a great environment, and people will return over and over, bring friends, and even host special events there. Environment has a profound impact.

KEEPING SHARP

It doesn't take an elaborate or expensive environment to be successful.

Elaborate Environments

Too many ministries start with environment before addressing more important factors. The quality of the teaching, the relationship a teacher has with the students, and engaging kids creatively according to their learning styles is primary, but environment can help or hinder those efforts.

Sometimes leaders get discouraged or intimidated when they see the incredible environments or sets that other churches create. While environment is important, it is not the *most* important thing. I have had amazing sets with tech and puppet windows built right in. I have also done ministry where I made backdrops and props out of cardboard that I painted and assembled with tape.

The most important aspect of environment is love. If the kids feel loved and the leaders are having a great time, the environment means less and less.

Bottom Line

If you have the funds and space to go crazy with environment, by all means do so! It will help take things up a notch. When you can't, remember Jesus had no set. Yet he was able to show God's love. Jesus met needs and taught the truth in a way people could relate to. At the end of the day, love is the most important environment!

THE CLASSIC TOOL THAT STILL WORKS!

When I was mentored by my mom in how to plan a Bible lesson, she shared with me an old formula known as the Hook, Book, Look, and Took Method. When I got to Bible College, I was issued a book titled *Creative Bible*

Teaching by Lawrence O. Richards (Moody Press, 1973). I discovered my mom's source for this time-tested method.

I have a degree in Bible theology from Moody Bible Institute, a master's in Christian Education from Trinity University, and decades of pastoral ministry. With all this, I still go back to the formula my mom taught me.

The best lessons will always reflect the old Hook, Book, Look, and Took. *Old doesn't always mean obsolete!* Hook, Book, Look, and Took are four classic tools as timeless as the hammer, screwdriver, pliers, and tape measure. Use them often!

The Hook

We all get hooked.

- The first five minutes of a movie are designed to draw the viewer in for the next two hours.
- The opening chapter of a book will determine whether someone reads the whole thing.
- Thirty second commercials know the importance of the first five seconds.
- Who hasn't clicked on clickbait? These ads tease our curiosity when we are supposed to be doing something else online.

Hooks can lead us to something good, and at times they distract us toward things that are counterproductive. Regardless, hooks work!

So how do you hook kids at the beginning of your lesson? While the specific hook should be determined by your lesson objectives, you can do many things to capture their attention.

Let's look at some suggested hooks for the familiar Bible story of David and Goliath.

Questions

Well-planned questions can get your kids thinking about the topic of the day.

- If everyone else was doing the wrong thing and you could step up and do the right thing, would you?
- What if you get laughed at?
- What if it was dangerous and there was a chance you could die? Would you still do it?

Games

Open with a game! It involves all the kids and gets them having fun. If the game illustrates the main idea of the lesson, that's even better.

- Option 1: Build a giant Goliath out of wood. The kids shoot foam sling shots at the giant.
- Option 2: Fill a large bucket with foam peanuts. Slip five stones in the bucket. The kids see how quickly they can dig through the bucket and find the stones.

Skits

A skit can grab the attention of the audience. Instead of acting out the Bible story, act out a real life scenario that illustrates the topic. You can even halt the skit at the point of crisis, tell the Bible story and discuss the application, and then resume the skit to illustrate and reinforce the lesson.

A boy at school is picked on by a bully who is making fun of him because he is a Christian. Others are standing around doing nothing as the boy is taunted. Another boy walks up holding a Bible, wearing a Christian T-shirt, and eating a banana.

Pause the skit and ask the kids what the boy should do. At the end of the lesson, resume the skit. Have the boy tell the bully to knock it off.

When the bully charges, the boy drops his banana peel. The bully slips on it and falls down defeated. Talk about how a banana peel doesn't seem like something that would win a battle, but a sling shot didn't look like something to defeat a highly trained soldier who towered above David. But God was able to bring the victory!

Riddles

A riddle or quiz can engage the mind as they try to figure out the answer. It needs to be on topic and fit the lesson, but it's a sure way to get them thinking.

What is bigger than God and more evil than Satan? Rich people need it; poor people have it; and if you eat it you will die.

Let the kids wrestle with this. They will have all kinds of silly answers. You can drag it out for a while, even through the entire lesson before you reveal the answer: Nothing.

Nothing is greater than God. Nothing is more evil than Satan. Rich people need nothing. Poor people have nothing. And if you eat nothing, you will die! David knew that nothing (and no one) was more powerful than God. This gave him the courage to face Goliath.

Challenges

Sometimes you can provide a challenge to get the kids thinking about the topic of the day.

Find a really tall, big, and strong man to help you with this. The strong man stands on the stage. Challenge kids to come up one at a time and move him. They can pull on his arm, push him, or try to topple him. Of course, most will fail.

Then, toward the end, choose the smallest child in the room and tell him or her to pray and ask God for help and then push with only one finger. The giant man falls all the way down! Talk about how many of the kids didn't even try because they knew it was impossible. Others failed trying to do it on their own strength. But when the little one asked God for help, they were victorious.

Illusions (Magic Tricks)

Children love illusions!

I often joke that Jesus was the first gospel magician because he used miracles to gather a crowd.

The only difference was he didn't have anything up his sleeve. His miracles were real. We can still do our own miracles, and don't worry, the kids know you don't have any powers! They just like trying to figure out how you did it!

The following illusion is called Heavy Air.

1. Before the lesson, cut a small hole in the bottom side of a plastic cup. Make the hole big enough for your thumb to fit in.
2. Show kids the empty plastic cup, using your thumb to cover the hole.
3. Tell kids you're going to fill it with heavy air. Pretend to pour heavy air from an empty water pitcher into the cup.
4. Act like the pitcher is heavy and the cup is getting heavier as you fill it.
5. Place the cup on a clipboard and cover it with a cloth. Slide your thumb into the hole in the cup. Hold the clipboard with your fingers.
6. Walk around the room, challenging children to lift the cup from the clipboard. They won't be able to lift the cup because you're holding it to the clipboard with your thumb.

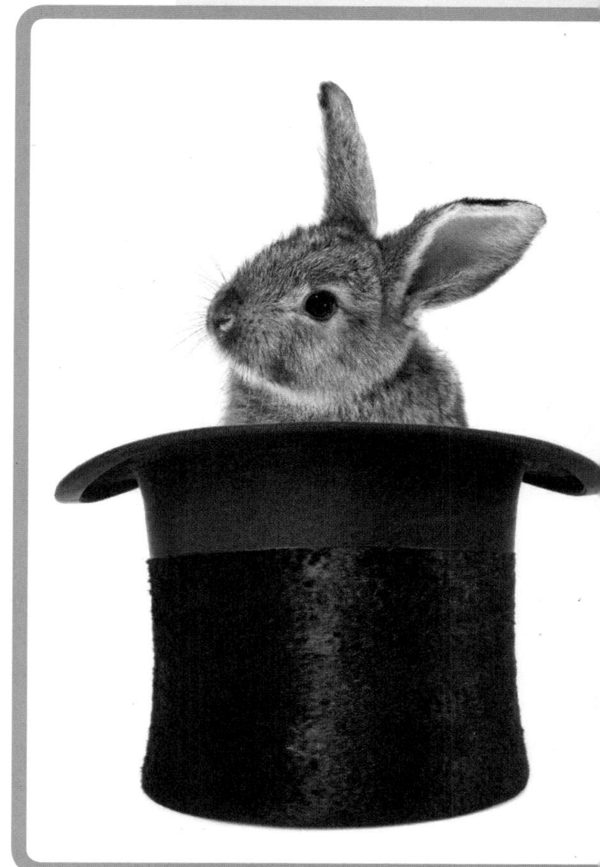

7. Finally, ask the youngest or smallest child to lift the cup. Before they do, slide your thumb out of the hole, enabling the child to lift the cup.

8. Talk about how God once used a small child to do something none of the bigger and stronger adults could do.

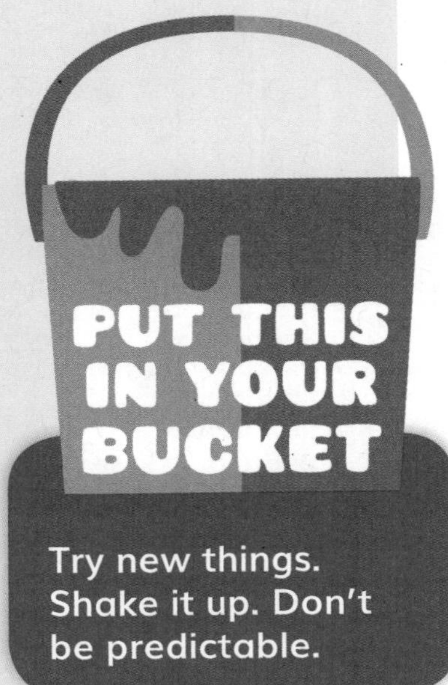

Try new things. Shake it up. Don't be predictable.

Last Word on The Hook

These were a few ideas of hooks for the story of David and Goliath. There are certainly others. The goal is to come up with something that immediately does two things:

- First, it captures attention and engages children in the program.
- Second—and this is critical—it introduces the topic of the day and gets them thinking about the main point.

And it does all this without them realizing it! A fun activity without a point is a waste of precious time. Everything you do, even the fun games or activities, should be building toward your educational goals.

Finally, be sure you try new things. Shake it up. Don't be predictable. Create an environment where kids don't want to miss church because you always have something new and interesting going on!

The Hook Practice

Here are ten well-known Bible stories. Think of a hook that you could do for each.

The Bible Story	A Possible Hook
Adam and Eve	**Sample:** Provide modeling clay as kids arrive. Challenge them to create an animal that doesn't exist. Ask them to give it a name. Show some of the creations during the lesson when you talk about how God created so many different types of animals.
Noah and the Ark	
The Crossing of the Red Sea	
The Story of Joseph	
The Story of Queen Esther	

Daniel in the Lions' Den	
Jonah and the Big Fish	
Jesus Makes a Blind Man See	
Peter Walks on Water	
Jesus Feeds 5,000	

The Book

The Bible is the Book, and no lesson should be without it. Kids need to read from and learn about the truths in the Word of God. While you can share the message of the book creatively through videos, dramas, games, and other fun activities, there should be times you simply read from the Bible.

Even if you keep it short, kids should see the Bible opened and read from. In a day and age when there is a digital version of everything, don't let the Bible become just a digital resource. It is wonderful that we can access the content of the Bible anywhere and anytime on our phones, but the digital version doesn't show the size and location of biblical passages.

There is something powerful about reading from a physical Bible. Kids see what a big book it is. They learn to understand the order, flow, and location of various books. And they can treasure their own Bibles more than they ever will a digital version.

Follow the suggestions below to bring the Bible to life!

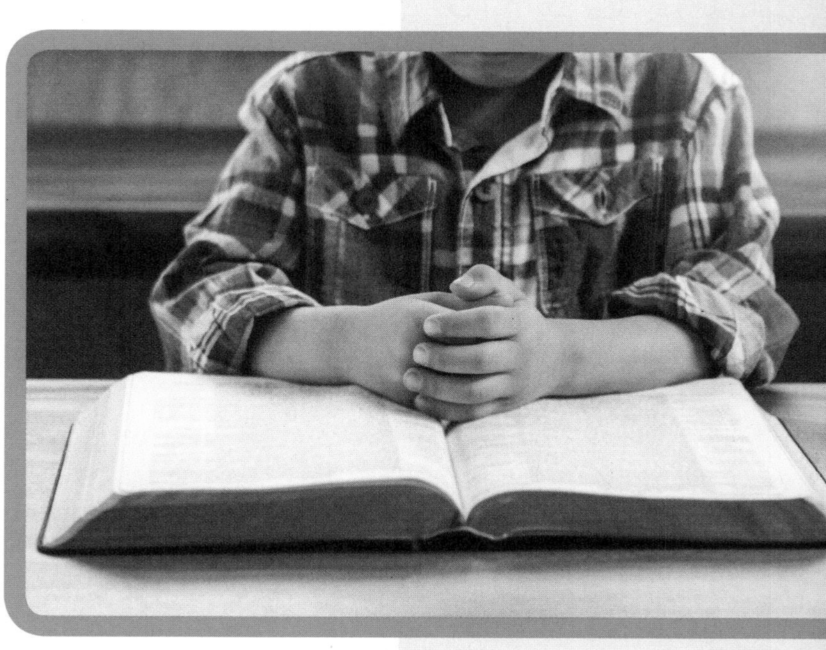

Read It

When you read the Bible, read it passionately and with authority. If there are various characters in the passage, change your voice.

Let Them Read It

Have kids look up passages and read silently. Or have a strong reader read it out loud for everyone else.

Act It Out

Pretend to be Paul sitting at a desk and reading out loud while writing one of his letters. Or ask an actor to

tell the Bible story in the first person. There are many ways you can bring the passage to life by showing the person who wrote the words or lived the story.

Video

Create a video with powerful images and have the Bible text scrolling below the images. Underscore it all with appropriate music. This can bring a passage to life in a fresh way.

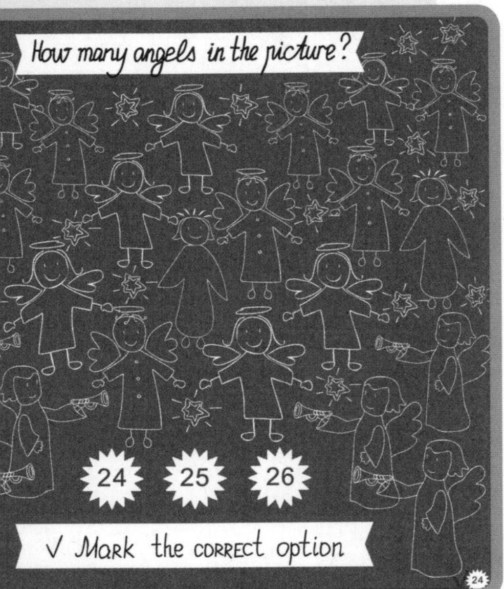

Puzzle

In small groups, provide puzzle worksheets based on Scripture. The worksheets might have:

- Bible passages with key words missing
- Codes to fill in
- Word searches

Memorization

There are endless ways to help children memorize a passage of Scripture. This is powerful as they are hiding God's Word in their hearts as the psalmist challenged (Psalm 119:11).

- Make an acronym of the first letter from each word. Or make acronyms from key words from the verse.
- Make a pictograph for each word. Create a rebus.
- Write it over and over again. Doodle as you write.
- Play hangman.
- Act it out.
- Print out the verse and have kids read it aloud. Then cover (or erase) one word and say the verse again. Continue until all the words are covered (or erased).
- Sing it out.

Break into Groups

Sometimes, especially if a passage is longer, it is better to break into smaller groups. Children may have an easier time focusing on the Scripture and not being distracted by others as the passage is read. Also in groups, children can take turns reading so that everyone participates.

Scripture to Music

One of the most powerful ways to communicate Scripture is through songs that use biblical text as lyrics. Not only does it help make the content enjoyable, but many will remember these passages years later.

Many well-loved verses have already been made into songs. If your verse has not, just make up a tune! Or have kids try to fit the words to a well-known tune such as "Mary Had a Little Lamb" or "London Bridge." Even if they can't get the words to fit the tune, they'll be memorizing just by trying!

The Book Practice

HOLY BIBLE

The Bible can be an intimidating book. It's ginormous! Think of four ways that you could help children engage with the Word of God besides simply reading it. You can take one of the ideas from the previous page and expand on it or come up with your own!

Idea 1

Idea 2

Idea 3

Idea 4

Consider sharing your best idea in the Kidology Facebook Group. Mention that this idea was inspired by *Kidology's Ultimate Toolbox*. You just might win a prize! Just find us on Facebook!

The Look

Once your students are Hooked and have read or heard passages from the Book, it is time to dig a little deeper. The Look is when kids learn why the passage is relevant.

The Look answers the questions:

- So what?
- Why are we learning this?
- Why is it important?
- What difference will it make in my life?
- How should I respond to my new knowledge?

When developing this segment of your lesson, develop some key questions to answer as a part of your teaching. Here are some different approaches you can use to develop these questions.

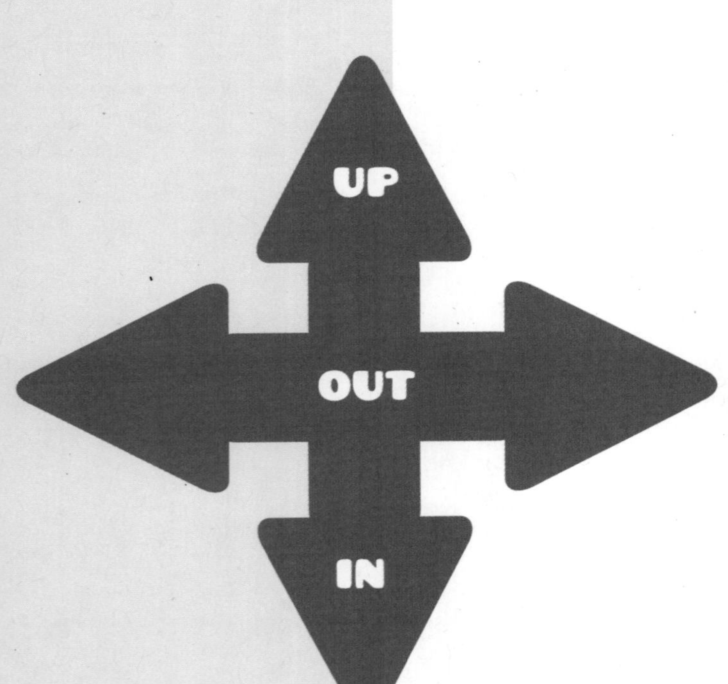

Up, In, and Out Approach

- **UP** What does this passage teach us about God?
- **IN** What does this passage teach me about myself?
- **OUT** What should I do as a result of this passage?

S.P.A.C.E.

Each letter from the word *space* offers a question to be answered after studying Scripture. Most passages, unless they are purely historical data, will touch on one of these.

S Is there a SIN to stop?

Sometimes we are exposed to a sin in our life that we need to acknowledge and repent. I originally learned this as "sin to forsake," but to avoid explaining the meaning of forsake to children, I adapted it to "sin to stop." While forsake is a stronger word, there is no mystery to what stop means.

P Is there a PROMISE to claim?

Perhaps there is a promise in the passage that we can claim for ourselves. Many of the promises in Scripture are conditional. If we do something, God will respond. Our application may be to take him up on his offer and enjoy the results of the promise.

A Is there an ATTITUDE to adjust?

We've all had a parent say, "I don't like your attitude!" It seems our heavenly Father could say the same at times. Our attitude is how we approach a topic or person and often determines how we will respond. There are times that an attitude change is just what is needed to see change in our lives.

C Is there a COMMAND to obey?

Often, Scripture is bluntly clear. When the Bible says, "Thou shalt not," there is no confusion. When we are confronted by a command issued by our creator, the proper response can only be simple obedience.

But sometimes we don't fully understand why we should obey. And sometimes it's just plain difficult! But we are to obey anyway. When we do, we learn that obedience is the quickest way to remain in the favor of and under the protection of our powerful and loving God.

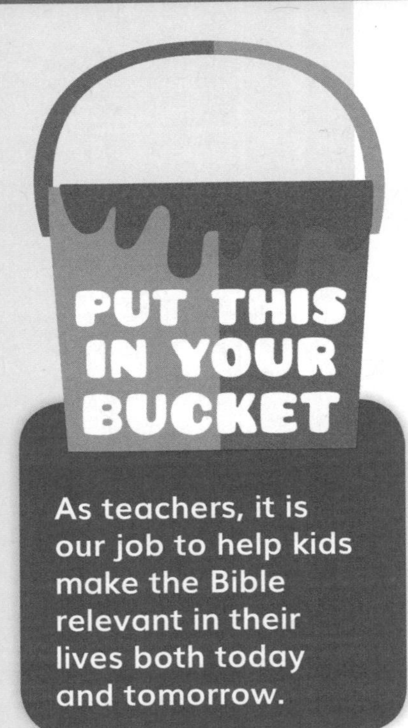

As teachers, it is our job to help kids make the Bible relevant in their lives both today and tomorrow.

E Is there an EXAMPLE to learn from?

I originally learned the *E* as "an example to exemplify." However, there are examples in Scripture that we should *not* follow. Whether it is Peter denying Christ, Jonah running away, or Moses hitting the rock when he was commanded to speak to it, we can learn from bad examples just as much as good ones. When reading a narrative passage, ask, "What can I learn from the people in this story?"

The Bible is an ancient book, but it is an eternal book. While it contains a wealth of historical information, it is loaded with timeless truths and practical principles that are as relevant today as they were the day they were written. As teachers, it is our job to help kids make the Bible relevant in their lives both today and tomorrow.

IS THERE A...

SIN to stop?

PROMISE to claim?

ATTITUDE to adjust?

COMMAND to obey?

EXAMPLE to learn from?

The Look Practice

What are three of your favorite Bible stories? List them on the next page and then prayerfully write about what that Bible story teaches. Ask yourself the **S.P.A.C.E.** questions.

After reflecting on these stories, I wouldn't be surprised if you don't find yourself itching to teach each one!

Bible Story 1

Bible Story 2

Bible Story 3

The Took

After Hooking your students, guiding them to the Book and taking a deeper Look, it is time for the Took! This is the application—action taken by kids as the result of the lesson. This is the challenge, the objective, the target you want kids to shoot for. What should kids do as a result of the lesson?

The Took should be something concrete and specific. Something they can do in the following week. It is not a generality, such as "be more kind" or "obey your parents more." They should be able to respond with a "yes" or "no" when you ask them if they did it.

While the application of a spiritual concept may be easy for adults to figure out, this doesn't come naturally to children. They need help coming up with something they can do. You are helping them create a goal for the week.

Keeping Sharp

A lesson application must fit the same criteria as the goals from section one.

A SHARP TOOK:

Specific—Give the children something specific they can do or try this week.

Healthy—It should be something that applies to the lesson they learned.

Adventurous—Make it both challenging and fun!

Realistic—Don't expect too much. Make it small so they can succeed!

Perceptual—How will they measure their progress?

A True Story

A mother once called me to ask what my lesson had been about on the previous weekend. Before I answered, I asked what prompted the question. She answered that her youngest boy did something very unusual, and she guessed it was because of something he learned at church. I explained that I taught on the Golden Rule, "Do to others as you would like them to do to you" (Luke 6:31).

At the end of the service, I asked all the children to close their eyes, bow their heads, and think of something really nice that someone could do for them. It needed to be something realistic, not "give me a million dollars." After, they raised their hand, signifying they had their idea in mind.

 **ONLINE RESOURCE:** Check out "You Are a Bible Character" on Kidology.org. Just like the characters in the Bible, our kids are average people who can experience our amazing and extraordinary God in everyday life! Visit Kidology.org/toolbox

I said, "Your assignment this week is to do that thing for someone else."

Some kids cried out, "No! You tricked us!"

I then asked the mom what happened with her boy. She told me that her youngest boy, Gabe, got some money from his grandmother for his birthday. They headed off to a toy store.

On the way, Gabe asked, "What is Matt saving up for?" Matt was his older brother.

Mom, not knowing the reason for the question, answered, "He is saving for a Spider-Man action figure."

Gabe said, "Then that's what I'm getting."

At first, his mother thought he was buying it to make his brother jealous. She told him he needed to pick something different and that it wouldn't be nice to come home with the toy Matt wanted.

Gabe replied, rather matter-of-factly, "Oh, I wouldn't do that, Mom. I'm buying it *for him*."

Surprised, she asked, "Why would you spend your birthday money on your brother?"

It was his reply that caused the mom to call me. He said, "Because I think it would be cool if Matt bought me a toy, so my assignment is to do that for him."

When we give kids a Took, we take the lesson from conceptual to practical. We give God a chance to work in their lives and demonstrate to them that *he is real*! They get to see that the same God who worked in the lives of Bible characters is still willing to work in their lives today!

The Took Practice

Here are the same ten well-known Bible stories that you practiced to make a Hook. Now it is time to take the story from the pages of the Bible and into the lives of your students! Think of a Took that you could challenge your kids with in order to help this historical story impact their lives in the following week.

The Bible Story	A Possible Took
Adam and Eve	
Noah and the Ark	
The Crossing of the Red Sea	
The Story of Joseph	

The Story of Queen Esther	Sample: When you see someone doing something that is wrong, have the courage to tell them gently that what they are doing doesn't please God.
Daniel in the Lions' Den	
Jonah and the Big Fish	
Jesus Makes a Blind Man See	
Peter Walks on Water	
Jesus Feeds 5,000	

Lawrence Richards writes:

It's best to avoid thinking of these as mechanical steps. They're more like four parts of a continuous, systematic but exciting process. In class the students probably won't even notice passage from one part of the process to another. No part is marked by routine; each is full of opportunity for flexibility and interaction. Yet each of these parts in the process has its own—and essential—role. (Creative Bible Teaching, p. 154)

Bottom Line

If you follow this lesson-prep formula, you'll always teach powerful and effective lessons. Each of these segments are critical and necessary. While they will often flow in this order, they don't always have to.

As you prayerfully plan your lessons, be alert for the Holy Spirit to give you creative ideas. Even if you use a published curriculum (which most teachers do), you still want to identify:

- What will you do to get their attention? (**The Hook**)
- What is the passage you are teaching? (**The Book**)
- How will you help your students dive into the content? (**The Look**)
- How will they apply the lesson to their lives? (**The Took**)

The next time you teach, be intentional in planning a Hook, Book, Look, and Took into your lesson. You'll see for yourself how powerful and effective they are.

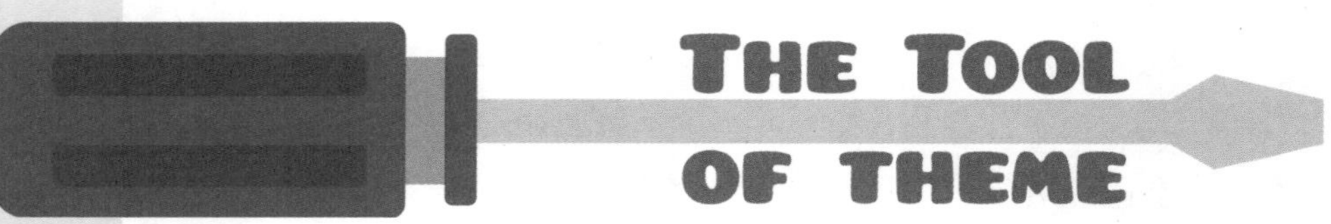

The Tool of Theme

Crafting a Theme

When it comes to teaching, one of the secrets to success is a well-crafted theme. Whether you are theming the overall ministry or a current teaching series, a well-planned theme gives everything a place and helps organize your efforts.

How do you come up with a fun and effective theme? I like to use the classic questions "who, where, when, and what" to come up with ideas.

WHO?

Consider role models whom you could theme a ministry after. A "who" can lead to a teaching series that focuses on a Bible character like Jonah or Esther.

Keep in mind, "who" doesn't have to be an individual, but can represent a group of people. If your "who" is athletes, do an Olympics theme—or sky-diving! I've done a skydiving theme when I taught about bravery and faith.

If your "who" isn't a Bible character, you can tie that role model to biblical themes.

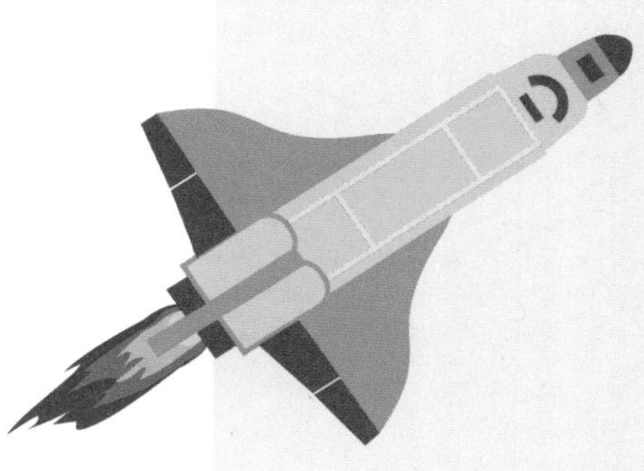

WHERE?

Kids love to learn about new places. You can transport them anywhere through their imaginations.

Here are some "where" theme ideas to get you started:

- Mountains
- Beach, island, or under the sea
- Outer space or the moon
- Playground
- Town square
- Volcano (I called mine "Kidzuma")
- Sports arena

Brainstorm about a really cool place to go. Then create that space in your ministry. Your kids will love it!

What?

This is the most general concept that can result in practically anything! I've seen movie themes, sports, science, video game themes. At my church, the kids still talk about one series where we transformed our room into the world of Minecraft, complete with a portal that teleported actors from stage onto a screen (via videos we filmed in advance).

Other "what" themes:

- Toys like plastic building blocks, puzzles, or board games
- Glow-in-the-dark
- Superheroes—Jesus is the ultimate superhero!
- Elephants, dolphins, armadillos, horses—what's your favorite animal?
- Trains—"Train up a child in the way he should go: and when he is old, he will not depart from it" (Proverbs 22:6 [KJV]).

When?

Similar to taking the kids somewhere, this concept allows you to take them "somewhere." Time travel is possible with imagination!

Some "when" themes:

- Bible times
- Future days
- 1950s, '70s, '20s . . . Just pick a decade!
- The Old West
- Prehistoric times

Brainstorming Themes

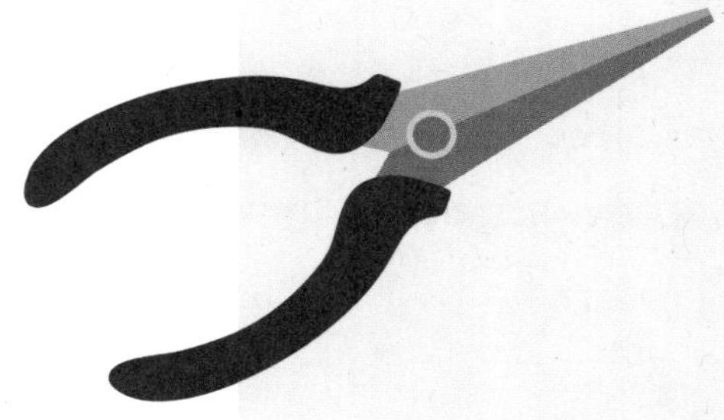

Without getting too detailed, think through the "who, where, what, and when," and see how many ideas you can create. You can copy some of the ideas mentioned on the preceding page to help get the creative ideas flowing. You just might come up with the next great idea that many other churches are inspired to use, too!

Who

Where

What

When

Below, list some of your favorite theme ideas from the brainstorming you did on the previous page. Include other ideas that occur to you, or even draw a doodle or two.

Classroom Management Tools

Teaching with Discipline

In children's ministry training, one of the most requested subjects is discipline. Believe it or not, the kids don't always behave the way we'd like! But I've never liked teaching discipline workshops. Most discipline is reactionary. It's in reaction to something—or someone—gone awry.

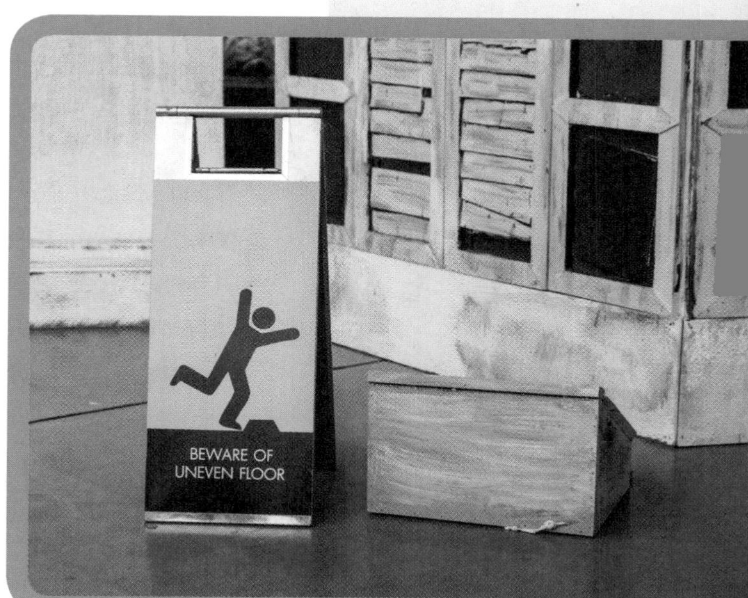

It's like dealing with uneven floors, cracked walls, or cracked window frames when the issue is that the house wasn't built correctly in the first place. In many ways, the same is true with discipline.

If you don't fix the foundation issues with your house, your floors will continue to be uneven. In the same way, if you don't fix what's wrong with the foundations of your program, you'll continue to see disciplinary problems as a result.

Often, children's ministry workers want to know how to fix issues with children instead of recognizing and addressing the foundational issues that enable those problems to pop up. Instead of discipline, I prefer to discuss classroom management, or better yet, discipleship. After all, our goal isn't well-behaved children. It is helping children become more of what God designed them to be.

Along the way, kids will make mistakes, but that is all a natural part of the learning process. Many of the discipline problems we encounter in children's ministry aren't actually problems at all. They are simply a part of the process of helping kids learn what God expects of them.

Here are some tools that will help you maintain order, keep kids engaged, and minimize conflict.

An Engaging Lesson

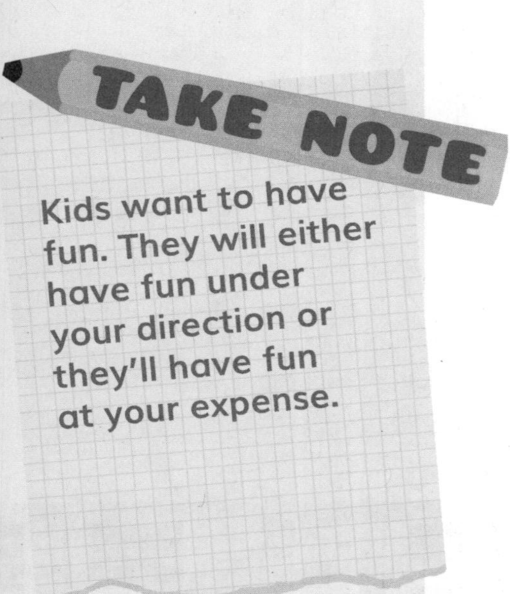

It is intentional that the entire first half of this third section was about how to put together an engaging lesson. The truth is a great lesson is the best way to make discipline problems disappear. There is an old children's ministry saying that goes, "If you don't have a plan for the kids, they'll have a plan for you!"

Kids want to have fun. They will either have fun under your direction, or they'll have fun at your expense. It isn't that they are trying to misbehave or be disobedient; it is simply that they are wired to move. God made them that way! An effective teacher channels that creative energy into learning experiences. As a result, there are very few discipline issues.

Many teachers who have trouble controlling their class need help creating lessons that will interest and engage the children. Therefore, the first step to managing the classroom is to create an experience that the children want to be a part of. Of course, you won't always engage one hundred percent of the children, and that's where the next steps come in. But if you put the effort into creating fun and engaging lessons, you'll have very little trouble maintaining control of your classroom.

Clear Expectations

Few things feel worse to a kid than getting in trouble for something they didn't even know was wrong. It is important to have clear expectations in our classrooms and ministries. Rules should be short, clear, and comprehensive. They need to fit the program.

Be sure to make your rules fair and realistic. "No talking" is not only unrealistic, it is a bit cruel. Even adults lean over and talk during a sermon. Let's not expect something of children that not even adults can do. However, we can address the same concern with the rule, "Don't distract others." That would address talking to your neighbor better as it focuses on the real reason for the rule.

Post rules where they can be seen and referred to as needed. Rules do not need to be reviewed weekly. In some ministries, the first thing they do at the beginning of the program is to review the rules. I think that is a very negative way to start. It assumes bad behavior from the get-go.

We don't review the rules of the road every time we get in our car to drive. We learned them. There are signs and glimpses of police cars to remind us, but for the most part we just enjoy the drive. Likewise, let kids enjoy the service. Signs can help remind us, and the presence of leaders can encourage us, but we don't need to be constantly instructed on rules. They provide structure and order, but they shouldn't be the focus.

Remember, if you have an engaging lesson, there will be little need for rules. They can be referred to as needed or just one-on-one. However, reviewing the rules periodically is fine, just don't make it a major focus unless you are establishing rules as something new.

Sample Rules

Sunday Morning

1. **Be kind to each other.**
2. **Be a part of what's going on.**
3. **Be respectful of leaders.**
4. **Have fun!**

Midweek Club

1. **We walk around here.**
2. **We take care of our stuff.**
3. **We respect each other.**
4. **We have fun!**

Four-Rule Tip

Shorter lists have better results. I like to keep my rule lists to a maximum of four rules.

The first two rules can be tailored to the needs of the situation. See my Sample Rules for Sunday Morning and Midweek Club to the left.

The third rule is my "catch all" rule—anything that happens will fit under rule three. It can be as simple as "Follow directions."

My fourth rule is always the same: "Have fun!" It's good to remind kids that we'll only be able to have fun if we are following the first three rules.

Note the difference:

- The first set of rules is for a program where the kids are in a single room for the entire time.
- The second set of rules is a program that involves moving around the building and using church equipment.

The tone is different for each. In both, rule three is the "catch all" rule that can include just about anything. Design rules that fit your ministry needs.

KEEPING SHARP

Questions can be a powerful teaching tool, but a child must be able to answer however they want. If you lead with a question where only one answer is acceptable, you can create an environment where conflict is unavoidable.

Direct; Don't Ask

Never ask a child a question if their answer isn't valid. For example, consider what might happen if you ask, "Do you want to play a game now?"

What if half of them answer no? What do you do if a game is the next activity on your lesson plan? Do you say, "Too bad. We're playing a game now"? Half the kids will not want to play and will feel that you are disrespecting their wishes. The feeling is one you created by giving them a false choice.

It is better to direct: "OK, now we're going to play a fun game!" Even if half the kids are less than excited about the game, they know what's next, and your enthusiasm will catapult them into the activity.

Providing valid choices is fine. For example, "For the next segment, you can either join me in this fun game, or you can sit along the wall and cheer on the players!" This way, the children have a choice to play or watch and cheer. The expectation for both is clear.

Sometimes, when a child is misbehaving, we don't realize that they're reacting to our ambiguity. It is only fair to give clear expectations so that children know what is expected and what their choices are.

Be Positive

We think of discipline as correction and therefore as something negative. As a result, we end up telling kids what not to do. In doing so, we give them yet another opportunity to disobey, which can escalate the situation quickly. A wiser approach flows from seeing the confrontation from a different perspective.

Instead of correction, we are *coaching*. Instead of telling them what not to do, train them how to do something correctly. In other words, we should tell them what *to do* instead of what *not to do*. If the child does what we ask, they succeed. For example, instead of calling after a running child, "Don't run!" Begin chanting, "Walk, walk, walk!"

It is difficult for the brain to process directions that have negations in them: words like *don't*, *not*, and *no*. The child must first picture what we're talking about and then negate it. Giving positive directions (no negations) allows them to understand and respond much more quickly.

Failure Is Success

It took Thomas Edison over a thousand experiments to get his first light bulb to turn on. He was once asked what it was like to fail a thousand times. His response was, "I never failed! I successfully discovered a thousand ways not to create light!"

When a child does something wrong, instead of pointing out a failure, we can point out their success! "Megan, you have just discovered how not to get to sit in the front row. Let me show you a better way." Or, "Peter, good job figuring out how not to encourage Billy to share with you. Let me show you a better way to get a turn with that toy."

Kids are experimenting with life, and many of those experiments will fail. Our role is not to emphasize the failures but to guide them toward those light-bulb moment when they discover what works best.

The bottom line is to be positive. Correct with a smile and be friendly. You are helping a child succeed, not merely stopping behavior. Discipline doesn't have to be negative. When we realize we are helping kids succeed, it can be done kindly with a smile and be a positive interaction.

Give Positive Attention

Often when a child misbehaves he is seeking attention. Believe it or not, a child would rather get negative attention than none at all. When we take a child aside to talk to them about their behavior, we may think we are giving them a wonderful talk. They may think, "Wow, I'm getting one-on-one time with this cool leader!"

They may misbehave again, not out of a rebellious heart or insubordination, but out of a desire to get some more quality time with that leader. While the leader grows increasingly irritated at the repeated behavior, the child is getting increasingly happy with the attention. The secret is to provide positive attention proactively.

Train your leaders to notice a child who is acting up or not participating. They may just need some positive attention.

- Ask them how they are doing.
- Give them a high-five.
- Let them know how glad yo u are that they are at church today.
- Offer to sit with them for a bit.

After some attention is provided, the leader can say something like, "Hey, I'll be watching you. I'm so glad you're here. We'll chat again in a little bit. Right now, make me proud and join in. Don't worry; I'll watch and cheer you on."

Proximity

This one is quick and easy. If you see disruptive behavior or a child whose attention is beginning to wander, you can often nip it in the bud by moving in the direction of the child or standing and sitting near them.

This is one reason it is important that all of your volunteers understand that even if someone else is leading the children in a large-group setting, it isn't time for them to have coffee and chat together in the back of the room. They need to be actively engaged with and near to the children, sitting with them, and fully participating in all the activities.

TAKE NOTE

Volunteers need to be actively engaged with and near to the children, sitting with them and fully participating in all the activities.

Become a Name Dropper

If you have kids you know need attention, develop the habit of dropping their names as you teach. Don't put them on the spot with a question. You never want to embarrass a kid by asking them a question if you know they may not be paying attention.

You can simply say something like, "You know what I mean, Micah?" Or, "Micah, you aren't going to believe this, but the craziest thing happened this week." As you drop names, it engages that child and makes them feel special that you used their name. It will rivet their attention to what you are saying, even if it's temporary.

Yes to Rewards!

Sadly, the use of rewards in children's ministry has become a bit controversial. There are some good people who advocate that rewards have no place in children's ministry. While I understand the concerns that drive this decision, I can't help but feel badly for the kids in their ministry. I also find myself

And it is impossible to please God without faith. Anyone who wants to come to him must believe that God exists and that he rewards those who sincerely seek him.
Hebrews 11:6

wondering if these same adults use a credit card that offers them rewards.

I have tried to find a verse in Scripture that would discourage us from giving rewards to children. I discovered that our God delights in giving rewards and even uses the promise of reward to motivate us. If adults need rewards to do the right thing, how much more do children? While intrinsic motivation sounds wonderful, it is at best a lofty goal and at worst an unrealistic goal for children.

Ultimately, we want to train children to follow God for the right reasons. Yes, rewards can be misused or overused. But just because something can be misused doesn't mean we eliminate it altogether. Balance always takes thoughtful effort.

Share the Gospel!

This final point may surprise you, but expecting children to behave without the influence of the Holy Spirit is a bit unfair. Many of the behaviors that we expect from children are actually Fruit of the Spirit. They are behaviors that result from the Holy Spirit transforming how we think, act, and react to others.

We want children to love, to be gentle, kind, patient, and—of course—self-controlled. These are traits that we struggle with and with which we need the Holy Spirit to help us. If we need the Holy Spirit's help to be patient or kind, how much more so do children?

Most kids who have grown up in the church have been taught about of the Fruit of the Spirit, found in Galatians 5:22–23. They might have been taught a catchy "Fruit of the Spirit" tune. But few have memorized the Acts of the Flesh found in the same chapter (Galatians 5:19-21). Don't get me wrong, I'm not advocating writing a catchy song for kids to sing the Acts of the Flesh. Several of them aren't really appropriate for children's church. My point is that both lists are there for a reason. Many Acts of the Flesh list exactly what we wrestle with when dealing with children.

Since you likely don't have the Acts of the Flesh memorized, let me refresh your memory on the ones that relate to children's ministry disciplinary problems.

- Discord
- Jealousy
- Fits of rage
- Envy
- Selfishness

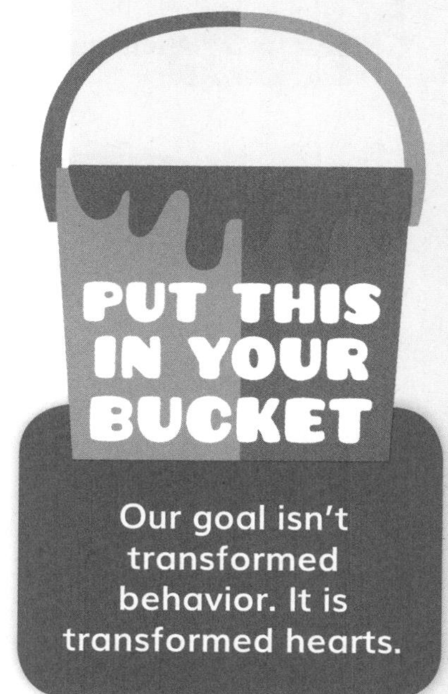

Our goal isn't transformed behavior. It is transformed hearts.

Why do I bring this up? Our main objective in children's ministry is not to create well-behaved children; it is to create disciples of Jesus. When I talk to a child about their behavior, I observe that while jealousy or rage was the issue, what I was hoping to see was a Fruit of the Spirit.

If I were to ask a child what the Fruit of the Spirit are, they might be able to list them from memory, or they might say something like, "They are what I'm supposed to do."

I enjoy explaining, "No, they are what God's Spirit will bring out of us naturally if we have the Holy Spirit in us. Have you ever asked Jesus to be your Savior? Have you confessed your sin to him so you can become a member of God's family? Invite the Holy Spirit to help you live the way God wants you to."

What a delight and joy it is to pray with a child and bring them to Jesus. Then, watch the dramatic change in their behavior. It won't be because they are trying harder, but because they now have the Holy Spirit in them helping them to be transformed! Never forget, our goal isn't transformed behavior. It is transformed hearts. Only that will change behavior long term.

4: Training Tools

Introduction

What Training Is Needed?

One of my favorite jokes is a made-up story of how I was taught to swim the old-fashioned way. The joke states that my dad took me out in a boat to the middle of a lake and tossed me in to the water. I then go on to say that getting back to shore wasn't the hard part. The hard part was getting out of the sack.

While the joke never fails to get a few groans, it makes people nervous because long before the sack enters the joke, they are worried about me swimming back to shore. *What kind of parent would do such a thing?* the listener wonders.

Yet, the same thing happens in children's ministry. Someone volunteers for the kids' ministry, and while we'd never put them into a sack, we might drop them into a classroom full of kids and effectively say, "Sink or swim!"

Three Types of Training

Basic Ministry Training

This level familiarizes volunteers with your church's ministry, goals, objectives, and vision. It covers practical knowledge like where to find supplies, how to communicate well, and how to keep up to date on important information. It also explains important child security policies for the protection of volunteers as well as the children.

Role Specific Training

This is training that pertains specifically to volunteers' jobs in the children's ministry. For example, working at the check-in counter, teaching a class, leading games, or being on the security team each have their own training.

Ongoing Advanced Training

This level is often neglected. Volunteers may have the basic training and the knowledge specific to their ministry, but there are always ways to improve. Ongoing advanced training helps your volunteers continually improve in their ministry skills.

Don't forget:

- People forget things and need refreshers.
- The situations and needs of your ministry will change over time.

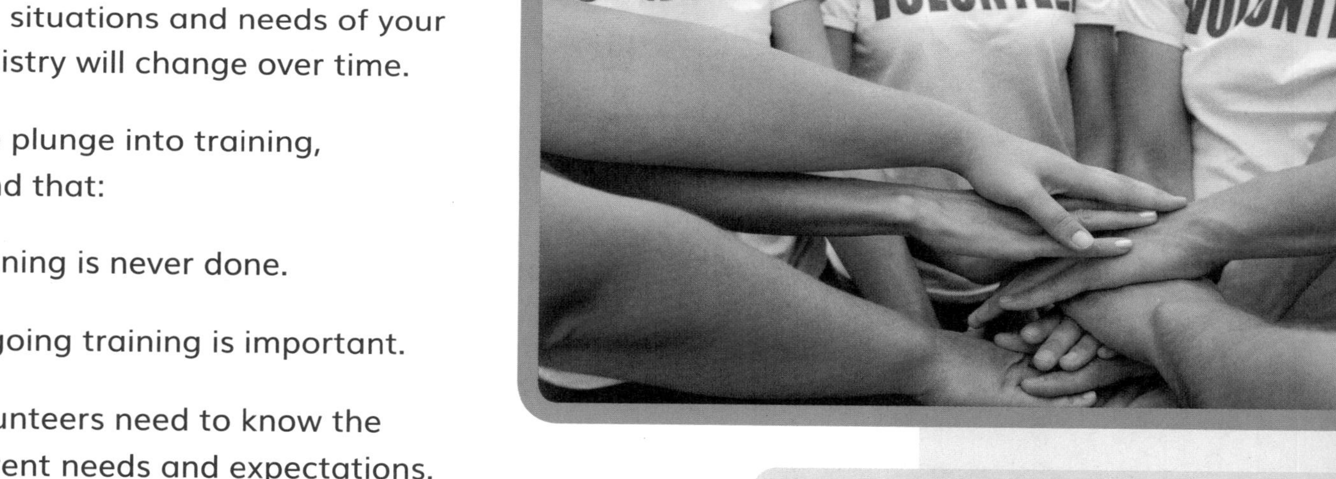

Before we plunge into training, understand that:

- Training is never done.
- Ongoing training is important.
- Volunteers need to know the current needs and expectations.

WATCH THIS VIDEO: The Power of a Strong Start
Visit Kidology.org/toolbox

Simply put, you need to train your volunteers if you want your ministry to succeed. The trade-off is great! Well-trained volunteers will:

- Remain longer
- Be more successful
- Enjoy what they do

Who wouldn't want a ministry with volunteers like that?

Training Tool 1: Basic Training

This level familiarizes volunteers with your church's ministry—its goals, objectives, and vision. It also covers practical knowledge like:

- Where to find supplies
- How to communicate well
- How to keep up to date on important information
- Important child-security policies

This is important training for all new volunteers, and it is important information to regularly review with established workers. As part of your basic training, be sure to review all of the following information.

Statement of Faith

We aren't just looking for volunteers to provide care. We are passing on our faith to our children. Therefore, it is important that our volunteers understand and agree to the theology we are teaching our children.

Provide your statement of faith to your volunteers. If they have any issue with the core doctrine, they may want to reconsider serving—especially if they are in a teaching role. There are some areas of theology that are not core theology—areas where there can be open debate. In those areas, it is best to explain that these topics are avoided in children's ministry. Such topics should be left to parents to discuss with their children if they wish.

In children's ministry, stick to topics essential to the faith. Avoid topics that can cause division.

Children's Ministry Vision

Explain why your ministry exists in the first place. Working with kids isn't always glamorous. There will be crying, yucky messes to clean up, and other discouraging things. When a volunteer asks themselves, *Why am I doing this?* they should already know the answer. You provide it with your vision statement!

Volunteers are doing more than providing childcare. They are ministering to children and laying a spiritual foundation. In God's timing, this will lead them into a relationship with God through Jesus Christ. The role of volunteers in this process is critically important!

Share the vision for the ministry and the goals your leadership team has developed, and let them see where their job fits into that overall strategy.

The next time they are wiping a running nose or waiting on a late parent, they will be more patient and gracious because they understand the bigger picture of children's ministry.

Where's What?

You might know right where to look for scissors or tape, but when a volunteer needs something, it can be a treasure hunt without a map. What is obvious to you can be overwhelming to a new volunteer. Providing a tour of the children's ministry area solves this problem.

If you have an organized resource room, consider providing a list of the supplies. Make it clear that they don't need to purchase their own materials. The fact that you took the time to show them also communicates how much you value what they do.

Child-Security Policies

We have a responsibility to minister in a safe and secure environment. Child-security guidelines are not optional. These guidelines not only help keep our kids safe, but they also protect our volunteers from any false accusations.

It is imperative that your ministry develop security guidelines and then clearly communicate them to your volunteers. Make sure they know you aren't merely providing helpful tips. This is a liability issue. Failure to follow the child security guidelines can result in removal from their volunteer position.

Never Alone Policy

Under no circumstances should a volunteer be alone with a child. This means adult volunteers. Middle-school and high-school helpers are great, but there should always be a minimum of two unrelated adults in a classroom at all times.

Why unrelated? Why can't a married couple serve in the same classroom? A married couple can serve together, but make sure there is another adult in the classroom as well. For liability reasons, it's best to have an unattached, unbiased adult in the room.

For example, what if the other kids have been picked up, there is only one child left, and the other volunteer says they have to leave? You should ask the other volunteer to stay anyway. In fact, this shouldn't be an issue if both volunteers are properly trained.

But if for some reason the other volunteer must leave (sickness, another meeting, etc.), there are other options. Your volunteers may:

- Ask another parent to stay
- Find another adult volunteer to wait with them
- Move with the last child to a public place

Be clear: **There can never be any exceptions to this rule.** News stories involving church staff or volunteers acting inappropriately with children occur because this rule was broken. The leadership must take action if this rule is violated.

Appropriate Touch Policy

We must always be wise in our physical contact.

Please understand that appropriate affection is important. We want kids to feel loved and accepted. High-fives, fist bumps, hugs, pats on the back, and other forms of casual affection are fine.

As kids get older, hugs should shift to the side. Avoid having kids sitting on laps, riding piggyback, or sitting on shoulders. We want to always be above reproach in our physical contact with children. When in doubt, don't do it, or ask a supervisor.

Never use physical discipline in correcting children, even if it is your own child, as observers may not know who your child is. Again, this is not only to protect the children, but to protect volunteers.

If volunteers are ever concerned about somebody's conduct, they should never hesitate to talk to the children's ministry staff. Assure them that the staff will listen and deal with it confidentially. It is better to report it and have it be nothing than for someone to wish they had said something later.

A volunteer may be worried that their report will remove someone from their position. Reassure your volunteers that a person will not automatically be removed if a concern is shared. Sometimes they just need some guidance, and your confidential input is helpful. Leaders are happy to coach individuals in appropriate conduct, and there are times when that is all that is need.

Safety Policy

Obviously, we don't want our activities to hurt a child. Ask yourself, "Does this look safe?" Sometimes, what we play may be perfectly safe, but it may not look safe to an observer. This could make others feel uncomfortable, even while we are confident that nothing could go wrong. There are times when we may choose not to do something because we do not want others to be uneasy, especially parents.

Accident Policy

Injuries do happen. They should always be reported to a supervisor—no matter how small the injury. In most churches, if the skin is broken, then an accident report should be filled out. The parent should always be informed regardless of how big or little the injury is. We would rather tell a parent about the incident than have them discover a boo-boo when they get home and wonder what happened. Parents are understanding and appreciative when we are upfront about accidents.

Check-Out Procedures

Most churches today use a secure check-in and check-out system to ensure that children are released only to an authorized person. This is usually the same person who dropped them off at the beginning of the program. Make sure you know your church's check-in and check-out system well, and train your volunteers. Help them understand the importance of these security procedures. Too often they aren't taken seriously. Volunteers need to grasp that they are the cornerstone of a secure check-in system.

While every system may be slightly different, most have certain aspects in common.

- No child should be admitted into a classroom without a check-in sticker, name tag, or whatever indicator your church selects. If a child doesn't have the needed security identification, ask the parent to go to the check-in center.

- No adults should be in the classroom without appropriate volunteer identification.
- Parents dropping off a child should not come into the room any farther than the doorway.
- Parents picking up a child must present the appropriate security identification.

One easy way to make sure children have the appropriate identification is to greet them by name. As you do so, note any special information. There may be allergy information that is very important. We do not want to cause an allergic reaction during snack time!

The most important part of a secure check-in system is that no child should ever be released to an adult without that adult having the appropriate security identification. Knowing the parent is not acceptable. You must check every time. If a parent does not have the needed security identification, do not release the child. Smile, be polite, but stick to the policy. Do not accept any excuses.

TAKE NOTE

The most important part of a secure check-in system is that no child should ever be released to an adult without that adult having the appropriate security identification.

Kindly send them back to the check-in center, and the staff there will resolve whatever the issue may be. Check-in staff can determine who is the authorized pick-up adult and reprint pick-up identification. A classroom teacher does not have the authority to bypass this policy. Only the check-in counter staff or church staff can do this.

Again, emphasize that this is for the volunteers' protection as well as the child's. No volunteer wants to be the person who released a child into the custody of adult who did not have legal permission to pick up that child. Yes, this can be awkward and inconvenient. But it is far less awkward than finding out later that you were used by someone to take a child illegally.

We do not know what is going on in the home. There may be a custody issue or a restraining order. Make sure your volunteers understand that because churches too often value friendliness over security, churches are one of the primary places where children are abducted by estranged parents. Determine that your church will not make that mistake. It sometimes takes only one lawsuit to close the doors of a church. We must have a sober understanding of the seriousness of this issue and communicate that clearly to our volunteers.

You can point out that these situations are rare, but once we start making exceptions on an individual basis, we open ourselves up to being vulnerable. We have to follow this policy across the board, every time, to protect every child.

Emergency Plan

Your emergency plan is the one thing you need that you hope you'll never use. It will be as unique as your church. It will answer questions such as:

- What do you do in the case of a fire alarm?
- Where will the kids go?
- What is your plan in the case of an active shooter?
- How do you conduct a lockdown?
- How and where will children be reunited with parents after an evacuation?

Thinking these questions through ahead of time and training your volunteers will prevent chaos in the event of an emergency.

Is critical for the leader to remain completely calm. Children will look to adults to determine how they should respond. A leader can be sent to assess the emergency. While they wait, the remaining leaders should have the children line up and be ready to leave the room. All belongings should be left behind. The only exception is coats in the case of cold weather.

Consider putting together some emergency kits that include blankets, flashlights, first-aid, and other items that could be needed. Place them in bags that are easily accessible to leaders in the case of an evacuation.

Include a map of your facility that clearly shows exit routes, where children will gather, and where parents can pick up children. Post these maps throughout the children's ministry area.

As children's ministry volunteers, they should always know the number of children in their care. Increase your count if children are added to your group. In the case of an emergency, you will not have time to count. When it comes to preschoolers, who love to count, just have fun with it.

When parents drop their children off in our children's ministry programs, they entrust us with their greatest treasure.

Knowing the number of children in your group is especially important if you end up moving children to another location during class time. Train your volunteers to count before leaving the room, in the middle of the move, and when they reach their destination. A supervisor should be able to ask a volunteer at any time how many kids are in their care, and they should be able to answer without counting.

When parents drop their children off in our children's ministry programs, they entrust us with their greatest treasure. We need to accept that trust with the highest sense of stewardship and take it very seriously. Children's ministry is incredibly fun, but it is serious business, too. We must make every effort to provide a loving, safe, and secure place where kids can come to know Jesus and grow in their knowledge of him.

Discipline Policy

A uniform approach to discipline is important. A clear chain of command is helpful so that parents have a single point of contact regarding any issues that may arise with their child. Making sure everyone follows the same process prevents confusion and reduces conflict. It assures parents that their children are treated fairly and that communication lines are open. It also protects volunteers from unnecessary conflict with parents

Adapt the following sample disciplinary policy as necessary to fit your own ministry.

Sample Discipline Policy

Due to the Never Alone Policy, disruptive behavior should be handled in the classroom, not in isolation with a worker and a child alone. The Children's Pastor and/or Ministry Coordinator will handle the correction if it is too much to do in the classroom.

The use of corporal punishment is expressly forbidden for all children's workers, including parents who serve in a classroom with their own children. Talk with the pastor if you need further explanation on this.

Establish simple rules for each classroom. State these positively.

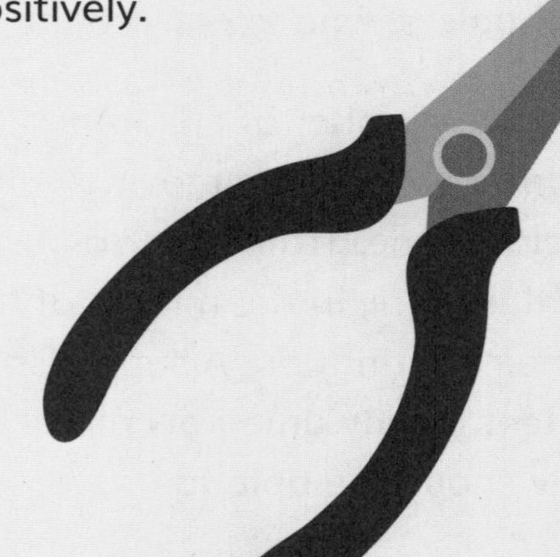

General rules for every class are:

- Respect those in authority.
- Use words to solve problems.
- Speak and walk softly indoors.
- Respect facilities, equipment, and supplies.
- Be consistent in enforcing your classroom rules.
- Never threaten a child.

Always maintain self-control in your classroom and with your students. You must never shout or exhibit angry behavior toward the children. If you feel you are losing control, contact your ministry coordinator or pastor for assistance.

Never embarrass a child with words or actions. Pay careful attention in times of correction.

Here are some things to do when a child becomes disruptive:

- Restate the rules to the entire class.
- Walk in the child's direction; stand near or over them.
- Gain eye contact with the student.
- Lightly touch the child on the shoulder letting them know that you care and are aware of their behavior.
- Redirect the child's actions.

- Change your activity. Perhaps the child is bored.
- Move the child to a different seat or location in the classroom to allow them the opportunity of greater success.
- State the positives of others' behaviors. Kids will rise to the level at which we have set the bar.

Consequence Structure

The following has been established for instances where a child repeats the same offence:

- 1st offence—Verbal correction. Tone is upbeat and friendly, but next steps will be clearly outlined
- 2nd offence—Talk with Ministry Coordinator
- 3rd offence—Conference with parent or guardian
- 4th offence—One week removal from program
- 5th offence—One month removal from program
- 6th offence—Conference again with guardian to see if this is the best place for them

Fighting

In incidents where a student is physically harmed or attempts to physically harm another, the following steps should be taken:

- 1st offence—Dismissal for the remaining time of service and a conference with parents.
- 2nd offence—Dismissal from service and conference with parents, one month removal from program.
- 3rd offence—Dismissal from service and conference with parents to determine if this is the place for the family.

In most cases, behavior will change on the first or second offence. When it is evident that you have an extreme case (such as fighting), which cannot be handled by classroom workers, contact your ministry coordinator or pastor for assistance.

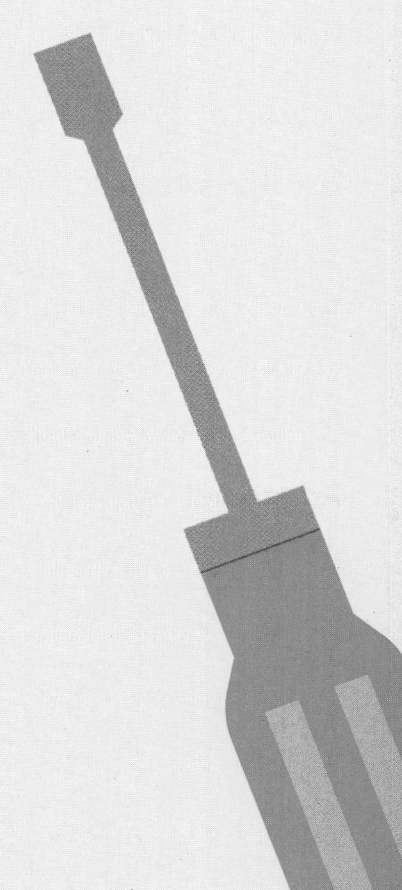

Injury Notification Form for Church Office

Name of injured child ______________________________ Date ____________

Age ______________________________ Gender ____________

Name of Parent(s) ______________________________ Phone ____________

Describe how child was injured. Include the location, names, actions of all children, and adults involved. Be as detailed as possible. ______________________________

____

____

Describe the child's injuries. ______________________________

____

Describe actions taken to treat the injuries. ______________________________

____

How and when was the parent notified? ______________________________

____

List the names and phone numbers of witnesses to the accident.

Name ______________________________ Phone ____________

Name ______________________________ Phone ____________

Name ______________________________ Phone ____________

Additional Comments ______________________________

____

Your name ______________________________ Phone ____________

Address ______________________________ Email ____________

Injury Notification Form for Parents

Date ____

Name of child ____

What happened ____

____

____

____

____

Your child was given aid by ______________________________ (name of adult)

Your child was helped in the following ways ______________________________

____

____

Please call me if you have any questions or comments.

Your name ______________________________ Phone ______________

Biting Notification Form for Parents of Injured Child

Date ____

Your child ______________________________ was bitten on the

______________________ today in the ___________________ class.

The skin was

- ☐ not broken.
- ☐ broken.

We comforted your child and

- ☐ washed the bite.
- ☐ put an antiseptic ointment on the bite.
- ☐ placed a bandage on the bite.
- ☐ held a cold compress on the bite.

We are sorry that this happened and have taken the following corrective steps:

- ☐ We moved the biting child away from the other children.
- ☐ We gently but firmly instructed the child not to bite.
- ☐ We alerted the parent(s) of the biting child about their child's behavior.
- ☐ Moving forward, we will closely observe the biting child in order to prevent additional occurrences.

Please call me if you have any questions or comments.

Your name ______________________________ Phone ______________

Biting Notification Form for Parents

Date ____

Your child __________________________ bit another child today in the

____ class.

We have taken the following corrective steps:

- ☐ We moved your child away from the other children.
- ☐ We gently but firmly instructed your child not to bite.
- ☐ We alerted the parent(s) of the child who was bitten about the incident. Your child was not named.
- ☐ Moving forward, we will closely observe your child in order to prevent additional occurrences.

Please call me if you have any questions or comments.

Your name ______________________________ Phone ___________

Financial Policies

Misunderstandings over money can be awkward and create conflict in ministry. Money needs to be handled with the greatest of care. It is important to establish guidelines for how money is collected, counted, turned in, requested, approved, and reimbursed.

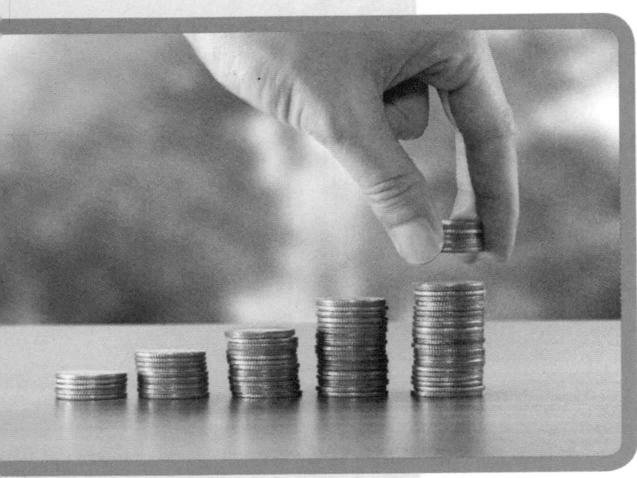

You never want to create a situation that presents temptation for someone, or worse, create an environment of suspicion when it comes to the handling of money. When money is collected, always make sure it is counted by two unrelated people, reported, verified, and securely deposited. Children's ministry collections are generally small, but the amount is not as important as integrity. Scripture admonishes us to be faithful with little if we desire to be entrusted with much (Luke 16:10).

Also, let volunteers know what is provided and what they can reasonably expect to spend for their area of ministry. Otherwise, you might have someone turn in a receipt for something that isn't in the budget and explain that you cannot reimburse them. Conversely, you might have people spending money and not know that they can be reimbursed. Being clear ahead of the time is the best way to prevent any hard feelings or resentment that can result from misunderstandings.

Code of Conduct

When it comes to managing volunteers, it is best to be proactive. Be upfront about what is expected rather than reactive to what they do that frustrates or disappoints us. How will you deal with volunteers who

- Don't show up when they are scheduled?
- Ignore training opportunities?

- Dress inappropriately in a classroom?
- Use bad language?

While we are in the process of disciplining our volunteers, we also realize that they are serving as role models to the kids. There is a higher standard we expect from those who lead and serve our kids at church. Our parents have an expectation that those who are watching their children are serving as a positive influence as well.

What is a Code of Conduct?

- Expectations of volunteers that are explained to them before they serve
- A declaration of faith
- An agreement to the church doctrine
- A commitment to serve for a set time frame (including advanced notice of expected absence)
- Commitments to Christian conduct in private life

On the next page is a sample that I use in my church.

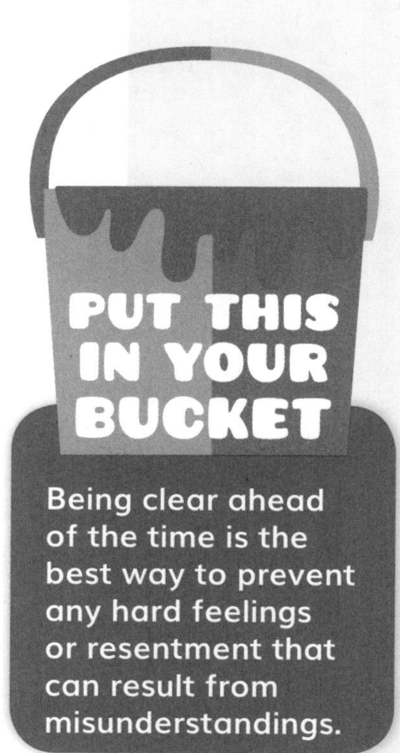

The Ten Standards of Excellence

A Children's Worker Should Be...

1. A Christian

Our ultimate goal in children's ministry is to lead kids to Christ and then help them grow in their Christian life. Therefore, our volunteers themselves should have a personal relationship with Christ. If you are unsure about where you stand in your relationship with God, do not hesitate to talk to one of the pastors. The pastors would be delighted to open God's Word and share with you how you can know for sure that you are saved and a child of God.

> *This is how God loved the world: He gave his one and only Son, so that everyone who believes in him will not perish but have eternal life.* (John 3:16)

2. A Regular

A volunteer should be a regular in church attendance and involvement, not only in children's ministry functions, but also in regular worship services and other church events.

> *Let us not neglect our meeting together, as some people do, but encourage one another, especially now that the day of his return is drawing near.* (Hebrews 10:25)

3. Encouraging in Speech

Our words should be encouraging, uplifting, and positive. No insults, cut-downs, gossip, slander, or any talk where someone may be hurt—especially in the presence of children. Humor should reflect a walk with God.

> *Speak as though God himself were speaking through you.* (1 Peter 4:11)

> *Obscene stories, foolish talk, and coarse jokes—these are not for you. Instead, let there be thankfulness to God.* (Ephesians 5:4)

4. An Example in Christian Character

Because volunteers should be examples and positive influences, they should refrain from gray area activities. They should be sensitive to convictions from others in both their actions and conversation. In their personal life they should be committed to Bible study, prayer, and Christ-like living.

> *You yourself must be an example to them by doing good works of every kind. Let everything you do reflect the integrity and seriousness of your teaching.* (Titus 2:6–7)

> *Don't you realize that your body is the temple of the Holy Spirit, who lives in you and was given to you by God? You do not belong to yourself, for God bought you with a high price. So you must honor God with your body.* (1 Corinthians 6:19–20)

Being an example includes being *modest in dress*. Without our defining exactly what you may wear, just be sure that your clothing glorifies God, not yourself. Don't allow your dress to distract others from spiritual things.

> *I want women [and men] to be modest in their appearance. They should wear decent and appropriate clothing and not draw attention to themselves. . . . For women [and men] who claim to be devoted to God should make themselves attractive by the good things they do.* (1 Timothy 2:9–10)

5. Responsible in Leadership

This involves attending meetings and training, or if unavailable, communicating ahead of time. Leadership responsibility also includes planning church events or outings only with the prior knowledge and approval of the children's pastor. Respect church procedures by following them.

> *Respect everyone, and love the family of believers.* (1 Peter 2:17)

6. Faithful in Commitments

When a volunteer gives their word, they should honor it. If they say they will do something or be somewhere, they will follow through. If something unexpected happens and they cannot show up, they must communicate as soon as possible with those who will be affected by their absence.

Now, a person who is put in charge as a manager must be faithful. (1 Corinthians 4:2)

The trustworthy person will get a rich reward. (Proverbs 28:20)

7. Pure in Relationships

No teacher or volunteer is *ever* to be alone with a child. This is not only for your protection and the church's protection, but it is especially for the protection of the children. Also remember: We are not only to avoid sin, but even the appearance of sin.

- Only women assist girls in the washroom. Only men assist boys.
- Ministry room doors must be open at all times.
- Volunteers should never give a child a ride home without having another unrelated adult present.
- Hugs are best from the side.
- Do not place children in your lap.
- See our Appropriate Touch Policy for more details on what is appropriate touch.

Talk to younger men as you would to your own brothers. Treat older women as you would your mother, and treat younger women with all purity as you would your own sisters. (1 Timothy 5:1–2)

Among you there must not be even a hint of sexual immorality, or of any kind of impurity, or of greed, because these are improper for God's holy people. (Ephesians 5:3 NIV)

8. Respectful of Authority

Always be respectful of church leaders in word, action, and attitude.

Obey your spiritual leaders, and do what they say. Their work is to watch over your souls, and they are accountable to God. Give them reason to do this with joy and not with sorrow. That would certainly not be for your benefit. (Hebrews 13:17)

Now we ask you, brothers and sisters, to acknowledge those who work hard among you, who care for you in the Lord and who admonish you. (1 Thessalonians 5:12, NIV)

9. In Partnership with Parents

The spiritual upbringing of children belongs first to the parents. The church's role is to supplement the training from home.

- Always seek to work with parents.
- Welcome parental input, and listen to their concerns.
- Never side with a child against a parent or contradict a parent in front of a child. You are on the parent's team.

If you have a concern about a parent or a home situation, talk to the children's pastor immediately. Report any signs of abuse to leadership.

Direct your children onto the right path, and when they are older, they will not leave it. (Proverbs 22:6)

10. Teachable in Spirit

This may be the most important trait of any volunteer who is seeking to serve the Lord. We all have weaknesses, but if we remain teachable, we will always be improving. We must be willing to listen to constructive criticism and prayerfully consider the input of others. We don't need to always agree, but if we fail to listen, we rob ourselves of an opportunity to grow.

Fools think their own way is right, but the wise listen to others. (Proverbs 12:15)

Get all the advice and instruction you can, so you will be wise the rest of your life. (Proverbs 19:20)

All children's ministry staff and volunteers are expected to uphold and follow these standards of excellence. Any questions or concerns from or about a volunteer should be addressed with the children's pastor.

Sharing the Gospel with Children

The number one goal in children's ministry is to see children know Christ as their personal Lord and Savior. Yet, children's ministry volunteers often do not know how to share the gospel with children or lead them in a prayer to ask Jesus be their Savior. Make this a part of your basic training, and encourage your volunteers to share the Gospel often. Look for opportunities to invite children to receive Jesus as their Savior.

While there is some debate about whether children can come to Christ, Jesus settled that firmly in Luke. "Let the children come to me [Jesus]. Don't stop them!" he said to his disciples (Luke 18:16). Jesus later said that adults need to come to him as a child, meaning that faith and dependence is the source of salvation (Matthew 18:3).

He even warned that it would be better to have a millstone placed around your neck and be dropped into the sea than to hinder a

Put This in Your Bucket

At a pastors' conference, one of the speakers asked each pastor to imagine they had come across a horrible car accident and a man was dying. He continued, "After calling the authorities, you now have mere moments to share the gospel with the dying man. What does this man need to know in order to go to heaven?"

As the first volunteer pastor tried to explain the gospel, the speaker—having a bit of fun—interrupted and said, "Too long, the man's dead." Pastor after pastor tried, and each got the same interruption.

Finally, the speaker said, "You are making it too complicated. Can you think of an example in Scripture where there was a dying man and another man shared the gospel with him?"

It was a bit embarrassing how long it took these senior pastors to figure out which scriptural passage the speaker was getting at. The example in question was from the crucifixion of Jesus.

Jesus offered no long, theological explanation. The thief acknowledged his sin and asked to be saved. Jesus assured him he would be with him in paradise. That was it (Luke 23:39–43).

As adults, we tend to over-complicate things. Jesus made a point of telling us that kids get it, and we need to be more like them (Matthew 19:14). We need to understand the gospel as they do—a simple admission of sin, an acceptance of forgiveness, and a decision to follow him. The rest is bonus!

child from coming to him (Luke 17:2). So, I don't see much room for debating whether or not we can share the Gospel with children.

How to Share the Gospel by Age

Sharing the Gospel with Children under the Age of Four

For very young children, the concepts of the gospel are challenging to grasp. The idea of someone dying for them is beyond their ability to comprehend. Theologically, we consider these children below the age of accountability.

The Bible is clear that all people are sinful from birth (Psalm 51:5) and commit sins even at a young age (Romans 3:23). Also, salvation is by God's grace through faith alone in Jesus Christ, (Ephesians 2:8-9). Yet, it is clear that very young children may not be able to express a saving faith in Jesus. How do we share the gospel with these little ones? We start by laying a foundation of truth that will help prepare them for a decision when they are older.

Using their five fingers, help them learn five simple truths. Hold up each finger, and have the kids repeat the phrase. For the thumb, the child can close the fingers and do a thumbs-up. In this simple process, there is some solid theology. There is an acknowledgment of their creator, his love for them, their sin, God's forgiveness, and a declaration of our ability to choose to follow God. There is a subtle difference in the final statement.

You'll notice they aren't saying, "I *say* yes to him," but, "I *can say* yes to him." It is a statement about what *can* happen in the future. It is fine for the child to say, "I say yes to him!" But this training is designed for a future decision to accept Jesus as Lord and Savior.

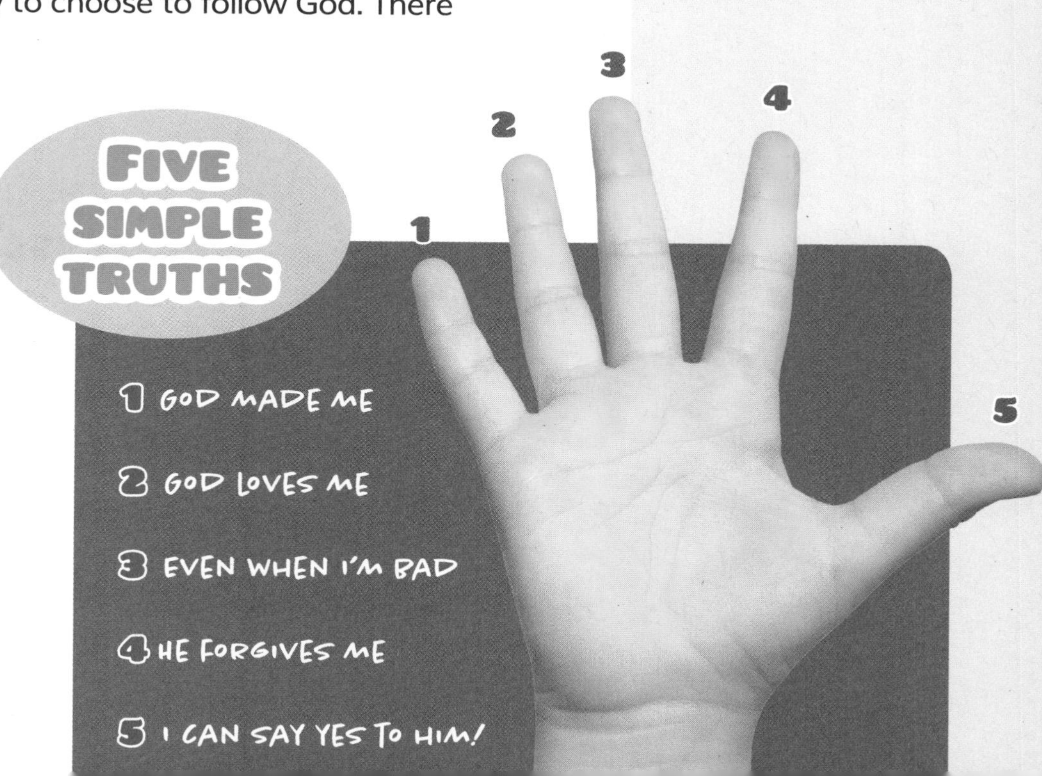

Sharing the Gospel with Preschool Children, Ages 4–6

Some people question whether preschoolers have the mental or spiritual maturity to make a decision to follow Christ for the rest of their life. The gospel message is so complex and has so much theology packed in to it, how could such a young child make such a significant decision? It's a valid question.

The *Wordless Book*

My favorite gospel presentation for preschoolers is called the *Wordless Book*. It works for any age, but it's ideal for kids who can't read. As its name suggests, it has no words! It also has no images. It contains just colored pages.

Most versions of the book have four pages: black, red, white, and gold, as well as a green cover. But other versions have green as a page, and some also include blue.

You can purchase wordless books, make your own, or use any objects that are the colors you need. Teachers have often moved beyond paper to using balloons, gloves, stuffed animals, markers, boxes, or anything they can find that display the colors of the wordless book—even beach balls!

The table on pages 223-224 offers an overview of what colors are used, what the colors represent, and Bible verses associated with each color.

WORDLESS BOOK

The original *Wordless Book* was written for adults. It was a sermon by Charles Spurgeon in 1866, later published in 1911, and it had only three colors.

The evangelist D.L. Moody added the gold color in 1975, and Child Evangelism Fellowship popularized the modern five-color version by adding green. Others have added other colors, most often blue.

Prayer for Salvation

After presenting the pages and their meanings, provide an opportunity to become a member of God's family. Tell the students that you and other adults will meet and talk with them now, immediately after the lesson, or any time they want.

When a child comes forward, take them to a private place to speak one on one. Ask if they know they are a sinner. Ask if they believe Jesus came to save them. If they answer yes to both questions, then ask if there is any reason why not to receive God's salvation through Jesus right now.

Below is a sample prayer you can lead them to pray:

> *Dear God, I know I am a sinner and am lost without you. Please forgive me! I believe you sent Jesus to die for me, and that he rose again! I ask Jesus to come into my life and help me be the person you want me to be. Help me to live for you! Thank you for forgiving me! In Jesus' name, amen.*

KEEPING SHARP

Some children ask about children who die young or before birth. In these cases, theologians point to 2 Samuel 12 where King David's newborn son was sick and about to die. David mourned, prayed, and fasted on behalf of his infant son. When his son died at only seven days old, David stopped grieving. His attendants asked him why he stopped mourning.

David replied, "I fasted and wept while the child was alive, for I said, 'Perhaps the LORD will be gracious to me and let the child live.' But why should I fast when he is dead? Can I bring him back again? I will go to him one day, but he cannot return to me." **(vv. 22–23)**

David concluded that he would see his son again someday in heaven. While the Bible does not directly state that children who die prematurely will be in heaven, there is no reason to believe that God would not save those who cannot make a faith decision. God's mercy extends to all sinners at a time when they cannot help themselves: *"God showed his great love for us by sending Christ to die for us while we were still sinners."* **(Romans 5:8)**

Color	Represents
Black	The black page stands for sin. The Bible teaches that all have sinned and fall short of God's perfect standard. Everyone is guilty of sin and must pay for their sin! It also is effective to compare the black to darkness, and talk about what it is like to be lost in the dark, unable to find your way. NOTE: Avoid saying "black is sin" or "black is evil." Instead, talk about the color black reminding us of darkness or being unclean.
Red	The red page stands for the blood of Jesus (1 John 1:7) which was shed for our salvation. First Corinthians 15:3–4 says that Jesus died for our sins, was buried and rose from the dead three days later. Jesus died to take our place, and rose again to prove his power over death! It is through faith in Jesus and through acceptance of his gift of salvation that people are saved and through nothing else (Ephesians 2:8–9). Jesus offers the salvation we need!
White	The white page stands for the cleansing of salvation. Once we accept Christ, we become a new creation (2 Corinthians 5:17). God saves us instantly through our faith in Christ. He washes away all of our sin and makes us white as snow before him (Psalm 51:7; Isaiah 1:18). This is the promise of God: he will forgive us all our sins!
Gold	The gold page stands for heaven. Some people begin with this page; I prefer to start with man's need and place the gold page here as another benefit of receiving Christ. Jesus has gone to prepare a wonderful place for those who choose to accept him as Savior (John 14:1–3).
Green	The green page or cover stands for the Christian's need to grow! Plants need three basic things to grow: sunshine, rain, and good soil. For Christians to grow, the three things they need are prayer, nourishment from God's Word, and healthy fellowship with other believers. All three of these must be present in the life of a believer in order for them to live a truly victorious life.
Blue (optional)	The blue page stands for baptism. Blue reminds us of the water used in baptism. When we are baptized, we are telling other believers that we are also members of God's family. This blue page is also a reminder that Jesus asked us to tell others about him, and baptize them as believers.

The Wordless Book

Bible Verse

For everyone has sinned; we all fall short of God's glorious standard.

Romans 3:23

This is how God loved the world: He gave his one and only Son, so that everyone who believes in him will not perish but have eternal life.

John 3:16

They are reborn—not with a physical birth resulting from human passion or plan, but a birth that comes from God.

John 1:13

The wall was made of jasper, and the city was pure gold, as clear as glass. . . . The twelve gates were made of pearls—each gate from a single pearl! And the main street was pure gold, as clear as glass.

Revelation 21:18-21

Rather, you must grow in the grace and knowledge of our Lord and Savior Jesus Christ.

2 Peter 3:18

Anyone who believes and is baptized will be saved.

Mark 16:16

Online Resource: Using the Wordless Book to Share the Gospel; Kidology.org/toolbox

Sharing the Gospel with Elementary Children (Grades 1–5)

In his book *Transforming Children into Spiritual Champions,* George Barna reports that children between four and fourteen are thirty-two percent more likely to come to Christ than during any other time of life. Sharing the gospel with elementary children is not only important, it is strategic!

Salvation becomes a pivotal point in a person's life. The sooner a pivot is made, the greater the impact. This decision can impact who they marry, where they go to school, and even their career. What a privilege to be a part of that incredibly significant life decision!

There are many methods to present the gospel. Use whatever method you enjoy the most. The important thing is that whatever presentation you use must include the core elements of the gospel, which are:

- God made us to enjoy a relationship with him
- We've sinned / fallen short of his standards
- Jesus died for us / taking our place / paying the penalty for our sin
- God offers salvation through Jesus
- We can accept salvation through Jesus (It isn't automatic, it must be accepted)
- Salvation comes through admission of sin and choosing to follow Jesus

The Bridge

There are many ways to share the gospel with children, but the illustration of a bridge remains my favorite. The bridge Illustration explains that there is nothing we can do to bridge the gap that our sin creates between us and God. Jesus' cross bridges that gap and allows us to come to God.

This illustration can be visualized in a number

of ways. Here are two suggestions:

- Draw it on a chalkboard or white board
- Act it out. Challenge kids to jump across an impossible space. Then lay down a cross made of paper they can walk on.

ABCs of the Gospel

Likely the most common summary of the gospel message used with children is the ABCs of the gospel:

Admit that you have sinned (and deserve to pay the penalty for your sins).

People who conceal their sins will not prosper, but if they confess and turn from them, they will receive mercy. (Proverbs 28:13)

Believe that Jesus came and died to pay that penalty for you.

Believe in the Lord Jesus and you will be saved (Acts 16:31).

Choose Jesus and commit your life to him.

Whoever wants to be my disciple must deny themselves and take up their cross and follow me (Matthew 16:24 NIV).

> **Keeping Sharp**
>
> Originally, in the ABCs of the Gospel, the letter C stood for "Confess Jesus as Lord." While this is still a valid choice, it requires extra explanations about the meaning of the word confess. This word is so associated with confessing sins that people forget its larger meaning. Confess literally means to say or declare. So when we confess Jesus as our Lord, we aren't asking for forgiveness. We declare our faith and allegiance in the Lord's authority. To make it simple for children, many leaders substitute "choose" or "commit," which kids already understand.

Training Tool 2: Role Specific Training

This training pertains specifically to a volunteer's job in the children's ministry. For example, working at the check-in counter, teaching a class, leading games, or being on the security team.

Review Job Description

Every role should have a job description. We covered this in detail in Section Two, Leadership Tools. You probably gave the volunteer the job description when they considered the role. This training ensures that the volunteer:

- Reads it
- Reviews it
- Asks any questions

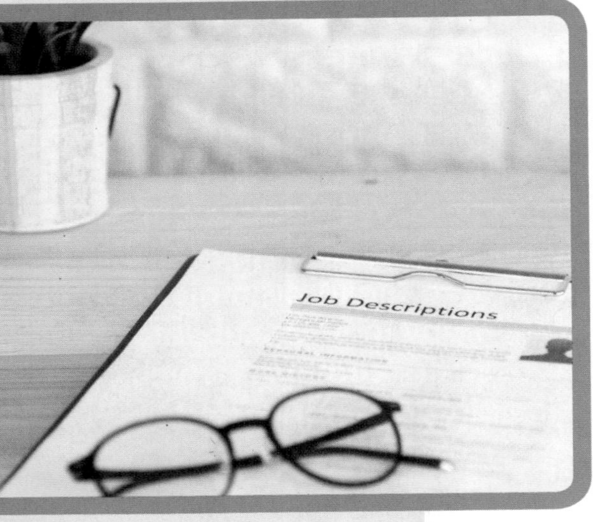

In a volunteer ministry, someone may not be able to do everything in the job description. You may want to

- Modify the job description
- Split the job into two positions
- Allow the person to skip those parts of the job

It is critical to make those adjustments proactively. It's better to modify the job description up front and keep a volunteer than to lose them because you are frustrated by their inability to do everything you want them to do.

For example, at my church, teachers should:

- Arrive fifteen minutes before the children. This gives them time to set up, prepare, and focus on the children as they arrive.
- Welcome the kids instead of fussing with materials. This not only sets the children up for a better experience, but it also gives parents assurance that their children are in thoughtful hands.

Volunteer Retention

One of the keys to long-term retention of volunteers is to provide a friendly and helpful orientation.

Once, I had a wonderful leader who was unable to get to the classroom early for personal reasons. Because I knew this ahead of time, I was able to recruit a greeter to engage with the kids until she arrived. Rather than firing her for being late consistently, I adapted to her situation.

It takes intentionality and a review of the job description at the beginning to avoid awkward situations later. There may be a few times that a volunteer will graciously remove themselves after reviewing the job description. They may realize they are unable or unwilling to do what it requires. While we never want to lose a volunteer, it is better to begin with clear expectations.

TAKE NOTE

Volunteer retention is the best recruiting tool!

Provide Orientation

Too often, we get a new volunteer and drop them into a sink or swim situation. Most volunteers are gracious and will stick with a role for the season. But if they have a bad experience, you may never get them to volunteer again. I've heard far too many potential volunteers say, "been there, done that," or worse, "I did my time in children's ministry." Yikes! This lets me know this person had a bad experience.

They were likely under-prepared, under-equipped, and under-supported in their previous experience. I make it my goal to give them a completely new experience that will keep them coming back to serve. One of the keys to long-term retention of volunteers is to provide a friendly and helpful orientation before they are scheduled to serve.

When you get a new volunteer, your job is not done. Never just add them to the schedule and move on to the next pressing need. I recommend a four-phase orientation process for new volunteers. While this requires some extra work and attention, you'll keep volunteers longer. Every volunteer you retain is one less you need to recruit. Volunteer retention is the best recruiting tool!

The Four Phases of Orientation

When someone volunteers for a role, explain to them your four phases for ministry placement. Reassure them that you won't just throw them into the fray. Even seasoned volunteers will be glad to know that you have a process for orientation.

While they may never admit it to you, new volunteers do wonder, "Will I like this? If I don't, how do I get out?" While they don't want to let you down, they also want to have a positive experience.

Validate their concerns. Tell each new recruit, "Before we assign you to a volunteer role, it's important to us that the job is a good fit for you. We want you to truly enjoy serving." This will give them great peace of mind.

Phase One: Observation

Explain to new volunteers that the first thing you'd like them to do is observe.

Schedule them as an additional worker with no responsibilities other than to be present. They can help by distributing snacks or helping with a game, but the key is that they observe. Afterward, talk to them about how everything went.

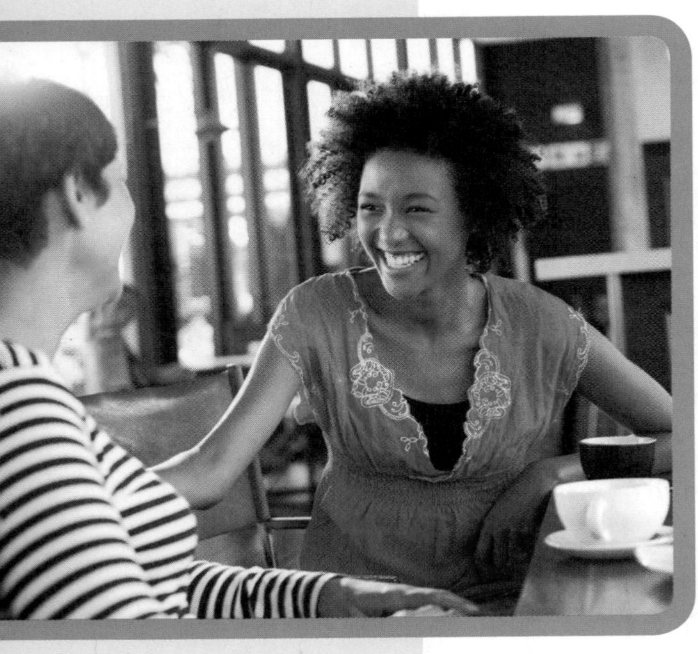

An in-person discussion is ideal, but if you don't catch them after their service, call the next day while their memory is fresh. If all went well, ask if you can schedule them for a trial period. Emphasize again how important it is that they are serving in a way that uses both their unique giftedness from God and their enjoyment.

Phase Two: Trial Period

The length of the trial period will depend on your church and the program needs. I recommend new volunteers serve at least twice in a trial role. If they are serving weekly, you'll follow up in two weeks. If it is bimonthly, or even monthly, you'll still follow up after they served twice.

Although we want the trial period to be long enough that the volunteer gets past "feeling new," don't make the trial period too long. The goal is that by the end of the trial period, they will either feel competent in what they are doing or realize it's not a good fit for them. If the job is not a good fit, your goal is now to move them into a better fitting role.

Phase Three: Review and Evaluation

After continuing in their role after the trial period, call for the review and evaluation of a volunteer's role. Many of your volunteers will be surprised by the contact. If it is a good fit, they have already considered themselves a regular volunteer and will gladly accept further assignment. If they aren't enjoying it, try to find out why. There may be a way you can modify what is expected of them or make an improvement to the ministry that other volunteers will appreciate as well.

If someone is in a bad fit, we are keeping them from where God wants them. Giving people an easy out if it's not a good fit honors them and will build credibility with volunteers. They will be far more likely to help out in the future, even in roles that aren't ideal, when they know you understand them.

I once had a volunteer who loved serving during the first service but was often late to the second service since parents were late to pick up their kids. This was good and fair feedback. In response, we recruited a transition team whose responsibility was to relieve first service volunteers when the service was over. Once the second service started, the transition team was free to go home. Many volunteers even stayed to serve longer or stepped into understaffed spots. It became a blessing to first-service volunteers.

Giving people an easy out if it's not a good fit honors them and will build credibility with volunteers. They will be far more likely to help out in the future, even in roles that aren't ideal, when they know you understand them.

Whether they are happy in their role or not, seek feedback during the review and evaluation. While you can't fix everything, you'll do your best to accommodate

Phase Four: Ministry Placement

They've been oriented. They have observed. They have completed a trial period and provided feedback. Now, it's time to join the team. Celebrate them! Announce them to children, volunteers, and even parents. Post their picture and a short biography in your newsletter or on social media.

Assign a Time Frame

Here is an important principle: Assign volunteers for a defined period of time. Whether it is three months or a full year, you honor them by defining when the role is over. At the end of their service, thank them and invite them to serve again.

This does many things to benefit you as well as the volunteer.

Volunteer Benefits:

- If their situation changes and they need to take a break, often they will still complete their committed time frame. This keeps a volunteer serving longer than they might have.
- Definite time frames honor volunteers, showing that you put their needs above your own. When they have that easy out, they will be back.
- If they have to muster up the courage to quit an indefinite assignment, you may never get them back. Often, because they usually quit months after they really wanted to, they end up feeling trapped. People don't step back into traps.

Ministry Benefits:

- Definite time frames help you move volunteers that aren't a good fit. It is easier to say, "Thanks for serving, I've got someone else for that role for next period, and I've got an idea of something else you might want to try." Or, "It seems like it has been challenging for you to meet the requirements of this role, would you like to take the next period off until things settle down for you?"
- They help prevent an over-developed sense of ownership in a volunteer's role or classroom. Yes, we want volunteers to feel ownership over their area of ministry, but never to the point that they are no longer serving as a healthy member of the team.

Phase Five: Check Up

Never stop checking in with people about their volunteer role. This surprises and delights volunteers when they discover that you are more concerned with their well being than just plugging names into a schedule. Listen to feedback, learn from it, and improve the ministry as you are able from feedback you receive.

Types of Training 3: Ongoing Advanced Training

The best organizations in any field are the ones that provide ongoing advanced training to their team members. Is this easy? No. It is especially difficult in a volunteer organization where people already have busy lives. Nevertheless, training is essential to the growth and health of any organization. So how do you provide ongoing training and encourage your volunteers to participate?

Let me provide a blueprint on **PREP**ing your volunteers for success! They need **P.R.E.P.** to be their best! Make it **P**ractical, **R**elational, **E**njoyable, and **P**eriodic.

P.R.E.P. Training

Practical

Relational

Enjoyable

Periodic

People's time is one of their most valuable assets. Don't ask them to give up their precious time for training that doesn't meet these standards.

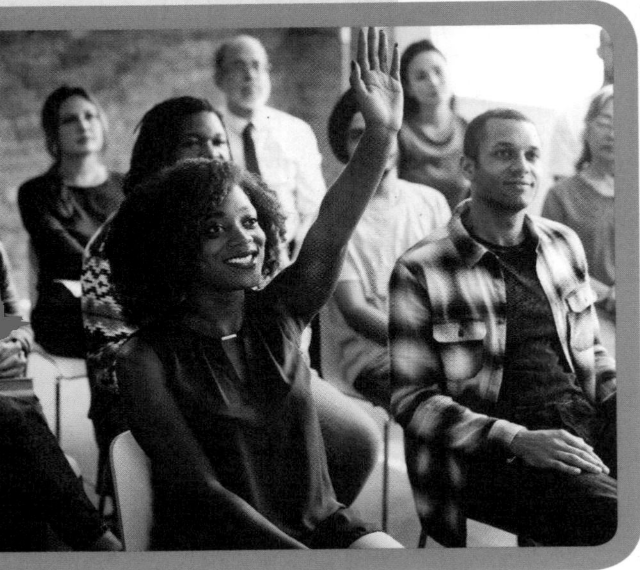

Make It Practical

Training needs to be practical. It must address real and present needs that they have as volunteers serve. If you plan a training session on the history of educational methods through the centuries, you'll likely be by yourself in a room.

Training needs to appeal to your volunteers. Ask your volunteers for topics they would like addressed. Don't expect every volunteer to come to every training opportunity. They will participate in the training that relates to their unique needs and interests.

At the end of a training the question isn't what did they learn, but what are they going to DO with what they learned? We want better volunteers, not just smarter ones.

Make It Relational

Volunteers aren't thinking during the week, "I wonder when the next training session is?" Life is crazy busy and people are being pulled in every direction. A training workshop can sound like just another demand on their time. However, everyone needs fellowship and enjoys people.

- Make your training social.
- Personally invite people.
- Allow people to interact, not just sit and watch or listen to someone talk up front.

People need to leave having learned something and having related to others who share their investment with children. You may never have the attendance you'd like at training events. If you make them relational, those who attended will spread the word and your attendance will steadily grow.

Make It Enjoyable

People love to laugh. They love to be appreciated. They enjoy a good meal and being with others. Similar to making your training relational, it must also be enjoyable.

If there are no smiles or laughter at a training event, you haven't created something worth attending. Play games, provide entertainment, and give away funny door prizes. People need to leave happy that they came. Those who missed it need to hear that they missed out!

A training event will either build momentum and motivation or it will erode it. The difference is up to you. Plan something you'd go to if you were a volunteer.

Make It Periodic

Training shouldn't be a once-in-a-life time experience! Make them periodic. How often will depend on your church culture and demographic.

- Once a year isn't often enough.
- Some churches have a weekly dinner for volunteers before a midweek program. This makes dinner easier on families.
- Sometimes they provide a short encouraging and equipping program before heading off to serve.
- Others do something once a month, or on every fifth Sunday if they want to have something once a quarter.

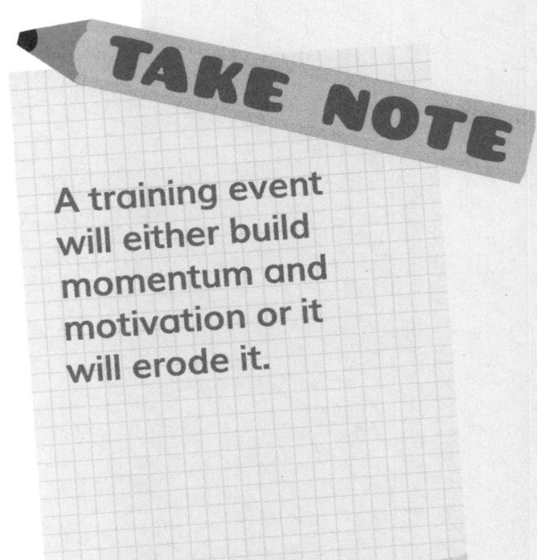

Work with your leadership team to determine what is best for your church.

Below are some of the common times and ways many churches provide training:

- **Fall Orientation:** Welcome and introduce new volunteers to your existing team. It's a good opportunity to remind those returning volunteers of important polices, alert everyone to changes, and update volunteers on exciting things in the upcoming year.

- **Christmas Social:** These get-togethers can provide a fun opportunity to equip and encourage.
- **Spring "Recharge" Event:** Just when volunteers start to feel weary, revitalize them with good news of all that's going on in the ministry.
- **Summer Socials:** Keep relationships growing.

Methods of Training

Break the mold. Training doesn't have to always look the same. If all you do is a dinner and speaker, it is time to try something new! If it doesn't work, it's no big deal. At least you tried something and likely engaged at least some of your volunteers. You may be surprised and end up discovering a new way to equip and encourage your volunteers!

Here are some ideas for different ways to train your volunteers.

Live Workshops

Don't write this off too quickly. In today's busy world, inviting volunteers to a luncheon for training will never get one-hundred percent of your volunteers there. But even if you only get half of them to a training, that is still *half* of your volunteers getting equipped and encouraged!

E-Newsletters

We live in a world of emails! Why not use them for nugget-sized training? If you see an issue you'd like to address with your volunteers, a short training blurb in your regular communication can address it quickly and easily. Use 24 Quick Volunteer Tips, which start on page 243.

Helpful Booklets

Put helpful tools into your volunteers' hands. A little booklet on discipline or a guide to sharing the gospel makes for a fast read. Make your appreciation gifts to volunteers something with a return on investment by assisting your volunteers in their service.

Video Training

We all know how popular videos are. Your volunteers spend time each week watching videos on social media. Most of those videos are likely a waste of time, as entertaining as they may be. Create short training videos, or share videos others have made. A two minute video may be a greater success than a two hundred word email.

Text Messages

According to a study by Pew Research Center in February of 2018, an estimated ninety-five percent of Americans carry a cell phone. Seventy-seven percent of those are smart phones. Younger Americans do more on their phone than they do on a computer. Tablet use is surging and text messaging is becoming integrated with tablets as well. You may even have volunteers wearing smart watches that deliver text messages. It is wise to tap into this connectivity.

No, you can't present a full training workshop via text message. But you can send short training reminders. Every week, in addition to a simple reminder to volunteers that they are scheduled to serve, I remind them of our core values. You can also send simple training messages, such as:

- Remember, our goal is to make Sunday the best day of our kids week!
- Make sure every single child feels noticed, welcomed, and loved.
- Don't forget, if a child is wearing a smile-face sticker, they are a guest. Be sure to give them focused attention.

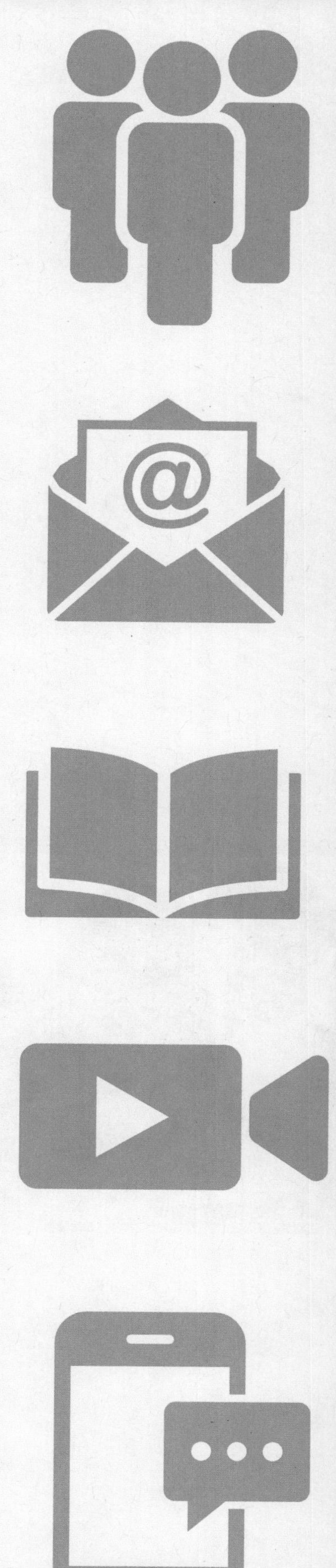

- Watch for kids that seem down or quiet. There may be something going on in their life. Ask how they are doing and how you can pray for them.
- If there is anything I can do to make your volunteer experience better, please don't hesitate to let me know. I'm here to serve you as much as the kids.

Social Media Group

I highly encourage children's ministry leaders to launch a closed social-media group for their volunteers. This is a private area where you can post announcements, event information, celebrate successes, and offer training resources. You can also measure engagement of your volunteers. While not everyone may have an account with a particular social-media site, choose a commonly used site, and most of your volunteers will be there. It's a powerful way to connect with volunteers who are likely on social media daily.

Spotlighting Success

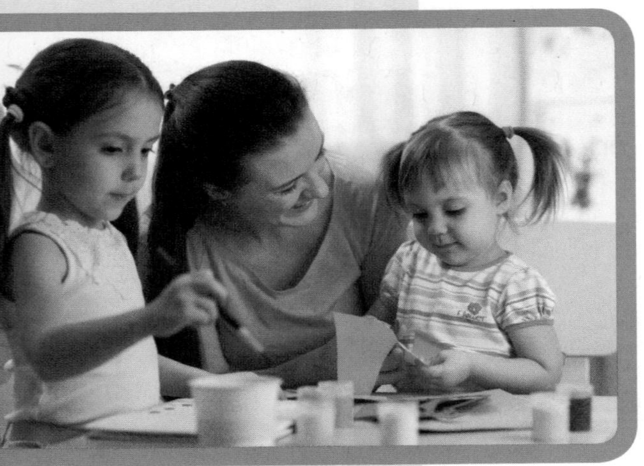

In leadership, we often focus on what is going wrong and fail to point out when our volunteers are doing things right. One of the best ways to train positively is to spotlight volunteers who are doing a great job. It shows other volunteers what success looks like.

For example, share a picture of a volunteer kneeling down to talk to a child. Mention that this is the best way to make a relational connection. You will be training others on how to talk to kids. Just telling volunteers they should talk to kids at their eye level has little impact. Seeing it done right is far more effective.

24 Quick Volunteer Tips

Volunteer Training can be overwhelming.
You might have heard the old joke:

Question: How do you eat an elephant?

Answer: One bite at a time.

How do you get your volunteers all trained?
One little training bite at a time!

How to Use the Quick Volunteer Tips

Instead of sending all your volunteers this complete list of tips or asking them to sit through a training session where you discuss each one, consider disseminating the information one tip at a time.

If you share one tip a week, you'll repeat a tip approximately twice a year. That's just enough of a time lag to serve as a good reminder to those who have seen them before.

Here are some ideas for sharing the tips:

- Each week, include one of the tips printed on a sheet of paper with other materials (such as attendance sheets or name stickers) you provide for your teachers.
- Turn each tip into a poster and place them prominently in your resource room or other staff gathering place. Rotate the poster periodically so people don't stop noticing them.
- Send one out in a weekly email or social-media post.
- Go the old-fashioned way: Mail them!

However you choose to share the tips, please include the source. Just add a short line such as, "Reprinted with permission from *The Kidology Ultimate Children's Ministry*

Toolbox." (Permission is limited to these volunteer tips, shared one at a time, by the original purchaser of this book. If you have any questions about making photocopies from this book, please refer to the "Conditions of Use" on the copyright page. Thank you for respecting copyrights!)

Tip 1: A Complete Lesson

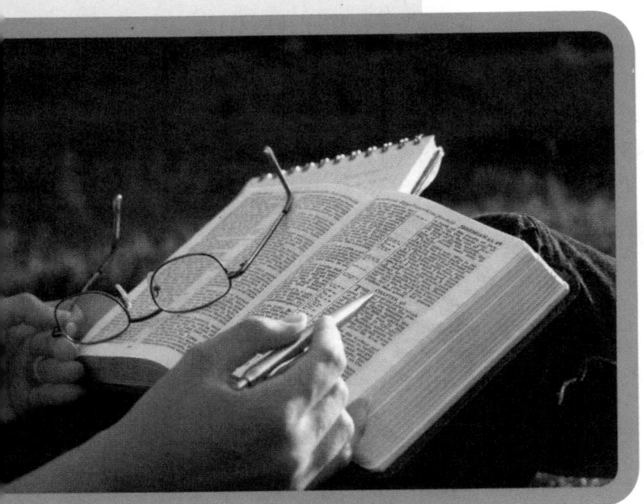

Teaching can be overwhelming—especially if your leader's guide is loaded with ideas and activities for you to do. It can be hard to decide what to do in the short time you have with your students.

Here is a little secret: You don't have to do everything in the lesson! Good curricula will give you more than you can do so you have options.

What makes a lesson complete, if it isn't completing everything in the leader's guide? Below are three essential elements to any lesson.

- **Verse:** You should have a key verse or two for the lesson. Read it. Have the kids read it. Explain it. If it is short enough, have the kids learn to recite it.
- **Bible Story:** You should have a Bible story to tell. Read it. Get the kids involved with it: acting it out, doing motions for key words, etc. Illustrate the story with props or visual aids to make it more engaging. Teaching from the Bible is vitally important.
- **Learning Activity:** You should have an activity that illustrates the point of the story and verse. *Doing something* is what makes abstract concepts stick in the minds and hearts of kids. Kids are concrete relational, which means they only perceive through the five senses. Whether it is a game, object lesson, student guide, craft, or other activity, use something that will help kids connect the verse and story to their own real life.

If you have done these three things, you have completed your task. As a bonus, include prayer as a way to close the lesson, reiterate what has been learned, and ask God to continue the learning process after they leave. Kids need to see adults pray.

Tip 2: Now What?

The purpose of teaching is to change the lives of your students. It isn't simply to give them more Bible knowledge. Always prayerfully extend a challenge to your students to put into action what they learned during your lesson in the following week. Many curricula provide challenges as part of their materials. However, if your curriculum doesn't, make up your own!

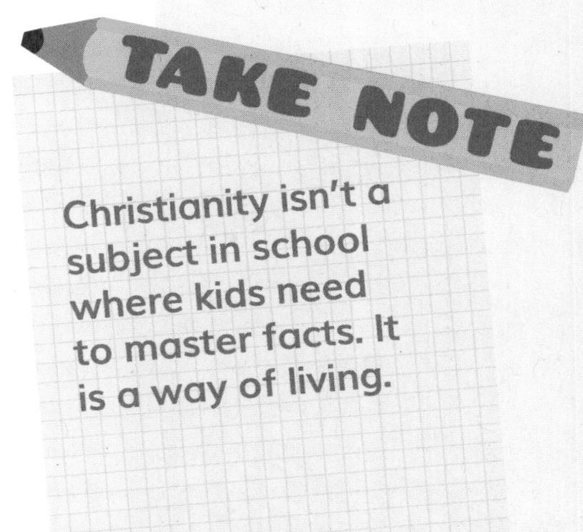

Challenge kids to:

- Respond gently when they are angry
- Forgive someone
- Send a note of encouragement
- Invite a friend to church

At the beginning of class each week, start with reviewing the previous lesson and the challenge they were given then. Give kids a chance to share what they have done. Keep it low pressure, as kids won't always do the challenges. But as you consistently challenge and follow up, they will eventually report on what they did.

This gets your lesson out of the classroom and into real life. Parents may contact you because they observe their child do something unusual and wonderful during the week. They'll suspect it had something to do with your class.

Be sure you do your challenges as well. Be willing to share your efforts. Christianity isn't a subject in school where kids need to master facts. It is a way of living. They should follow Jesus and live out what they learn. How can they do that if you don't guide them with some practical ideas and challenges? Be prepared for some amazing stories as you challenge kids and follow up.

Tip 3: Punishment vs. Discipline

As you have certainly discovered, discipline is an art that we need to master as we work with children. Kids are energetic and wiggly and prone to test our boundaries. However, there is a difference between punishment and discipline.

Punishment

- Benefits the punisher
- Flows from anger
- Response to being annoyed, bothered, or disrespected by the child
- Seeks to rebuke or embarrass the child
- Brings negative feelings to both the child and leader
- Forcefully removes child from the activity

Discipline

- Benefits the one being disciplined
- Flows from love
- Recognizes the child's value in God's eyes
- Seeks to encourage and correct the child
- Brings about positive change
- Does not result in raised voices or pointing fingers

Using a positive, gentle response to inappropriate behavior is extremely effective.

- Have clear rules
- Reinforce them with calmness
- Speak with a gentle but firm spirit

Children will naturally start to follow this type of correction.

The occasional problem child will need some extra grace. This requires proactive help, such as changing where they sit, providing a helper to be near them, and some personal incentives to work on cooperating. It is rewarding when you see progress in a child's behavior, and know it is because you are gently guiding them to be the child they truly desire to be.

Love conquers what punishment never will!

Tip 4: Make Learning Fun and Interactive

Too often, you can find yourself with a group of kids who are content to let someone else answer questions or participate in activities. This is when it is important to mix a simple game with learning.

Here are some simple ideas to get you going:

- Take a small trash can and place it on a table. Whoever contributes an answer (even if it's wrong) gets to throw a ball in a basket. The point is to increase participation.
- On the floor, use tape to make a giant tic-tac-toe board. Challenge kids to get three in a row. The way to do so is have a kid stand in a space on the board after answering a question or otherwise participating.
- Have all the kids line up on a wall. Read true-or-false sentences aloud. If they think the sentence is true, they raise their hand. If they think the sentence is false, they keep their hands down. Those who are correct take a step toward the opposite wall. Once a child reaches the other side of the room, they get a treat. Continue until all the kids get a treat.

When kids are physically involved, it may feel more chaotic. But the kids will be listening better and will remember more because their entire body was involved in the learning. Be creative. Make up your own games. It will get a little noisy, but they'll be learning!

Tip 5: Get Kids to Talk

Or How to Get Beyond "Uh-huh" and "Yeah."

Does this conversation sound familiar?

"How are you doing today?"

"Fine."

"What did you do at school this week?"

"Nothing."

"Nothing? You had to do something! Anything interesting happen at school today?"

"Nah."

Kids are great at answering questions with only one word. So how do you get kids to talk? First of all, *you* have to resist the urge to talk. Kids need to be convinced that you actually want to hear what they have to say. This takes some time.

Here are some tips to get kids talking:

Avoid questions that can be answered with only one word! Especially if that one word is *yes* or *no*.

Ask questions that are open ended. These questions require them to think and have an answer unique to them. Open questions start with things like, "What do you like about . . .," "What would you do if . . .," "Why do you think . . .," etc.

Ask for their advice. "What do you like best about church?" This can be followed by, "If you were the teacher, what would you do?" Accept whatever they offer. You don't have to actually do what they suggest, but you can enjoy the suggestion.

A common response that I receive is, "Give us candy every week." I just respond, "Oh, I'm sure everyone would love that, but then we wouldn't have time for games!"

In that answer, I'm demonstrating that I'm on the same page with them, even if I know it won't happen.

Follow short (or one word) answers with more probing questions.

If a kid's favorite subject in school is reading:

- Ask what kind of reading.
- Ask what book or books they've read recently.
- As if they like a popular series and consider reading it yourself. In the future, you will be better prepared to converse on that series of books.

Bonus Tip: Ask questions about things in the culture of kids. Asking a child to explain a video game has fueled many conversations!. Conversations about things that interest kids will open them up big time.

Tip 6: Direct, Don't ask.

Provide real choices. One of the mistakes adults make is asking children their opinion when they don't have a choice in the situation. Choices are important to kids.

In the adult world, we use questions to give polite instructions. A wife may say to her husband, "Honey, would you help with the dishes?" What she really means is, "Help with the dishes."

These instructional questions confuse children. If you announce, "Would you like to sing now?" the children may answer, "No." They're not being silly (or maybe some are!), but sincere. They really might not want to sing now.

This puts the leader in a tough spot. Do you say, "Well, we are doing it anyway. I wasn't really asking"? A better option is to avoid the situation in the first place by enthusiastically and simply instructing, "It's worship time!" See the difference?

However, you can offer legitimate choices at the same time you give instructions.

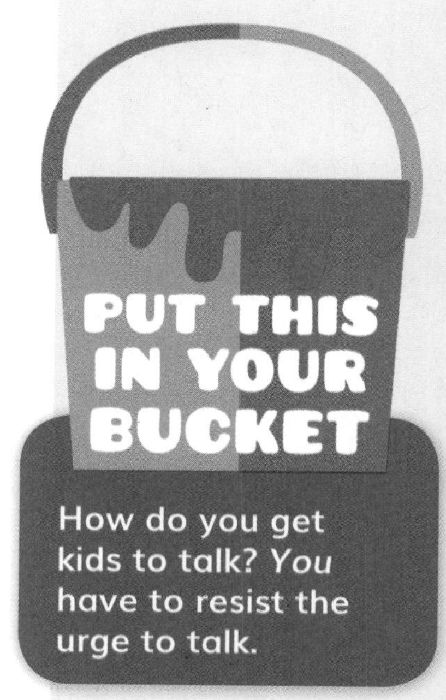

How do you get kids to talk? *You have to resist the urge to talk.*

- "Choose a partner for worship time."
- "Pick a good seat as we are about to hear a fantastic story!"
- "Go pick the table where you would like to do the craft."

When we give children both real choices and clear instructions, and do it with enthusiasm, they will gladly follow and have a great time partnering with us in the learning experience.

Tip 7: Plan Your Questions Thoughtfully

Two priests once argued about whether it was OK to pray while smoking. Since they disagreed so strongly, they decided to write to the Pope to get his answer.

When they met again to report whether or not the Pope backed up their side, to their surprise, the Pope had agreed with both of their positions.

The priest who felt you should not smoke while praying wrote and asked, "Is it OK to smoke while praying?"

The Pope replied, "No, because prayer is serious business, and it demands your full attention."

The priest who thought it was fine to smoke while praying asked, "Is it OK to pray while smoking?"

The Pope replied, "Of course. You can pray any time, and God will hear you."

Obviously, how you frame a question can determine the answer you will get.

If you ask children questions that they can answer with a simple yes or no, you won't get them thinking about the topic. You need to ask open-ended questions that don't have an obvious right or wrong answer. These are called *analytical* (requiring some thought) or *personal* (answer relates only to the one answering) questions. If you take the time to write out strategic questions ahead of time, you will end up having great conversations with your students.

Tip 8: Engaging Your Students with Prayer

Do you start or close your class or small group time with prayer?

Prayer is one of those things we can be guilty of talking about more than doing. Not only is there power in prayer, there is also an impact when kids hear us pray. It teaches them how to pray.

- Prayer can help kids focus and bring their attention to the topic at hand while emphasizing the importance of your time together.
- Pray with your kids, and ask God to give your group wisdom. Your kids may surprise you with a more focused attitude during this time of discipleship.
- When kids ask you to pray for them, show them that you are serious about prayer by praying for them right then and there.

If kids see how important prayer is to you, it is far more likely they will begin to follow your example.

If kids see how important prayer is to you, it is far more likely they will begin to follow your example.

Tip 9: Aim High

If you aim at nothing, you are sure to hit it!

- What is your goal when you are teaching?
- Is there some information you want kids to learn?
- Is there a behavior you want to see change in their life?
- Is there something you want them to be able to do as a result of your lesson?

Whenever you teach, be sure you are absolutely clear on your aim for the lesson. It can be a different type of aim for each lesson, but it must be obvious. Your curriculum may suggest several, but it is best to hone

If we truly believe that we are changing lives and not providing childcare, then we must determine our aim with each lesson and measure our success.

in on one. Some weeks you may focus on a particular verse. Other weeks may be about character traits.

Ask yourself, "What's the one thing I want kids to walk away from the room with?" The answer will be your aim.

Once you have determined that aim, choose learning activities that will create the target for that aim. Every goal should be measurable. How will you know that you hit what you were aiming at?

Things like "Know the plan of salvation" or "Learn a new Bible verse" sound like worthy aims. But how do you measure what another person knows? You can't crack open their brain and look at what got deposited there during your lesson. However, things like, "Repeat the ABCs of salvation after me" or, "Repeat the memory verse without prompting" are measurable.

Write down your aim and how you will determine if you have succeeded. It may be that you won't find out until the following week.

If we truly believe that we are changing lives and not providing childcare, then we must determine our aim with each lesson and measure our success. Not only will we be more effective teachers, we will also be encouraged as we see the impact of our efforts!

Tip 10: Grow Like a P.R.O.

To really grow, we have to let God work inside of us. Trying to grow on our own won't yield good results. Teach kids to rely on Jesus like a P.R.O.

- **P**ray—Begin by asking God to seek your heart and show you where he wants to work. As the Holy Spirit reveals areas that may need to change, confess them to him.
- **R**epent—True repentance shows a change of our hearts, minds, and intentions from our way to God's way.

- Obey—We want our kids to obey God's will and follow his Spirit. Spiritual growth will come as our hearts learn that obedience is a gift of love. It should be the first choice of those who belong to Jesus.

We all know that few of our students will "go pro" in their favorite sport. But using this phrase that they relate to can help them "go pro" in their spiritual growth.

Tip 11: Traits of Effective Teachers—Enthusiasm

Why is enthusiasm so effective? For starters, it keeps students' attention—and the more they are listening, the more they are learning. Enthusiasm validates the content and gives credibility to the teacher. If a teacher lacks enthusiasm, it makes the content sound unimportant. Or, worse, it makes the teacher look unqualified to teach. Either of those conclusions, even at a subconscious level, will stifle learning.

How do you show enthusiasm? Smile! Be confident! Teachers must be convinced of their own value if they want their students to be eager to learn. A new teacher can compensate for lack of experience by being enthusiastic.

Ask yourself not, "How enthusiastic am I?" but, "How enthusiastic do my students think I am?" Then, think of some ways to increase your enthusiasm while teaching!

Tip 12: Traits of Effective Teachers—Clear Communication

To teach effectively, we must communicate clearly. But teachers often forget to evaluate how well the students understand the lesson. Just because you *said* it doesn't mean you *taught* it. Teaching involves a transformation in the student. It can be as simple as new knowledge they didn't have before, but it ought to go further in changing the way they think and behave.

How do we know if we've been teaching or talking?

The first key is to ask effective questions. The first secret to asking questions is to ask the question and wait.

That's right. Wait.

Studies have shown that after asking a question, most teachers wait *less than a second* for an answer ("Your Secret Weapon: Wait Time;" *teachervision.com*). If no answer comes—in less than a second—they give the answer. Students will certainly allow the teacher to do this. However, if a teacher waits for an answer, the same awkward silence that urges them to provide the answer will prompt students to venture a guess.

Ideally, wait three to five seconds. Count them in your head as you wait. Then, after someone answers, wait three to five seconds again. If you don't jump in and start talking right away, someone else just might have something to say.

The next key is to learn to ask a variety of questions, ranging from questions requiring recall to questions that require thought and personal analysis. The latter type of question enables answers with no risk of being wrong.

The final key is to help a student modify their answer until it becomes acceptable. Always thank a student for participating and acknowledge something good about their answer, even if it was far off. Avoid saying "No," or "Wrong," or "Bbbzzztt! Try again." A negative response will shut down not just that kid, but every other kid who saw them get shut down. Instead, say something that reinforces their attempt to answer and then provides the correct information. For example, "I can see why you might think that, but actually David was just a young boy."

1. ASK THEN WAIT

2. VARY THE QUESTIONS

3. STAY POSITIVE

Accept answers as a gift, and you'll receive many more. Planning questions ahead of time will result in more thoughtful and intentional questions. Through an effective use of questions, your teaching will become clearer, and your students will learn more!

Tip 13: Traits of Effective Teachers—Know Their Stuff

Effective teachers have a firm grip on the subject matter they are teaching. It is critical to prepare and know your material—even more than you plan to share. In the week before you present the lesson, use teacher guides or curriculum as a basis for your own study. When you share what you have learned, students will engage more. It also prepares teachers to be flexible in their teaching methods.

Teachers do not need to know everything on a subject, but they should have a firm grip on the material and the big idea they are trying to communicate. I often say to students, "You probably aren't old enough for this, but . . ." and they rise to the occasion, eager to be challenged and to learn something new. Try it!

Tip 14: Traits of an Effective Teacher—High Expectations

One of the most profound secrets of effective teaching is that students rise to the level of their teacher's expectations. This is called the Pygmalion Effect and was discovered in a famous study by Robert Rosenthal and Lenore Jacobson (*Pygmalion in the Classroom*, 1968). In the study, teachers were asked to administer a test to their students. They were told that the test would determine the top twenty percent of their class. The teachers assumed that the students were the "lab rats" of the experiment. In reality, Rosenthal and Jacobson were watching the teachers.

One of the most profound secrets of effective teaching is that students rise to the level of their teacher's expectations.

After all the students were tested, Rosenthal and Jacobson gave the teachers fake statistics. They randomly picked students to be in the top twenty percent, regardless of the students' actual test score. Naturally, the teachers believed the scientists. Eight months later, that random twenty-percent group ended up being top of their class. Why? Because the teachers expected more from them. They challenged them more than the others who they perceived had less potential.

Teachers who expect great things often act to fulfill their own prophesy. How do you communicate high expectations to your students? Be willing to try challenging things and expect your students to succeed. If they are struggling, be the one who believes they can do it. Children are natural pleasers and will work hard to live up to what you think they are capable of.

I once challenged the kids in my class to memorize an entire book of the Bible. Within a month several kids knew the book of Philippians by memory and could quote it with ease. Had they never been challenged, they would have never undertaken such an endeavor. What will your challenge be? How will you encourage your students and celebrate their success? If you want to be a great teacher, expect great things from your students.

Tip 15: Notice the Gentle Tugs

In Luke 8, Jesus was ministering to the crowds when he suddenly felt someone touch his garment. He felt power go out from him. A woman came forward and admitted she had touched him. Jesus was busy doing his Father's work, but he wasn't too busy to notice the gentle touch of a woman in need—a woman who didn't feel she could interrupt or ask him for help. So she settled for a hidden touch.

While we certainly won't have power flow out of us, we need to be like Jesus in this story. Every time we lead our classes or programs, we find ourselves busy doing what our Father has given us to do. But we must not miss when children seek a little attention from us. They may not feel they can interrupt or ask, but they will tip us off with small gestures. They may try to hold our hand, or sit next to us, or linger around. We must be sure that we stop and minister to these children right in the moment of their need. It might be a kind word, a listening ear, or a promise to pray that will provide healing to that child in the moment.

Teachers who expect great things often act to fulfill their own prophesy.

Tip 16: Your Story Matters

Do the kid's in your class know your personal testimony? Of course, I'm not talking about adult things they are not ready to handle. But I am talking about the amazing things God has done in your own life.

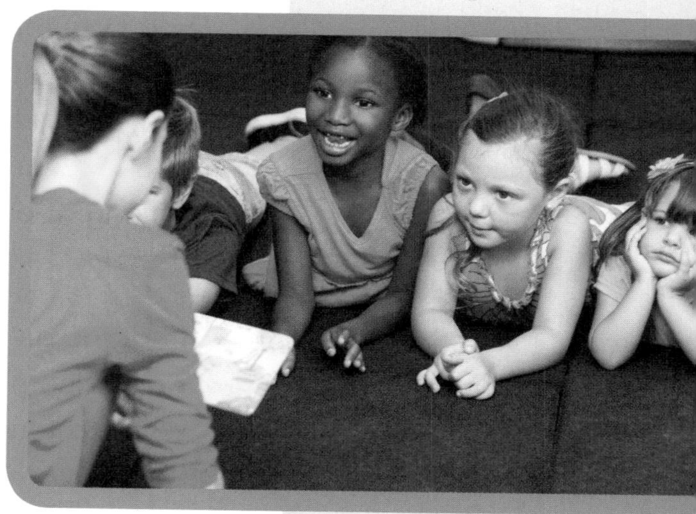

Tell the kids what God is doing in your life. Start small by relating a Bible story to your own life. For example, "Saul was a totally different person after meeting Jesus. When I met Jesus, I became a new person, too. I used to have such a terrible temper, but God changed me from the inside out. I still get angry sometimes, but I handle it completely differently."

KEEPING SHARP

When children hear a story about someone long since dead, it remains distant and less relevant than if they hear the impact of the Bible on someone they actually know.

When children hear a story about someone long since dead, it remains distant and less relevant than if they hear the impact of the Bible on someone they actually know. There is a reason Jesus told stories—stories connect people to truth and to the storyteller. Be sure you share real-life stories from your life. You will find your students connecting with you and then to the material in a much more effective manner. You are the best proof of the reality of God to your students.

Tip 17: The Eyeball Game

I make it a point to look every child in the eyes when I am teaching. I call it the eyeball game, but it is only a game in my mind. If a child isn't looking at me, I will come back to them. If I need to walk out and among them to look into the eyes of every child, then I do that. If I need to gently put my hand on the shoulder of a child to get them to look up, then I do that. If I need to kneel down to see their eyes, I do that. No child is missed. I have no Bible verse to back this up, but I think this is how Jesus ministered.

When you look someone in the eye, you connect with their soul. When you are in a crowd and listening to a preacher or speaker and make eye contact—even for a moment—there is suddenly power in that moment! Their words suddenly are for you. I bet you remember what they were talking about at that moment. Perhaps you even wonder if they intended to look at you at that very moment.

Imagine giving children that same feeling when you are welcoming them. You are glad *they* are there! You want to teach *them*! You have a message for *them* from God's Word. God has something they need to hear. Don't underestimate the power of the eyeball game.

Tip 18: A Laughing Class Is a Learning Class

You've heard the family that plays together stays together. Well, I propose an extension of that principle: The class that laughs together learns together.

Let's face it, from a child's perspective, Sunday is supposed to be a day off from school. And then somebody went and invented Sunday school. Whatever you call your Sunday experience, it's more listening, learning, and being led by grown-ups.

The secret is to have so much fun that they don't even realize they are learning.

- Play games
- Act out stories
- Create a reward system
- Use Bible trading cards

Ask yourself, "How much laughter is in my class?" You may need to up the Laugh-O-Meter a bit. Search the web for kid jokes, and open with a few each week. It's easy to have fun, and it also makes you a more effective teacher.

Tip 19: Call and Respond!

Always be looking for ways to rally attention while making it fun and active for your kids. One fun strategy is to use a call and respond activity. This is a short, interactive activity that helps engage kids while reinforcing the lesson of the day.

Teach it at the beginning, and then repeat the sequence throughout the lesson. Of course, it can be altered from week to week to keep kids on their toes.

"If I say _____ (or do_____,) then you say_____ (or do______)."

Some examples:

- Leader: CLAP, CLAP, CLAP, "JESUS LOVES ME."
  Kids: CLAP, CLAP, CLAP, "NO MATTER WHAT!"

- Leader (in a funny voice and rhythm): "HELLO, CLASS."
  Kids (mimicking voice and rhythm):
  "I'M LISTENING, TEACHER."

These call and respond strategies are excellent for regrouping, transitioning between activities, or simply adding some fun into your lesson.

Tip 20: When a Child with Special Needs Visits

Getting to know people with special needs can be difficult. It takes time. Generally speaking, it is similar to knowing any other person in our ministry. Sometimes they present a communication challenge. Other times, there are behavior issues. Often, there are physical impairments that tend to make us feel uncomfortable. Wheelchairs, crutches, or seeing sticks tend to be obstacles in our everyday environments.

Start by welcoming the child warmly. Get them involved in a simple task you can compliment them on (whether or not it was done well). Activity takes their mind off of the newness they are feeling.

Also, assess whether they can manage on their own or if they need someone to come alongside and help them. Your leadership can be helpful in determining the next steps, but at the start, love and patience are key.

Much of getting to know special-needs people is trial and error. It's okay if you need to move in and out of a classroom, change activities frequently, or give tangible rewards (stickers, high fives, hugs) to let them know how great you think they are doing. You are getting to know what it takes to love them. Be positive and loving, and show interest in them.

Tip 21: Ask for Guesses, Not Answers

Years ago, I had a little boy in my class named Trevon. Whenever I asked a question, regardless of the Bible story, his hand would shoot up. He always answered with an enthusiastic, "Moses!" Some teacher must have hit it out of the park telling Trevon the story of Moses.

I felt bad for him. One Sunday, I decided to rig the Q and A for Trevon. Though it had nothing to do with my lesson, I asked, "Who did God give the Ten Commandments to?"

Of course, Trevon's hand shot up again! I smiled as I called on him. Trevon hesitated. "Jesus?" He answered.

I was dejected. "No, Trevon, it was Moses." I felt terrible. I thought I had set this little guy up for success, but instead, I had caused him to fail yet again. I shared this story with a mentor that week.

He said, "Karl, that's because you are asking for answers instead of guesses."

You see, a guess can always be affirmed. I could have been saying, "Moses? What a great guess! He was a mighty man for God in the Old Testament, but I was thinking of someone in the New Testament." No matter how far

No matter how far off the answer, I can now affirm the child's thinking and effort while guiding them toward the correct answer.

off the answer, I can now affirm the child's thinking and effort while guiding them toward the correct answer.

"Michael Jordan? Wow, he is amazing on the basketball court, but I'm thinking of someone who was amazing in the time of Jesus. In fact, Jordan might be known as 'Air Jordan,' but this disciple of Jesus walked on water! Not even Michael Jordan can do that. Any guesses?"

Start asking for guesses, and your students will keep trying and contributing. As a result, they will both learn and be encouraged.

Tip 22: Expressive Facial Expressions

Want your storytelling to have greater impact? Be expressive! It takes intentional effort at first, but it will come naturally over time. Every emotion and expression is reduced as it travels the distance from you to your audience.

- A smile one-on-one is a straight face to a group.
- A laugh close up is a chuckle to an audience.

How do you compensate for this? Take your expressions up a few notches when you are in front of a group. You will feel like you are too loud or too expressive, but your intent will be recognizable.

This is hugely important when it comes to children. If you want to express happiness or excitement, your face needs to really show those emotions. If you want to express sadness, surprise, or anger, show them at two hundred percent, and your audience will be drawn in.

Tip 23: Get Real

If you want your lessons to truly impact your students, you must tell them how the story affects them *right now*. Think of tangible ways to relate the lesson to their lives. What exactly are you asking the kids to do that day or that week?

A mistake we often make is to end our lessons with something open-ended and vague. For instance, instead of, "Let's all be more forgiving," be specific.

> "Who do you need to forgive right now? Who do you need to ask for forgiveness? Before today is over, go to that person and ask them to forgive you. Every night, ask God to help you forgive that person who hurt you. Next week, we will all talk about it. I will do this also, and let you know how it goes."

Do you see the difference? Most children are not great with the abstract or the subtle. Give them something small, concrete, and doable. This is what takes your lessons from "a story long ago" to "God's Word changing me now."

Tip 24: Exaggerated Gestures!

If you aren't exhausted at the end of a story, you aren't telling it right. Keep your audience engaged through exaggerated expressions and gestures.

Super-size it! Want your message to have impact? You'll want to blow up everything you do. When I coach my volunteers on puppets or drama, I dare them to be too loud or too silly or too zany. Rarely have I ever had to ask for *less* of something.

I'm not talking about exaggerating the facts and being dishonest. I'm talking about exaggerating your motions, your voices, and your descriptions, so you are larger than life.

If you aren't exhausted at the end of a story, you aren't telling it right. Keep your audience engaged through exaggerated expressions and gestures.

Encouraging Volunteers

> **Online Resource:** See Karl's blog post: You Don't Have a Recruiting Problem, You Have a Relationship Problem. Visit Kidology.org/toolbox

Everyone Needs Encouragement

When volunteers leave a ministry, it is often because they failed to connect and build relationships. If people don't feel encouraged in what they are doing, their volunteerism will be impacted.

The mission statement of Kidology.org is to "Equip and encourage those who minister to children." If you equip without encouraging, you provide only knowledge. People are less likely to act on new information alone. If you only encourage, you may give courage, but they won't know what to do with it. Equipping tells them what to do. Encouraging says, "You can do it!"

Ways to Encourage Volunteers

- Compliment them when you see them doing something great.
- Thank them verbally for serving.
- Celebrate them on birthdays, holidays, and out of the blue!
- Send handwritten notes in the mail or send a quick email.
- Give little gifts of appreciation.
- Be responsive to their needs and suggestions.
- Give them a shout out on social media.
- Brag about them! It'll get back to them.
- Spend time with them socially, not just in service.
- Call when you aren't asking for something, just to check in.

What else can you do?

5: Outreach Tools

Introduction

Reaching Them All

WATCH THIS VIDEO: Asking Why before When and What
Visit Kidology.org/toolbox

When Jesus concluded his work on Earth, he left with a final mandate in Matthew 28:19-20,

Go and make disciples of all nations . . . teach these new disciples to obey all the commands I have given you.

This mandate is two-fold. First, reach the lost. Then, disciple them.

Most of our programs inside the church are designed for the second half of the great commission—teaching kids everything Jesus commanded us. Children come to know Christ as their savior in our programs, but often they already know the gospel from their parents.

If I were to ask you what your primary goal is, I'm confident most would respond, "To introduce kids to Christ." Yet, many children's ministry leaders don't:

- Know *how* to share the gospel with children.
- *Train* their volunteers to share the gospel with kids.
- *Regularly* provide opportunities for kids to accept Christ.
- *Follow up* and *disciple* kids who make a commitment.
- *Intentionally* reach out to kids who don't already go to church.

TAKE NOTE

Warning: An intentional outreach strategy may mean doing *less* to reach the lost.

If our number one goal is to lead kids to Christ,

- We must answer the question, "How many kids have we led to Christ in the last year?"
- We must prioritize the gospel in our ministries.

What Does Prioritizing the Gospel Look Like?

An intentional outreach strategy may mean doing *less* to reach the lost. If we are too busy running programs to focus on the lost, we need to refocus our energies. This doesn't mean the things we are doing aren't good, but it may mean that we are letting lower priorities slip above our mandate from Jesus.

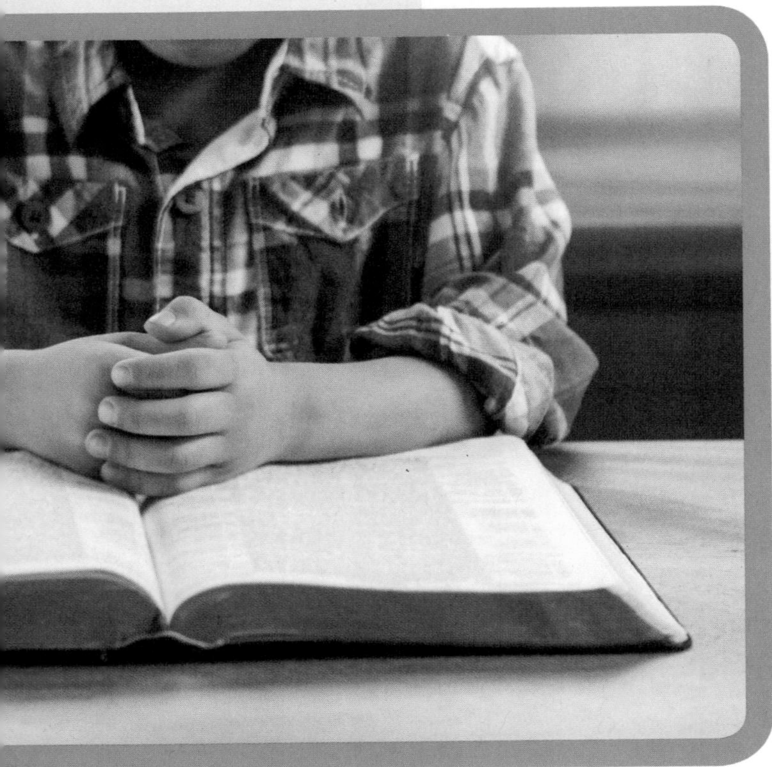

To reach the lost, we must first be ready to receive them and guide them to Jesus within our ministry. We need to clarify our vision, build our leadership team, recruit volunteers, and hone our ministry. Just as we clean the house before company arrives, we need to tidy up in our ministries to prepare for our guests!

Then, we must get outside the building and reach them where they are. If you are serious about reaching lost kids in your community and world, start with a serious evaluation of your current ministry. How well are you reaching the kids God has already given you? Then, focus on the others.

Reaching Kids for Christ

Reaching Kids Inside the Church

How well are you reaching the kids God has already given you?

1. Know how to share the gospel.

Have a favorite method. As the leader, you must be able to confidently explain the gospel. If this area needs improvement, don't delay. Memorize a presentation that you can do quickly. Then, be ready!

2. Train your volunteers to explain the gospel.

Include this in your basic training as well as your ongoing training. Provide a tool, such as a book or booklet, volunteers can follow. But allow them to use a different method if they choose. If one hundred children visit your church, each volunteer will be ready, able, and willing to share the good news!

3. Share the good news regularly.

It is almost embarrassing to include this step. Don't we share the gospel every Sunday? Many churches do not. Sundays can be geared toward teaching the stories and life-principles of the Bible rather than the gospel message. This is good stuff, but it's aimed at students who already know the gospel and have accepted Jesus as their Savior.

Some churches do this weekly, but once a month may be adequate. Do what the Lord leads you to do in your ministry. The key is to make sure it is done regularly. Without intentional planning, months can slip by with missed opportunities to introduce a child to Jesus!

4. Provide opportunities to respond to Christ.

There is little point in explaining the gospel if we aren't going to give children an opportunity to respond to the good news. I've heard leaders explain that they don't invite kids to accept Jesus because they don't want to deprive parents of this privilege.

As a Christian father, I understand the joy of leading my own son to Christ. In fact, I have my own scriptural mandate to lead my children to God.

What about the children who don't have Christian parents? What if their parents are new believers or lack the knowledge and skill to lead their children? I was four years old when a volunteer at my church led me through a simple prayer to ask Jesus to be my Savior. I don't recall my parents being upset that she robbed them of this opportunity. They celebrated it as we should any child who makes such a life altering choice.

5. Prepare an intentional follow up strategy.

It's an exciting moment when a child prays and asks Jesus to be his or her personal Lord and Savior. Now what? It is important that we help children understand the decision they made. It is common in children's ministries for kids to accept Jesus over and over.

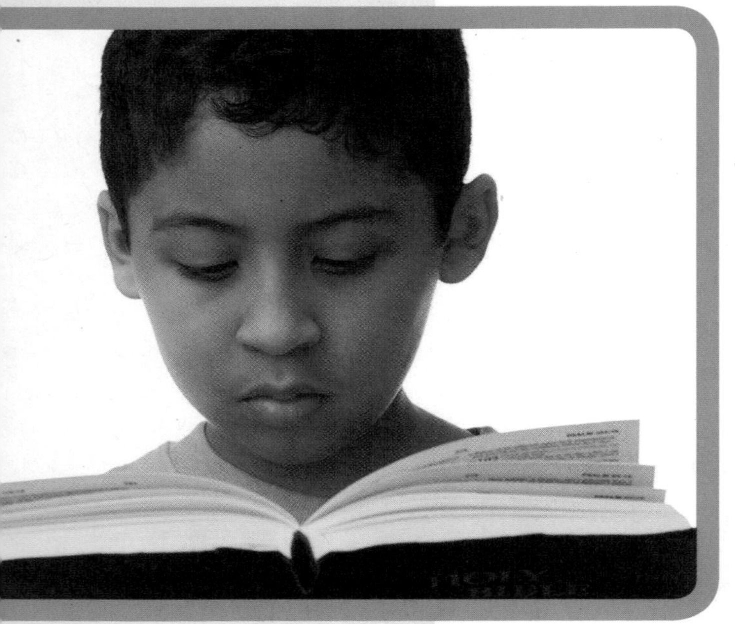

Part of the problem is that they don't feel a change. If a child comes forward, prays a salvation prayer, and goes back to their chair as though little happened, why wouldn't they feel they need a do-over? Unless we make that moment a significant memory, we may be confusing the child who doesn't fully grasp what they have just done.

There are many ways we can help to solidify this decision, help the children grow in their understanding of what happened, and create a spiritual anchor they can reflect back upon. Consider giving them a Bible. Use the dedication page in the front of the Bible to record the date and who gave them the Bible. There are many follow-up booklets that you can give to a child to help explain the decision they made.

Online Resource: Learn about follow-up tools from a Facebook discussion. Visit Kidology.org/toolbox and look for the Follow-Up Tools Discussion link.

6. How will you include parents?

Parents certainly have a significant role in their children's lives. Scripture is abundantly clear that parents are the primary spiritual leaders in their kids' lives. Anything we do at church is to support, supplement, and complement what is happening at home. When a child accepts Christ at church, we owe it to parents to communicate this to them and offer support.

What can we offer parents?

- Provide a clear explanation of the decision their child made.
- Provide a follow-up booklet that explains the gospel and what's next in the Christian life.
- Offer prayer support for the child and family.
- Share the gospel with the parents if they are not already Christians.

Reaching Kids Outside the Church

Once you are effectively reaching the kids within your church ministry, you are ready to start reaching outside the limits of your building and ministry programs. Don't wait until everything is perfect—you'll never get there. The key is to be ready for the guests you will get once you begin your outreach.

How can you reach kids who don't attend your church?

Online Resource: Available on Kidology is a twelve-lesson discipleship booklet (written by this author) called My Awesome Adventure. It takes kids and parents through fun, interactive, colorful, comic lessons that cover the basics of the Christian life. Learn more at: Kidology.org/toolbox

1. Equip your kids to share their faith. Make it short, fun, and easy.

Who interacts with kids every day who do not attend church? The kids in your ministry! The children in your ministry are already deployed to the mission field. Their classmates, neighbors, teammates, and others are kids you are trying to reach.

It shouldn't surprise you that kids get ministry opportunities all the time. Friends ask them about God, church, or their faith.

- Train your kids to see these moments as sent from God.
- Equip them with the tools and skills needed to respond.
- Assure them they don't need to know all the answers.

By talking with their friends about Jesus, they help draw them to him.

CALLED TO BE WITNESSES

Sometimes kids feel an unhealthy burden of responsibility when it comes to leading their friends to Jesus. I've had kids devastated when a friend didn't accept Christ. They thought that they had failed. Jesus said that we are to be his witness, right? Explain to kids the limits of being a witness:

A witness in court shares what they have seen, heard, or experienced. It is not their job to convince anyone of the truth. That is the job of the lawyers. The Bible says that it is the Holy Spirit who convicts. Let the Holy Spirit be the lawyer. All God wants you to do is share your own personal experience with Jesus and what he means to you.

Do you have a gospel tool or presentation that you can provide your kids? Have them available every week for kids to take. Take time to train your kids in using the *Wordless Book* or another gospel presentation.

ONLINE RESOURCE: For a sample of a fun incentive for kids to bring friends to church, check out a blog post Karl wrote on spinners. Visit Kidology.org/toolbox

2. Give your kids an incentive to invite friends to church.

Kids will struggle to share their faith, and that's OK. An incentive can encourage them to take that first step of inviting a friend to church. The incentive can be a small prize that you give to the guest and the friend who brought them.

Occasionally, someone asks me, "Aren't you bribing the kids?" First of all, a bribe is when you provide an incentive for someone to do something wrong. There is nothing wrong with bringing a friend to Christ, so it can't be a bribe.

My response to the question is to ask if adults are encouraged by rewards, points, or incentives. Incentives often determine where we eat, gas up our cars, or shop. Incentives encourage positive behavior until habits are formed.

Why expect anything different from kids?

For fun family events to host at your church, check out *24 Easy-To-Do Family Ministry Holiday Events* by Shelley Henning, available from RoseKidz at www.hendricksonrose.com.

3. Plan events that will draw kids (and families) to your church.

Unchurched families have preconceived impressions about church. They may think of the church as a place of judgment and hypocrisy. To break down those barriers, we need to offer events that help reshape families' views of the church.

- Keep things light and fun.
- Meet a need in the community.
- Build a bridge and establish trust.
- Break down misconceptions.
- Avoid high-pressure gospel presentations.

Reaching Kids Who Will Never Come to Church

Finding ways to get children and families through the front doors of your church is important, but there are many children who will never enter your building. Even if they wanted to, they may not have supportive parents or a means of getting there. Do we write them off? Are they someone else's responsibility?

The responsibility to reach the lost lies squarely upon the church.

I heard one pastor put it this way, "If your church were to suddenly close its doors, would your community even notice? Or would they fight to help to you survive?"

1. Create events where the kids are.

Jesus never invited people to the synagogue. He went where they were, met needs, and spoke the truth in love. Be courteous, but be bold.

- Where are kids?
- How can you create an event there?
- What can you do in a park?
- At a school?
- In kids' backyards?

Instead of Vacation Bible School at the church, what about asking families to host a small event in their backyard? The church can provide the needed materials.

KEEPING SHARP

If your church were to suddenly close its doors, would your community even notice? Or would they fight to help you survive?

2. Partner with others who are already reaching kids.

No need to reinvent the wheel. There are likely ministries in your community that are already ministering to children and families. Likely, they are praying for help.

You can provide more than just fuel for their ministry. You might be able to offer an upgrade! You can provide volunteers and perhaps even funding.

You may invest time, energy, and resources to reach kids for Jesus who never end up attending your church. But is that a bad thing? Is your goal church attendance or leading kids to Christ?

Nevertheless, don't underestimate the impact on your own ministry when the volunteers are focused on more than just the programs within the walls. They become a part of something bigger. That makes your children's ministry more attractive.

How do you find local ministries that impact children and families in your community? You can research online, but it's even better to talk to others in your area. Call other churches to see what they are doing. You may be able to team up. Find out what outreaches your denomination or fellowship may already be a part of. It's a lot easier to support something that is already established than to start building something.

3. Meet needs of kids and families in your community.

While Jesus had a teaching ministry, he also spent a great deal of time simply meeting needs. When we meet needs, we earn the right to be heard. Would Jesus have maintained the crowds if all he did was preach? Certainly not. His miracles, while amazing enough to draw a group, were meeting real needs. He wasn't levitating or doing escape tricks (he waited until the resurrection and ascension for those). He was meeting *real needs* of *real people*. Once he had an audience, he shared the good news!

Seek the Lord of the harvest with your leadership team, and pray about what needs in your community you can meet. You'll never lack ways to reach the lost with the good news of Jesus!

Types of events or activities that can draw in the community:

- Holiday events for families
- Easter egg hunts
- Vacation Bible Schools
- Summer church camps
- Sports, music, or drama camps
- Freedom festivals for July 4th or Memorial Day
- Fall festivals on or near Halloween
- Christmas events
- Meeting needs of the community
- After-school tutoring
- Support groups for kids (such as children of divorce)
- Ministries for children with special needs
- Fun events to which kids invite friends
- Game days
- Picnics
- Hiking trips
- Trips to local amusement parks
- Sack lunch Sundays (bring a sack lunch to church for an afternoon of activities)

Your Strategic Checklist

Here are some questions to ponder as you seek to reach *all* the kids in your community:

- Do I have a gospel presentation I know well and can do at any time?
- Do I need to train my volunteers in a specific gospel presentation?
- Do I need to provide a fun and easy tool for my kids so they can share the gospel with their friends?
- Do I regularly schedule times to share the gospel and give children a chance to respond?
- How am I going to draw new children (and families) to my church?
- What am I doing to reach children (and families) that would otherwise never visit my church?
- Is there something I need to stop doing to prioritize sharing the gospel in my community?
- What is one thing I am going to do as a result of reading this chapter?

Online Resource: For a list of helpful websites to give you ideas for community events, visit Kidology.org/toolbox

Special Events

When I first started out in children's ministry, I lived for special events. An open space on my calendar seemed to scream at me to plan something. Weekly ministry seemed like a chore on top of all the special events. Boy, did I have it backward. I not only wore myself out, I wore out my volunteers and families, too.

It wasn't until my third ministry position that the lead pastor said to me, "Karl, I don't want you to be driven by the calendar. I want you to be driven by our mission. If a special event helps us pursue our mission, I'm all for it. But I don't want you to feel any pressure to keep the calendar full of events."

I felt like a huge burden was lifted off my shoulders. How did he know that I started my planning by looking at a

For fun family events to host at your church, check out *24 Easy-To-Do Family Ministry Holiday Events* by Shelley Henning, available from RoseKidz at www.hendricksonrose.com

calendar? I started to ask, "What am I trying to accomplish? How can I best accomplish my goals?" Sometimes the answer is a special event, but other times there are more strategic ways to accomplish the same goal.

That is why we start with vision and mission and then break those down into S.H.A.R.P. Goals (see pages 50-54). If someone asks, "Why are you doing this event?" we ought to be ready with an explanation.

Should we do special events? Absolutely. But they must flow from our vision for the ministry and help us accomplish the goals we have set to bring that vision into reality.

Types of Special Events

Holiday Events

Holidays are a natural time to host special events. Whether it is Easter, Christmas, or Halloween, families are more open to attending church events during the holiday season. Easter Egg Hunts, Christmas programs, or Halloween alternatives can be attractive to families in your community and bring folks into your church who might never visit on a Sunday.

Don't forget the smaller holidays, too! Perhaps for Mother's Day, Father's Day, or Grandparents' Day you can find a fun way to help families engage with your church, even if it is just something unique on Sunday. For Valentine's Day, some churches have offered free childcare, so busy parents can go out on a date without having to pay a babysitter. Be creative, and you may just end up creating an event that is a big hit in your local community.

Outreach Events

Outreach events are occasions to meet a need in your community. Offer a special event for families who have children with special needs or something else that attracts the attention of families. From science shows, to sporting events, to family game-show events, you might find you can attract families to your church during seasons when there aren't any holidays.

Family Events

Families today are beyond busy. Planning family events can negatively add to their load or positively offer a rare chance to do something together. The key to planning successful events is to create opportunities that families already want to do but don't get a chance to do.

- Rent a theater to see a movie
- Host a game night
- Plan a camping trip
- Visit a zoo

Most parents feel guilty about not planning family time. We need to be careful that family events aren't adding to their stress, but offer an opportunity to enjoy some fun time together.

Relational Events

Church is often a place we attend and then leave. While relationships are one of the most important aspects of being a part of a church, sometimes our programming can hinder relationships from developing and growing. A brief handshake during the adult service or a coffee in the lobby rarely foster deep relationships. Some of the best events a church can host are those that are loosely structured and allow people to talk, laugh, and relate to each other.

Informal and spontaneous events can be effective as well. I may plan a lunch at a local restaurant weeks ahead but only announce it on Sunday. "Hey, my family is eating at Dion's Italian Restaurant after church. If you'd like to join us, please do! I'll be doing balloon animals for the kids."

Registration Limited!

One of the best ways to fill an event is to limit the number of people who can attend. Ironically, an "all welcome" event may result in low attendance, but a "limited to fifty people" event may fill up quickly!

By providing short notice, there is no pressure to come. If I announce it weeks ahead, people wonder if they have to RSVP and what the real agenda is for the meeting. Relational events can help friendships form and grow.

Intergenerational Events

When families arrive at church, they separate to their age-specific ministries. While this can be ideal for targeted education and worship experience, it does pull families apart.

There is also a concern about our seniors not mixing with the younger generations when they have so much wisdom, knowledge, and life experience to offer. Intergenerational events can help younger people connect with and benefit from those who have walked the journey of life longer.

I have done this by hosting a parenting forum where parents learn from each other.

- Ask parents who have finished raising their kids to host each table.
- Mark the tables with topics, such as discipline, dating, managing money, or chores.
- Rotate parents every fifteen to twenty minutes.

Everyone has valuable input to provide! There is no need for perfect parents, as even sharing mistakes or regrets can be helpful to younger parents.

Celebration Events

Everybody loves a party! You may have trouble getting folks to come to a teacher training luncheon, but if you host a party, you may have to cap the registration!

What do you have to celebrate in your ministry or in the lives of your church attendees? Some churches host a monthly party for kids who have a birthday that month. What about:

- Graduations?
- Baptisms?
- Baby showers?
- A VBS party a week after the event to celebrate and thank the volunteers?

Keep it light and fun, and be sure to feed people. Great prizes get people talking and make others wish they had been there.

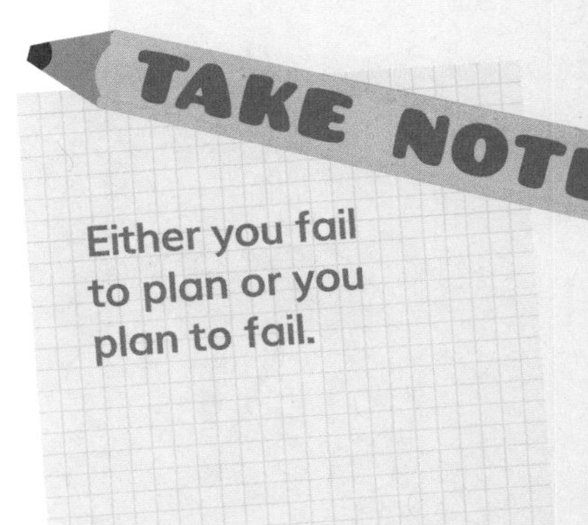

Either you fail to plan or you plan to fail.

Fundraising Events

Before planning a fundraising event, be sure to check with your church leadership on policies. Whether the event is for the children's ministry in general or for a specific need, fundraising events can be a quick and fun way to raise needed funds.

People are more willing to pay if they understand they are contributing to a cause. Getting volunteers can be easier when they understand they are helping accomplish a goal for the ministry.

Whether it's a car wash, a parents' night out, or a silent auction, planning an event can be a great way to put the fun back into fundraising.

Planning a Successful Event

Know Before You Go!

You're ready to plan an event. What do you need to do to pull it off? Understand that most of the work is before the event. The day of the event is merely execution. Either you fail to plan or you plan to fail.

The classic leadership book *The Art of War* by Sun Tzu contains many great proverbs. One of the most well known is, "Every battle is won before it's ever fought." The preparation for battle is more important than the battle itself. If someone wins a battle, it is because they planned well.

It's possible that in the preparation stages a leader cannot see victory. It is better to withdraw from a battle than to enter when defeat is assured. The same is true in ministry.

We may not like comparing events to battles, but the principles are the same. If the event goes well, you know it was well planned. Likewise, if an event is a disaster, not enough planning went into it. It may have been better to cancel the event than to attempt it without adequate preparation and resources.

Timing

Plan events well in advance. If you don't have adequate time to plan, you don't have adequate time to pull off an event. In general, you need at least three months to plan, prepare, and promote an event. A full year is ideal!

The Why, the Who, the What and the When!

How do you plan great events? The answer is to know what questions to ask! As the saying goes, if you want the right answer, you have to ask the right questions.

The WHY: Find Your Purpose

People don't rally around events. They rally around causes. Know why this event is important. Any document containing budget, staffing, or resources should point to the purpose of the event.

If you want the right answer, you have to ask the right questions.

Are you:

- Reaching the lost?
- Bringing in new families?
- Creating significant memories?

Whatever it is, keep it central, and people will step up to meet the needs.

Those who fail to articulate and promote the *why* will struggle with every other aspect of the event.

The WHAT: Know What Questions to Ask

A pastor once told me, "There are three things that are most important when planning an event: details, details, details." The key is to preconsider everything. The further ahead you think through details, the less stressful your event will be. No detail is too small! Ask as many questions as possible before the event. Then, use the answers to create checklists.

Questions about Preparation

- What supplies do we need?
- What supplies do we already have?
- What do we need to buy?
- How much will this cost?
- Where are we going to store things as we collect them?
- What do I need permission to use or move?
- How many people is it going to take to pull this off with excellence?
- How will we promote the event?
- Will any other events be impacted?

Questions about Event Logistics

- Who will get the supplies?
- What needs to be set up?
- What rooms will be used?
- What are the technical needs?
- What graphics or communication tools are needed?

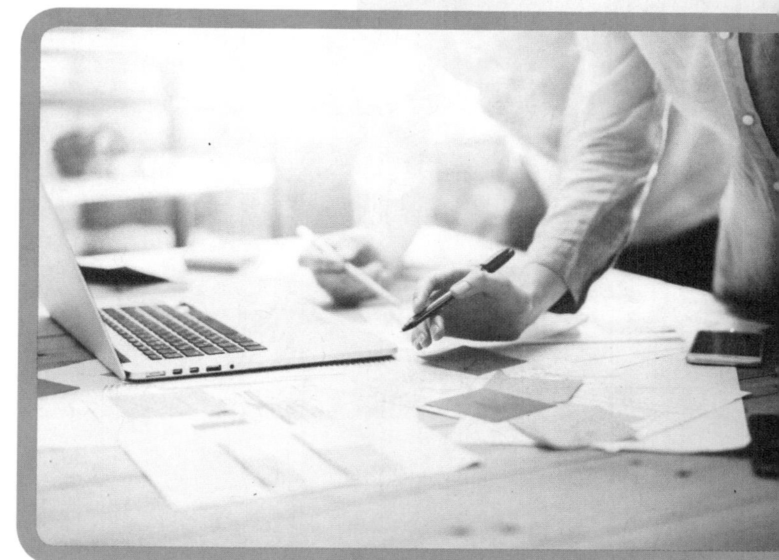

- Will people need to register?
- How and who will manage registration?

Questions about Break Down and Follow Ups

- How will clean up happen?
- How will we measure success?
- How will we follow up with people?

Before getting answers, you need to determine *all* the questions. You do not need to have all the answers right away, but you do need to identify all the issues. Ideally, this will be done in a group. Conversation is helpful as each person will provide a unique perspective. This takes time, but if you are intentional in advance, it will help make your event a success.

The WHO: Find Your Helpers

Next, you must determine how much help you'll need to pull off the event. Whatever you think you need initially, it's likely you'll need more.

Delegate

As a leader, you ought to delegate just about everything, including leadership. As the one in charge, you need to have the flexibility to be responsive to the surprises that are sure to pop up.

Deadline

Set a deadline for assigning specific roles for the event. You never want to cancel an event once it has been announced, but there ought to be an early stage of planning when only volunteers and leaders know about it.

Promote

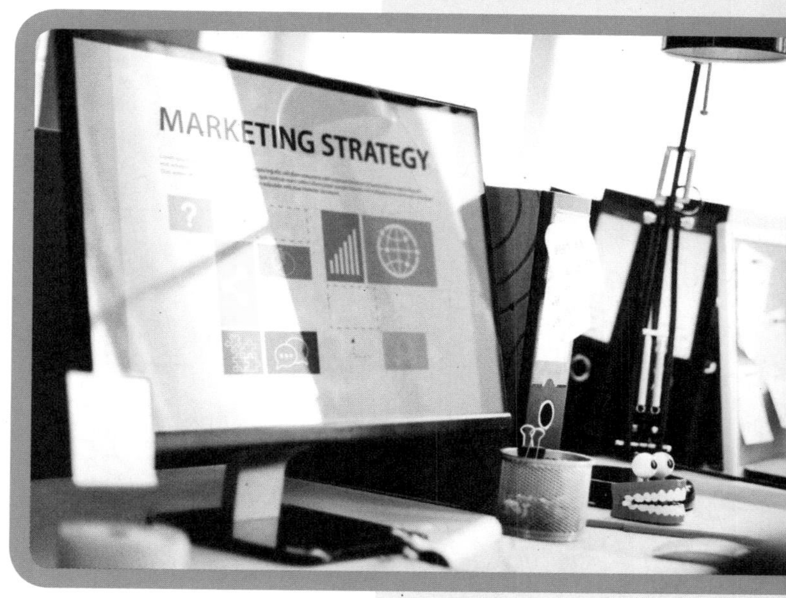

Once you determine you have the funds, people, and resources to pull it off, then you start promoting the event. This is an effective way to kick off your recruiting efforts. Announce, "We'd like to do this event, but before we can approve it, we need a core of leadership in place." Pitch your *why*, and start building a team that will make it happen.

What If It Doesn't Happen?

Don't be discouraged if you are unable to pull off an event. If God is in something, he will provide what is needed. When you don't get what you need, it often is God letting you know that this is not the time or the project he wants you to focus on. Release it guilt-free knowing that where God leads, he provides. And where he doesn't provide, he is guiding you toward a different strategy.

TAKE NOTE

On the following pages, you will find a Parent Permission Form and a Medical Release Form. Modify these forms to meet the needs of your ministry, and adapt them for each special event you host.

The WHEN: Make a Plan

The *when* is not the date of your event, but your preparation deadlines. Your plan isn't for everything to fall into place at the last minute. It is to have everything in place at the time of the event. Of course, we live in a world where nothing goes exactly as planned. Expect some last minute adjustments, ideas, or changes.

Still, how many last minute items could have been avoided if you had prepared in advance? There will always be surprises, but that is no excuse for a lack of planning.

As you prepare your checklist of things to do, include deadlines. Plan for additional margins. When it comes to signage or basic supplies, there is no need to do those things the week before an event. The more you can do earlier, the better.

ONLINE RESOURCE: A powerful event planning insight: The work will expand to fill the time allowed. Read more at Kidology.org/toolbox

PARENT PERMISSION FORM

Name of event ____

Location ______________________________ Phone ______________

Leaders Name___________________________ Phone ______________

Name__________________________________ Phone ______________

Date __________________________________ Time ______________

Cost $____

If your child will participate in this event, please complete, sign, and return this statement of consent and release of liability. As the parent or guardian you remain fully responsible for the actions and conduct of your child, including any legal responsibility which may result.

I hereby consent to have my child, ______________________________, participate in this activity.

If this activity takes place away from the church facilities, I understand that my child will be under the supervision of the person(s) designated above on the specified dates. I further consent to the conditions stated above regarding participation in this event.

In consideration of my child's participation in this event, I agree to indemnify and hold harmless ______________________________ (name of church) and its representatives, including chaperones, from any and all claims, including negligence, arising from or relating to my child's participation in this event. This indemnification and hold-harmless agreement does not apply to claims for intentional misconduct or gross negligence.

____ (date)
Parent/Guardian Name (print)

____ (date)
Parent/Guardian Name (sign)

Please return this form along with a completed Medical Release Form by __________(date).

Medical Release Form

Name of Child ____

Name of Event ____

I (we), the undersigned parent(s) or guardian(s) of the aforementioned minor, do hereby authorize adult volunteers of ______________________________ (name of church), as agent(s) for the undersigned to consent to any medical or surgical care deemed advisable by any accredited physician or surgeon in an approved emergency clinic or hospital for the treatment of my minor child, named above. I further release from any liability ______________________________ (name of church), any of its ministries or leaders in the event of an accident en route, during, or returning from the event specified above. This agreement does not apply to claims for intentional misconduct or gross negligence.

____ (date)
Parent Guardian Name (print)

____ (date)
Parent/Guardian Name (sign)

Address ______________________________ City ______________

Emergency Phone Numbers: Home ______________________ Cell ______________

Health Insurance Company Name ______________________________

Policy or Group Number ______________________ Phone ______________

If parent or guardian is not available in an emergency, please contact:

Name ______________________________ Phone ______________

Please list any allergies. Include medications, foods, etc.

____

____

____

____

____

Does your child have any medical or special needs, including medications? (Circle One)

No Yes

If yes, please explain. ____

____

Doctor's Name ________________________________ Phone ______________

Dentist's Name _______________________________ Phone ______________

Date of last tetanus shot _______________________ Birthdate ______________

Event Planning Worksheet

CATEGORY	NOTES
Name of Event:	
Purpose:	
Date:	
Time:	
Location:	
Schedule:	
Staff:	
Supplies:	
Marketing:	
Other Ideas: (Crazy Ideas!)	

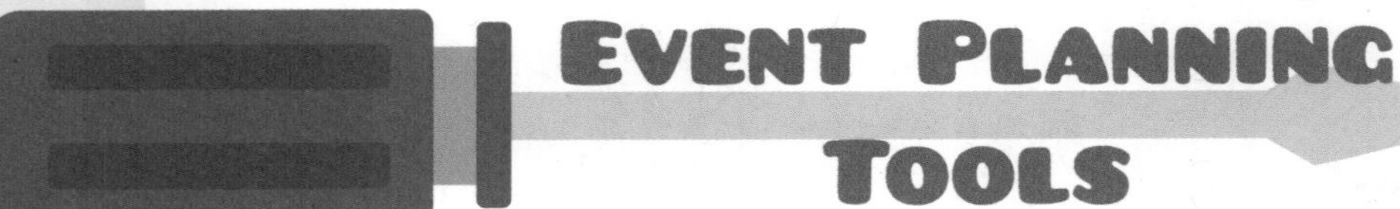

Event Planning Tools

Event Planning Worksheet

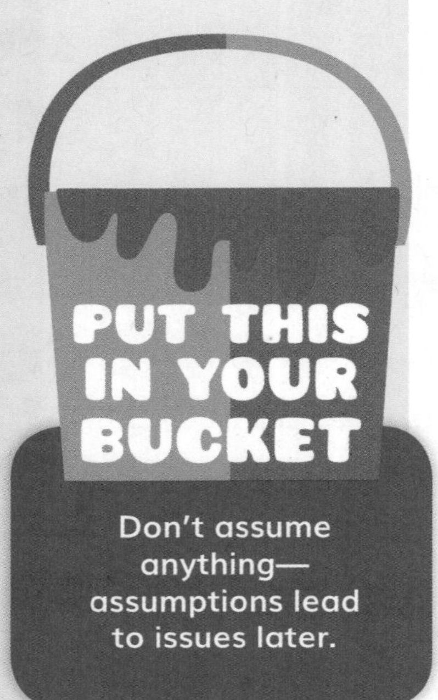

Don't assume anything—assumptions lead to issues later.

You'll find the Event Planning Worksheet on the previous page. This is your initial planning document. Once you have completed the worksheet, you may want to convert it to digital form. This way it can be shared with other leaders and volunteers.

On your Event Planning Worksheet, be specific about:

- **What** needs to be done?
- **Who** is this task assigned to?
- **When** does this task need to be completed by?

Every single task, regardless of how small it is, needs to be recorded. Don't assume anything—assumptions lead to issues later. If a task is large, break it into steps. Often people are overwhelmed by big tasks and can have a tendency to put them off. When they are broken down into steps, it appears more reasonable.

To complete the form, make notes on the following aspects of your event:

Name of Event

Be creative but clear. A strong name will foster curiosity and create interest. It won't confuse or raise questions.

Purpose

Always have a clearly articulated purpose for doing this event. This will help sell the event to others, bring focus to different decisions, and provide a framework for evaluating the event afterwards.

Date

Make notes to address the following considerations:

- Are there events close to yours that may force people to choose one or the other? You may choose to move your event or cancel others that or cause conflict for families.
- Are there conflicts in family calendars? Holidays? School days off or breaks that might result in people traveling?

Time

Make notes to address the following considerations:

- Is there adequate time to plan and prepare? Are you attempting this too soon?
- Will people be able to get food before or after an event?
- Do you need to provide food to make it easier for people to attend?
- Does it go too late? Parents may not want kids out too late on a school night.
- Is it too long? A great event that goes on too long causes people to leave feeling exhausted or tired. First impressions are important, but final impressions will impact your next event!

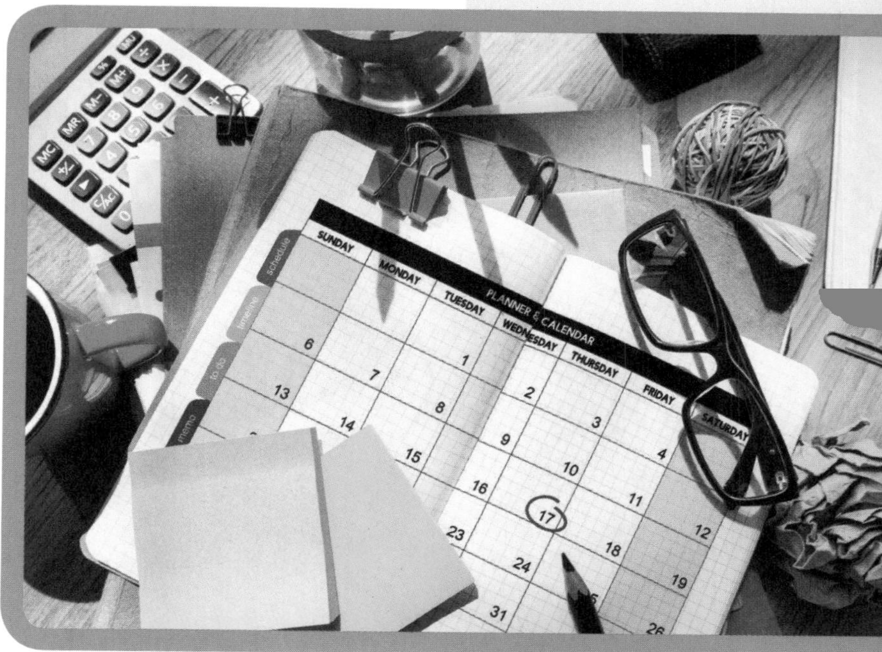

Location

Make notes to address the following considerations:

- Do you have enough space for the anticipated attendance?
- Are there enough restrooms?
- Would an off-site location be more attractive to your target audience?
- Is there adequate parking at the location you are considering?

Schedule

This is deeper than just the starting and ending time. Scheduling covers every aspect of the event from the set up, to the actual event, to the clean up.

Think through the transition times. How long will each component be? Provide natural breaks if it is a longer event.

Here are some things to consider as you determine the schedule:

- Are there any conflicting events within the church or outside that could hurt your attendance?
- Is the event too long or too short?
- Are there enough breaks?
- If food is provided, is there enough time to distribute and enjoy the food?
- Is there adequate transition time?
- Is there enough time to set up?
- How much time will you need for clean up?
- During the program, how long will each component be?

Staff

At the earliest stages of planning, estimate how many volunteers you'll need to pull it off. Expect this number to change (grow!) as you continue planning.

While every event will have different needs, here are some basic roles to consider:

- Who is the primary leader? It is best to delegate this and oversee this person.
- Who is doing set up and clean up? These can be separate crews.
- Do you need greeters?
- Is there event registration? Who will manage that both before and during the event?
- Should you have security at the event?
- How can you break up teams to focus on different aspects of the event? Each aspect should have a team leader and the necessary number of team members.
- Who is handling marketing for the event?
- Do you need someone to lead follow ups after the event?

Delegate as much as possible. You can still oversee, help, and advise volunteers.

As you think through many of these roles, you may find yourself thinking several times, *That's my job!* Consider delegating as much as possible. You can still oversee, help, and advise volunteers. The more you delegate, the more you will be able to help with unexpected issues. You will also be able to execute some of those amazing ideas that will pop into your head as the event gets closer!

Supplies

Every event requires stuff. Most of the supplies you need will be obvious, but it's the less obvious ones that will do you in!

Thoroughly think through your event and make a checklist so that there are no hindering surprises on the day of your event.

Here are some examples of things that might be overlooked:

- Paper supplies
- Trashcans and bags
- Extension cords
- Batteries
- Name tags
- Markers
- Chargers
- Copier paper and toner
- Cleaning supplies
- Stapler, scissors, tape
- First-aid kit
- Basic tool set
- Prizes and candy

Label items with masking tape. Write which rooms they came from so they can easily be put back.

Marketing

We'll discuss marketing in more detail later in this section, but for now, make a list of ways to target your audience. No need to list the obvious items, like church publications, website, or social media. Focus on listing new and creative ways to market your event.

A strong event planning document will require a significant time investment, but it will always pay rich dividends in getting approval, funding, and building a volunteer team.

Event Budgets

Events have many costs. There is the investment of time, energy, resources, facility, and money. Before an event is even finalized, a budget needs to be determined and approved. Think through everything you may need to purchase in order to pull off your event.

The more specific you are, the more trusting you appear—and the more likely you are to get the approval. Avoid large vague numbers like, "I need $1,000 to do this event." Those entrusted with the stewardship of funds see that as a lack of planning. They will be hesitant to approve such a request. If it is more than is truly needed, they fear money is wasted or just spent because it was approved.

Every ministry has limited funds. Your leadership still wants to spend the money where it can make the greatest impact. A detailed budget says, "I've thought this through and know what I need to make this event a success." A detailed budget also allows leadership to see where the money is going. They are more likely to get excited about providing the funds that are needed.

What Is Your Dream Budget?

Always present two budgets for any event. The first is your dream budget. It is your ideal finances to support what you'd be able to do. It should also explain the additional impact that you anticipate as a result of extra investment.

Secondly, present your minimum budget. This is the requirements for the event to take place. If the basic budget is not possible, you can't do the event. You may never get your dream budget, but it helps cast vision. It gets the leadership thinking about what could be done with more resources.

Your goal is to get a budget approved that is somewhere in the middle. There will be times that you'll be surprised to get your

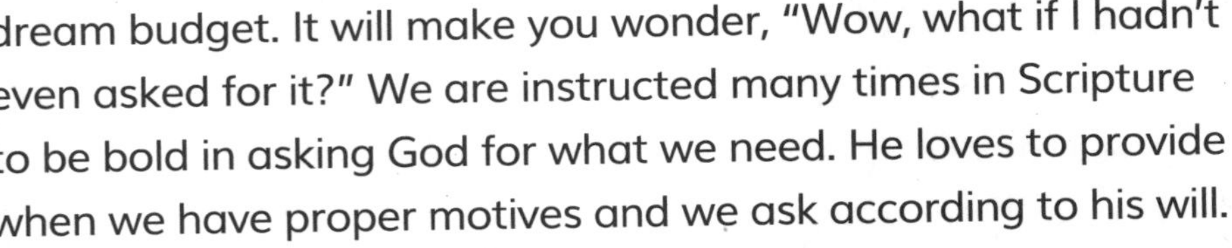

dream budget. It will make you wonder, "Wow, what if I hadn't even asked for it?" We are instructed many times in Scripture to be bold in asking God for what we need. He loves to provide when we have proper motives and we ask according to his will.

Budgeting Your Event

Sometimes volunteers are hesitant to help with an event because they assume they need to pay for their own supplies.

In the next few pages, you'll find the Event Budget Worksheet. Organize expenses into logical categories. This will help you spend your money wisely. If cuts are needed, this organization makes it easier to prioritize.

Below are things to consider as you put together your budget and complete the worksheet.

What?

Make a list of what to buy. Explain why it is needed.

Who?

State who will spend the money. When you are recruiting, you should be able to say, "Here is what you are responsible for, and this is your budget." I always tell people that they may certainly donate toward their area of ministry, but this is not the expectation.

If people want to donate toward an event, make sure this comes after their regular tithe to the ministry.

Where?

Detail where the various supplies will come from.

Many volunteers have store preferences when it comes to shopping for supplies. Create accountability by giving them a list of locations where they are likely to find the right things. This allows you to estimate your costs. Once your budget is approved, it may be difficult or impossible to account for extra expenses.

How Much?

This is where the rubber meets the road: How much will each item or category cost?

While you don't need to make budgets to the penny, avoid generic round numbers.

If you are concerned about not having the margin for unexpected expenses, include a line for miscellaneous expenses.

Let your leadership know that if this budget is approved, you won't be coming back for more. Your goal is always to come in under budget, which is why you are including some margin in the overall budget. This level of honesty also builds trust with your leadership and shows your ability to manage the finances of an event.

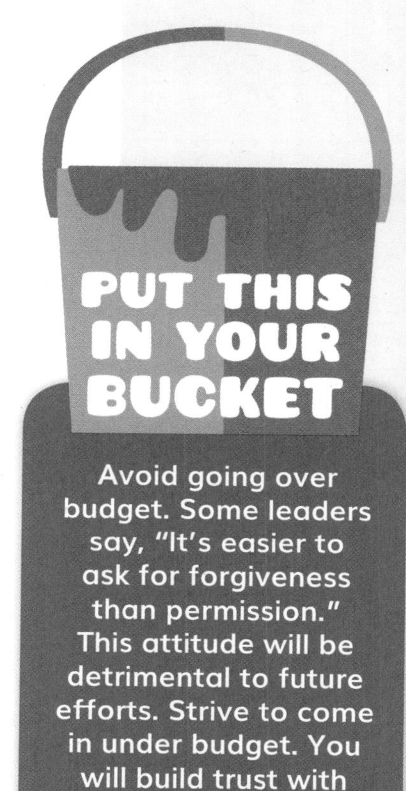

Avoid going over budget. Some leaders say, "It's easier to ask for forgiveness than permission." This attitude will be detrimental to future efforts. Strive to come in under budget. You will build trust with the leadership which could lead to more funds in the future.

Notes

A final column on the Budget Planning Worksheet is provided for notes. This is where you can provide any additional information to anyone reviewing your budget. It clarifies:

- Any unknown factors about the cost estimate
- Any options regarding choices
- Reasons for the choice that was made

For example, if the line is for a bounce house rental, make a note about your options. Write, "There is a small one for five hundred dollars, but we chose the big one for seven hundred fifty dollars because twice the number of kids can participate. This makes lines shorter, and it's cheaper than renting two of the smaller one."

The leaders may choose the less costly option when considering overall cost of the event, but at least they'll understand your reasons.

EVENT BUDGET WORKSHEET

WHAT	WHERE	WHO	COST	NOTES:
Category:				
Total for this category:				
Category:				
Total for this category:				
Category:				
Total for this category:				

WHAT	WHERE	WHO	COST	NOTES:
Category:				
Total for this category:				
Total Budget:				

Additional Notes or Explanation

Marketing Your Event

Marketing

How will you get the word out? There are the obvious methods you already use for church communication. But if you are trying to reach new people, you'll need to be creative. How are you going to mobilize your people to invite others? You'll want to use everything in your marketing toolbox and then brainstorm some specialty tools.

The Basics

- **Print materials:** flyers, posters, invitations, etc.
- **Digital marketing:** social media, email, texting, etc.
- **Relational marketing:** announcements, phone calls, visitation, etc.

Some Creative Ideas:

- **Print materials:** Try door hangers or paper airplanes!
- **Digital marketing:** Offer a prize drawing for those who share a social media post. Or use a specific #hashtag. You'll get others sharing socially!
- **Relational marketing:** Visit area businesses. Ask for donations and if you can put up a poster in their business. Offer to put their logo on your program. Then, mention them from the stage in thanking promotional partners.

Other Ideas

Encourage creative brainstorming. In your initial planning, be bold and even list crazy ideas that you aren't sure will be approved or even possible. This will get people excited about the event. You may be surprised when leadership jumps at one of your crazy ideas and takes the event to the next level!

Marketing Time Line

A marketing strategy is more than just what you will do to promote the event. It also determines the timing for maximum impact.

Start by identifying your target audience. Is it regular church attendees or new people? List ways that you can reach them.

- Start with methods that cast a wide net.
- As the event nears, narrow your focus and your efforts. Sometimes it is helpful to work backward, starting with what your final push will be or how you will follow up with people. While you may not have time to call everyone on the phone, you can start with mass email.
- Follow that with a targeted invitation in the mail that goes to anyone who hasn't responded to the email.
- Make phone calls the week or two prior to the event to those who haven't responded to the previous methods.

Create a timeline that shows what you will do during each week leading up to the event. There may be things you repeat, perhaps even every month. There will also be some efforts that are best done advance and others that are ideally done in the week or days prior to the event.

Event Marketing Plan Worksheet

List your marketing plans in order of execution. Indicate what to do, who will do it, and if there is a cost associated with the effort. You can record any notes, comments or exact marketing text in the notes field. Be sure to check off efforts as they are completed. Note the results of each tactic so you learn what is most effective for your target audience. Learn from this event to promote future ones even better!

When?	What?	Cost?

Who?	Notes

Event Evaluations

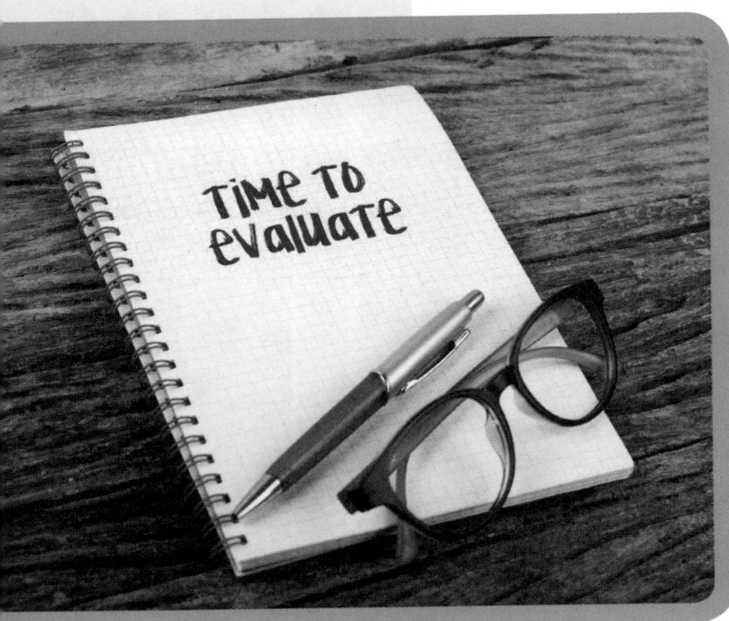

Always evaluate your events. You need to celebrate the things that went well and learn from what could have gone better.

- Do your own personal evaluation.
- Ask your leaders for input.
- Survey those who attended.
- Follow up with everyone who attended.
- Select a small sample group. Sometimes you'll get a better response from a small group who are aware they were specifically chosen.

Personal Evaluation

Take notes during the event and record your thoughts after the event while your memory is fresh. Use the Personal Event Evaluation on page 305.

- What did you do well?
- What could you have done better?
- What frustrated you?
- What should you have anticipated?
- What surprised you?
- What should you do again?
- What lessons did you learn?
- Who were your strongest leaders or volunteers?
- Were your goals accomplished?
- Did you have any surprises?

- What did you hear from others?
- If you did this again, what would you change?
- What should you never change?
- Are there any stories that came out of this event that are worth sharing?

Team Evaluation

Give your team a chance to share their thoughts about the event before they know your conclusions. Copy and distribute the Team Event Evaluation on page 306.

- Create a safe environment for sharing.
- Let them know you want honest feedback. It's OK to say you need both positive and negative feedback.
- Ask them many of the same questions listed above under Personal Evaluation.
- Compile the results.
- Give extra weight where you see consensus.

You will never pull off a perfect event, so learn what will improve future events. Don't forget to celebrate the event, the volunteers, the results, and the impact!

Guest Evaluation

As organizers, we sometimes see what we want to see. It is always helpful to seek objective feedback from those who attended the event and were not involved in planning it. Know that most feedback will be negative since positive feedback is rarely volunteered. Copy and distribute the Guest Event Evaluation on page 307.

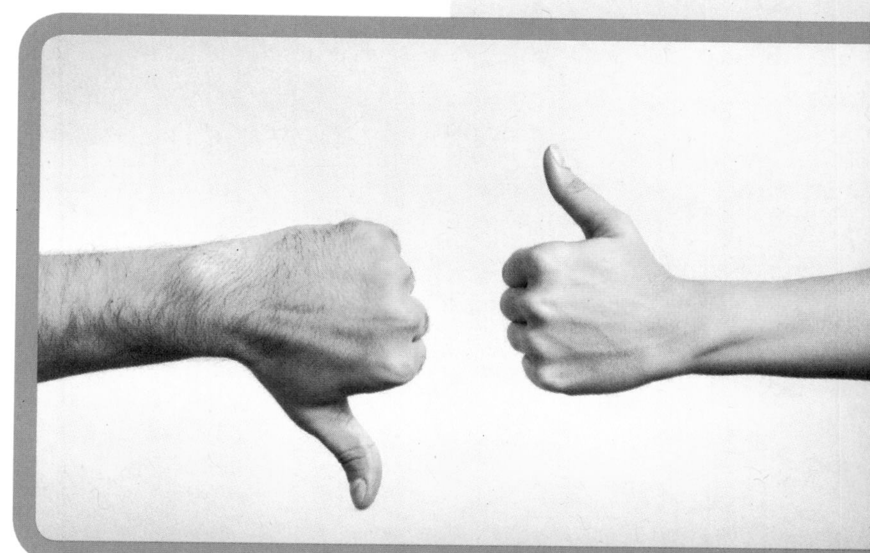

Your goal isn't to make everyone happy. It is to have the best event possible.

Common Concerns

Give common concerns or suggestions extra weight. Isolated or unique feedback can always be accepted with gratitude and grace. You do not need to implement every suggestion you receive. Your goal isn't to make everyone happy. It is to have the best event possible.

Keep It Short

Keep your survey extremely short. You'll get more responses that way.

Future Events

Every event has something to offer future events. See if you can write down at least three things you learned. Ask yourself, "How can this event help make the next one even better?"

Personal Event Evaluation

Write notes in each area that is applicable. Be honest, brief, and specific.

Name of Event:	
Date/Time:	Location:
Schedule:	Facilities:
Marketing:	First Impressions:
Print Materials/Graphics:	Program:
Set Up/Clean Up:	
Registration:	Follow Up:
Impact/Results:	
Ideas for next time:	

Team Event Evaluation

Write notes in each area that is applicable. Be honest, brief, and specific.

Name of Event:

What were the highlights?

What feedback have you heard?

What was your favorite aspect of the event?

What surprised you?

What did we overlook?

What should we NOT change?

What should we change?

Should we do this event again? Did it meet our goals and objectives?

Ideas for next time?

Guest Event Evaluation

Only Five Questions!

Thanks for coming to our event! You have been selected to provide us with some feedback so we can better serve you and families like yours in the future. Feel free to be brief, but please be as specific as possible. If you'd rather talk to someone about your experience, please don't hesitate to contact us. Your input is much appreciated.

1. How did you hear about our event?

2. What was your favorite aspect of the event?

3. What did we do well?

4. What could we have done better?

5. Would you be willing to give us a quote that we can use in future event promotions? We will only use your first name and last initial in any publication that uses your comment.

Thank you!

Follow-Up Strategy

You put a lot of prayer, time, effort, resources, energy, and hard work into your event. When the event is over and all cleaned up, you can finally relax! You are *done*.

Well, you did this event for a defined purpose, right? One of these purposes was likely to reach new people. You reached them! What a shame it would be if they only came to that one event, and you never saw them again until the next big event. Now is the time to reach out to them and follow up.

Email

Email is a quick and easy way to follow up. Thank people for coming. Ask them for a quote you can use to promote future events. If you want a feedback survey, provide a link to where they can provide quick feedback online.

Mail

Snail mail may be old fashioned, but that is precisely why it has impact. A letter in the mail says to the recipient that they are valued. You spent time and resources to thank them or get their feedback. You may get a stronger response than from email.

If you want people to mail something back, include a self-addressed stamped envelope. The money you spend on that stamp may be the nudge they need to reply, especially if they know they are part of a select group being asked for feedback.

Social Media

Look for feedback online. As people post pictures or comments online about your event, respond! Hit that Like button, retweet them, or comment on their post. Thank them publicly for coming and for their feedback.

Telephone

Connecting over the phone communicates value and genuine interest. If you have to leave a message, script your message ahead of time so it is focused, clear, and short. The person you call may never call you back, but they will appreciate your call nonetheless.

Here is a sample of a follow up phone call:

Hello! Pastor Karl here. I just wanted to call and thank you for coming to our event last week at our church. Our desire was to create a fun opportunity for kids and families to connect. I hope your family had a great time.

If you gave us your email address, we'll be sure you are the first to know about our next event. If not, please consider calling the office and leaving a message with your email address.

There is no need to call me back. But if you have any questions about our church or any feedback on the event, please don't hesitate to call or drop me an email.

Just so you know, our Sunday service times are 9:00 and 11:00. If there is a way we can pray for you or serve your family, please let me know. We're here for you! See you next Sunday!

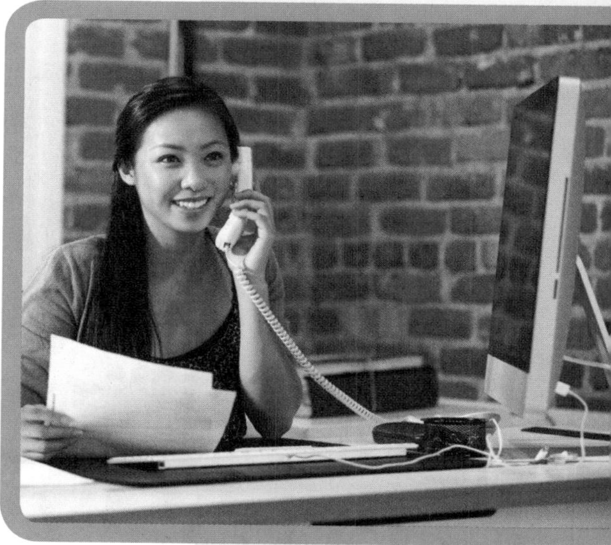

Personalize it with the name of your event and church. Keep it upbeat, positive, and most of all, short.

In Person

The most powerful way to follow up with someone is to meet with them in person. Programs and events might get people into a church, but they don't bring people back. Relationships are the glue that grows a church after an event.

Help your guests connect with real people at your church, and your event will result in ongoing growth, rather than just a spike in attendance. Knowing there will be someone to greet them and sit with them might be just what it takes to get an unchurched family to attend one of your worship services.

Focus on First Impressions!

Be thoughtful about the first impressions your event provides. It may be worth your time to get in your car and drive up to the church.

- What do you see?
- If this was your first time to visit, is anything confusing?

Walk into your front doors as though you've never been in the building.

- What do you see?
- Can you find your way around?

Consider how folks are greeted, guided, and what their final impression is as they leave. You are not merely promoting an event, you are promoting yourselves as a church family. You are giving people an idea of what the culture of your church is like. If everyone is in a hurry, scrambling with event details, and unable to calmly connect with guests, that communicates a hectic environment. People have enough of that already in their daily life.

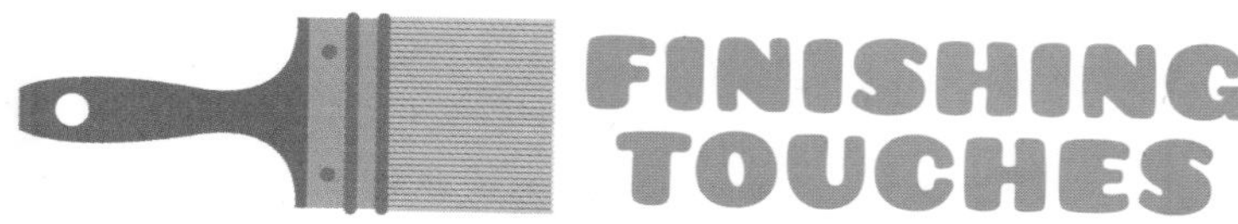

FINISHING TOUCHES

As the primary leader of an event, your goal should be to delegate every task so that you can greet people, welcome them, answer questions, and guide folks in a calm and relaxed manner. People notice when the leader is accessible.

Work to create that experience from the moment guests arrive on your church campus until they leave.

Visit the best-run restaurants, resorts, entertainment venues, or businesses, and you'll see the effort they put into first impressions. Take notes, and implement your newfound ideas in your ministry!

THE GRAND OPENING

INTRODUCTION

THE ULTIMATE GRAND OPENING

A final word from the author . . .

- Have you ever attended a grand opening?
- Have you watched a ribbon cutting ceremony as a building is opened to the public?

It can be pretty exciting. A lot of hard work went into that final moment. Now, everyone can enjoy the end result. The building is beautiful, clean, fully-staffed, and stocked according to its purpose. It can be an impressive sight!

In ministry, we never get that moment. We never get that event where we can say, "I'm all done!" While this may sound discouraging, it should instead encourage you!

We never get a grand opening because there are always new kids, new families, new leaders, new needs, new ideas, and new opportunities. Not to mention, new challenges! Even the most successful children's ministry is constantly in flux.

Sometimes our frustration in ministry stems from an unrealistic goal. If we believe we are in the process of perfecting something, we will always be discouraged. When we realize that we are in the process of building programs to build people—people who one day will be presented as perfect to God—we have reason to celebrate.

It helps us embrace our current challenges in light of the

ultimate goal: building people to know, love, and serve God. Our ministry may never be complete, but we do our best and then leave the rest up to God!

I pray you have found this toolbox helpful and inspiring as you seek to do your best to build something amazing for the kingdom!

- Review these tools often.
- Sharpen them.
- Always keep your eye out for new tools that will make your ministry even sharper!

Let us think of ways to motivate one another to acts of love and good works. And let us not neglect our meeting together, as some people do, but encourage one another, especially now that the day of his return is drawing near.

Hebrews 10:24–25

Prayerfully consider the Action Plan Worksheet on page 314. Remember that we are awaiting the grand opening of the new Heaven and new Earth! Paul declared in Philippians 1:6,

God, who began the good work within you, will continue his work until it is finally finished on the day when Christ Jesus returns.

I may never get to see your ministry, but I will get to meet you someday. As they say, "Here, there, or in the air!" See you soon!

PASTOR KARL BASTIAN

A.K.A. THE KIDOLOGIST
KIDOLOGY.ORG
KIDOLOGIST.COM

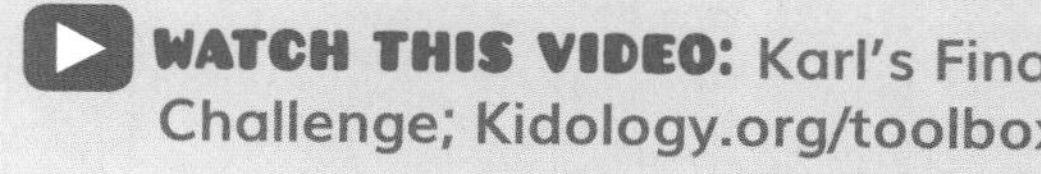

WATCH THIS VIDEO: Karl's Final Challenge; Kidology.org/toolbox

Action Plan Worksheet

Take this time to review what you've read. Use the next four pages to take note of what tools you've gained and what you'd like to implement in the future. Write some goals or a prayer for the future of your ministry.

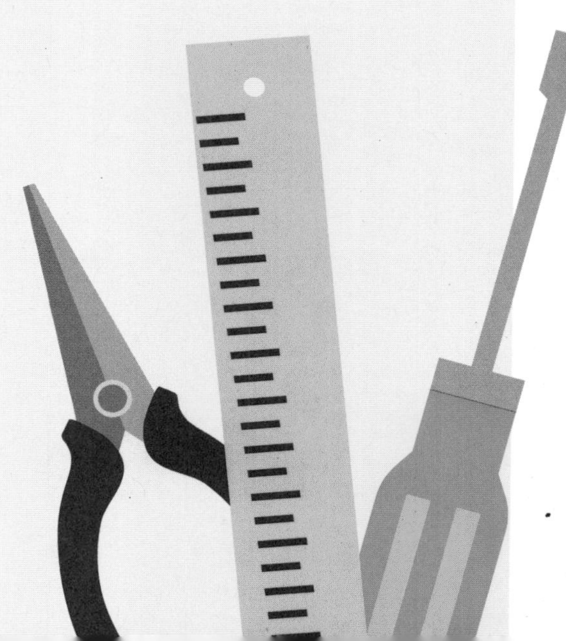

Addendum: Online Resources

Find all the following resources on the Kidology.org website. Go to Kidology.org/toolbox.

Video

Introduction

- Proactive Leadership

Section One

- First Things First

Section Two

- Lose the Cape!

Section Three

- The High Calling to Teach

Section Four

- The Power of a Strong Start

Section Five

- Asking Why Before When and What

Wrap-Up

- Karl's Final Challenge

Other Resources

Section One

- His Yoke is Easy and His Burden is Light

Section Two

- Does your CM have an Org Chart?
- Volunteer Interest Form
- Meet Our Newest Volunteer Poster

Section Three

- Candy Get Game
- You Are a Bible Character

Section Four

- Using the Wordless Book to Share the Gospel
- You Don't Have a Recruiting Problem, You Have a Relationship Problem

Section Five

- Follow-Up Tools Discussion
- My Awesome Adventure
- Kid Incentive Blog Post
- List of websites providing ideas for community events
- Work Expands